PUPPIES IN
AMERICA

LAWS, POLICIES, ATTITUDES AND PROCESSES THAT SHAPE THE LIVES OF

PUPPIES IN AMERICA

Assessing Society's Needs, Desires, Values and Morals

CARMEN M. CUSACK

sussex
ACADEMIC
PRESS
Brighton • Chicago • Toronto

2 4 6 8 10 9 7 5 3 1

First published in 2016 by
SUSSEX ACADEMIC PRESS
PO Box 139
Eastbourne BN24 9BP

and in the United States of America by
SUSSEX ACADEMIC PRESS
Independent Publishers Group
814 N. Franklin Street, Chicago, IL 60610

and in Canada by
SUSSEX ACADEMIC PRESS (CANADA)

British Library Cataloguing in Publication Data
A CIP catalogue record for this book is available from the British Library.

Library of Congress Cataloging-in-Publication Data
Names: Cusack, Carmen M.
Title: Laws, policies, attitudes, and processes that shape the lives of puppies in America : assessing society's needs, desires, values, and morals / Carmen M. Cusack.
Other titles: Puppies in America
Description: Brighton : Sussex Academic Press, [2016] | Includes biblio-graphical references and index.
Identifiers: LCCN 2015048164 (print) | LCCN 2016004593 (ebook) | ISBN 9781845197803 (hbk : alk. paper) | ISBN 9781845197810 (pbk : alk. paper) | ISBN 9781782842897 (e-pub) | ISBN 9781782842903 (mobi) | ISBN 9781782842910 (pdf)
Subjects: LCSH: Puppies—United States. | Puppies—Social aspects—United States. | Dogs—United States. | Dogs—Social aspects—United States. | Animal welfare—Moral and ethical aspects. | Human–animal relations hips—United States.
Classification: LCC SF422.6.U6 C87 2016 (print) | LCC SF422.6.U6 (ebook) | DDC 636.7/07—dc23
LC record available at http://lccn.loc.gov/2015048164

Typeset and designed by Sussex Academic Press, Brighton & Eastbourne.
Printed by TJ International, Padstow, Cornwall.

Contents

List of Illustrations and Figures

Sources and permission information for the illustrations is detailed in the Acknowledgments.

Acknowledgments

Special thanks to Ralphe C. for invaluable editing, I wish him the best. Thanks to Samuela Jones for playing, MY, RBBNMM, and Whisper Cusack for the topic.

The author and publisher gratefully acknowledge permission to reproduce illustrations copyright material detailed below, designated by "Courtesy of" or "Author". For other illustrations the author has provided best available source information. The author and publishers apologize for any errors or omissions in the list below and would be grateful to be notified of any corrections that should be incorporated in the next edition or reprint of this book. Substantive efforts were made by the author to chase down the sources of all the illustrations reproduced in this book.

Cover Photo: Courtesy of Matthew Waranius.

1.1   Author: Ralphe C.
2.2   Author: Carmen M. Cusack.
2.3   Author: Cecil (Cecil William) Stoughton, 1920-2008, Photographer (NARA record: 4538278); current location, National Archives and Records Administration (NARA).
2.4   Author: Beverly & Pack. Retrieved from: https://www.flickr.com/photos/walkadog/3574847368/in/ photolist-xmmyVw-4o1sG3-4o1u6E-hzRZx-6rU2zs-j623zh- oG1iJd-opxt7t-xC8Tso-oE1fGC-opxsXF-9BdaQF-v3GQej
2.5   Author: Seaman Brooke Sauers, U.S. Coast Guard (https://www.dvidshub.net/image/1792792). Public domain, via Wikimedia Commons.
2.6   Author: USCG Historian's Office (U.S. Coast Guard photo). Public domain, via Wikimedia Commons.
3.1   Author: Wcawikinfo. A crib full of 2-3 week old baby grey-headed flying-foxes in care of Wildcare Australia at The Bat Hospital.
3.2   Attributed to flickr user atul666. Baby seal asleep on a beach near Lincoln City, Oregon.

3.3 Author: Jens Buurgaard Nielsen (Jensbn~commonswiki). Black-capped Squirrel Monkey (*Saimiri boliviensis*) with baby. Picture taken in Apenheul zoo, Apeldoorn, The Netherlands (May 2006). Public domain, via Wikimedia Commons.

5.1 Author: Stamatisclan. A sandy Flemish Giant male napping beside a sable-and-white Shetland Sheepdog. Public domain, via Wikimedia Commons.

6.1 Author: Venpia(https://commons.wikimedia.org/wiki/File: %EC%9A%B8%ED%94%84%EB%8F%852.jpg). Public domain, via Wikimedia Commons.

9.1 Author: Wolvix1965. Erect penis of male German Shepherd.

9.2 Author: Carmen M. Cusack.

10.1 No information about the photographer located on the web.

12.1 Author: Staff Sgt. Nicole Mickle (https://www.dvidshub. net/image/493913). Public domain, via Wikimedia Commons.

13.1 Author: Carmen M. Cusack.

14.1 Photo credit: DiningAddiction.com. Available at http://www.diningaddiction.com/bau-house-dog-cafe/

15.1 Author: Carmen M. Cusack.

Introduction

A truism is that American "kids, like all kids, love the dog" (Nixon, 1952). Babies and puppies effortlessly play together; and bonds between humans and dogs often last a lifetime. *Laws, Policies, Attitudes, and Processes That Shape the Lives of Puppies in America: Assessing Society's Needs, Desires, Values, and Morals* discusses how American laws and policies are designed to honor dogs' importance to humans. American culture may expect humans to use laws and policies to treat all dogs, including puppies, like family members; and offer to some dogs better quality of life than is available for human companions. For example, some dogs may be humanely euthanized to prevent suffering throughout a terminal illness; however, medically assisted suicide for terminally ill humans is verboten in most jurisdictions. Preference and privilege for dogs is tempered against a weak bundle of protections classifying dogs as property not persons. Though dogs are immune from legal responsibility, and may not be maltreated, they are denied rights and remedies. Despite subordination throughout the history of human civilizations, dogs have been deified, glorified, and celebrated in religion, art, entertainment, and other facets of human societies, many of which have been inherited—in some form or another—by American culture.

Each chapter in *Laws, Policies, Attitudes, and Processes That Shape the Lives of Puppies in America: Assessing Society's Needs, Desires, Values, and Morals* is a limb in the central argument that innumerable outlooks, practices, and ideals contour puppies' and dogs' lives and status in the United States. Topics in this book mix law, social and behavioral science, criminal justice, history, anecdotes, food studies, and political science. Throughout *Laws, Policies, Attitudes, and Processes That Shape the Lives of Puppies in America: Assessing Society's Needs, Desires, Values, and Morals*, the terms "puppy" and "dog" may be used synonymously when shared and overlapping experiences are discussed; however, careful consideration is paid to puppies due to their lovability, trainability, vulnerability, and perfection.

Chapters One and Two discuss two of the most pervasive American mediums: art and transportation. Chapter One analyzes song lyrics; film; mythology; puppy-shaped art; and literature to propose that

American art reflects individual interpretation and a variety of cultural and subcultural influences, such that a generalized picture of puppies' lives in America cannot be ascertained. However, what is evident, is that human–puppy interactions provoke extreme emotions, such as exuberance, love, and disgust. Americans played momentous roles in the invention and promulgation of modern automobiles, airplanes, trains, bicycles, spacecrafts, and watercrafts. Chapter Two investigates puppies' presence and influence on these modes of transportation and their significance to the people, who navigate them and regulate them.

Chapters Three, Four, and Five discuss beasts dwelling inside civilization. Beasts may be humans, domesticated canines, or wild animals, who are unpitying or untamed. Chapter Three looks into respectful affairs between domesticated dogs and captive exotic animals seeming to defy prey-predator dichotomies. These relationships may also flout Americans' perceptions of puppies as being more like humans than wild animals even though dogs straddle humanity and the wilderness. Americans' treatment of dogs as members of the human family seems to be influenced by perception, as evidenced by their use of word "puppy" near exclusively to mean young dog although "pup" may describe young in numerous other species. In Chapter Four, puppy killers are analyzed according to intent, societal roles, and community relationships. Public response to puppy killing may be relevant to killers' status, authority, innocence, and wantonness. Cruelty, defensible killing, delinquency, and qualified immunity may seem to be defined by law and norms, but are often interpreted *post hoc* by courts and law enforcement agencies in contravention of public outcry. Laws forbidding or permitting killing, skinning, and trading dog hair and fur are discussed in Chapter Five. The federal government and several states limit or bar dog fur and hair markets, but the majority of jurisdictions are silent about intrastate sale, purchase, and trade. One reason may be that commodification of skinned dog fur and hair is taboo; and therefore, laws are unnecessary. Another reason is that many states have not had significant problems with dog fur and hair trade; however, fur from stray and farmed dogs has been imported from China, and Americans and Europeans have been misled by negligently and willfully mislabeled fur products.

Chapters Six through Ten look at complexities involved in interpersonal relationships, including families and handler-service dog relationships, in America. Chapter Six includes thorough analyses of how multifaceted areas of American civil and criminal law commodify, defend and shield, or inadequately protect puppies. Areas of law examined in Chapter Six include property, tax, estate and trust, administrative, animal, Constitutional, health, torts, and family law. Dog training is discussed in Chapter Seven. Children and adults suffering from debilitating phobias and mental disorders may rely on service dogs' assistance. Even though some neurotic dogs may require specific training to overcome neurosis, they may be suitable companions and service animals. Chapter Eight discusses policies and operations pursuant to America's War on Drugs affecting puppies, for example, who are poisoned by medical marijuana; implanted with drugs by narcotics smugglers; and sold by gang members, who deal drugs. Puppies, especially Beagles and stray dogs, may suffer animal experimentation in laboratories. Physiological similarities between babies and puppies; and sociosexual comparisons between puppies, dogs, children, and adults are discussed in Chapters Nine and Ten, which also examine findings possibly explaining parenting and bonding. Two sections in Chapter Nine may serve to compare Americans, who prefer dog "children" to having human children, with mass hysteria in rural India causing a false belief that contact with a dog may result in human impregnation by a dog; and one section in Chapter Ten compares compositions of baby milk replacer formula, puppy milk replacer formula, human milk, and dog milk to question whether interspecies wet nursing is viable and appropriate.

Chapters 11 through 14 comparatively delve into modern and ancient civilization to discuss how and why over the span of thousands of years, epochal norms and cultural standards have influenced, but not fundamentally changed humans' relationships with dogs and puppies. Seemingly timeless similarities provide evidence of humans' and domesticated dogs' inextricable and unchangeable interdependence. These chapters acutely analyze effects on working dogs and companion animals on technology; the meaning of justice; image, economic prosperity or misfortune; politics; and religion.

CHAPTER ONE

Art

Music

The term "puppy" has many definitions that extend beyond the description of a young dog. The word figuratively or literally may be interpretable by diverse audiences. "Puppy" may reference love, submission, frailty, or particular aspects of culture and interpersonal phenomenon discussed further in Chapters Three, Eight, and Thirteen. Some audience members may derive one meaning from lyrics while others interpret the same lyrics as having a distinct meaning. Interpretations may be individual, social, contextual, or cultural. Three examples of songs with lyrics using the term "puppy" are "Puppy Toy" performed by British musician Tricky (2008); "Craven Choke Puppy" performed by Jamaican musician Bob Marley (1992); and "Too Many Puppies" performed by the American rock band Primus (Claypool, LaLonde, & Alexander, 1990). Their diverse, yet overlapping, allusions may suggest various definitions and understandings of the word "puppy" within English-speaking cultures that could reveal or influence attitudes towards puppies (Heine, 2009).

Tricky's duet, "Puppy Toy," may describe people and dogs involved in dependent relationships. "'Again, we go round and round. I'll get the drinks. I guess it's always my round.' 'Can you get me that drink?'" (Tricky, 2008). The song could be interpreted by a dog handler to be about a service dog, who retrieves drinks (Grace, 2013; Youtube.com, 2010). "'Friends, girls, they come and go' . . . 'Got any cash?' 'She likes that money, boy! She needs a puppy toy'" (Tricky, 2008). The lyrics could be understood to describe a dog handler, who abstains from socializing, in order to afford toys for a service dog. A handler with post-traumatic stress disorder (PTSD) could interpret some lyrics to describe dissociative episodes and panic attacks. "'You stare and look confused . . . Won't love, won't care again.' 'Girl, you got a vicious tongue.' 'You're talking to me?' . . . 'Girl, you seem insecure' . . . 'Get your head right.' 'There's nothing wrong with me'" (Tricky, 2008). An assistance dog may lick a handler when traumatic memories have been triggered. At the beginning of a dissociative episode a handler suspiciously may view a service dog. A night terror related to PTSD is portrayed in a commercial for The Royal Dutch Guide Dog Foundation. In the commercial, a veteran is experiencing a nightmare in which he is wounded and trapped in carnage while another soldier is whimpering and licking him (KNGF, 2014). The veteran is stirred from his nightmare by his assistance dog, who is whimpering and licking him. The commercial demonstrates that service dogs momentarily may be confused with flashbacks. Even though Tricky's song was written by a British musician, the Dutch commercial illustrates that a lyrical interpretation applying to a service dog and handler's relationship may be understood by people fluently speaking English in other societies.

Bob Marley's song "Craven Choke Puppy" (1992) may be understood to have a number of different meanings in English and Jamaican Patois; thus, colloquial or symbolic use and interpretations of "puppy" could be multidimensional (Kripke, 1991). For example, Craven A is a brand of cigarettes sold in Jamaica. "Craven-a, go choke a puppy" could refer to poisoning and suffocation during animal testing, smoking, or secondhand smoke inhalation (Marley, 1992). The lyric could refer to deteriorative effects of teen rebellion on youth. The phrase "craven choke puppy" has been translated by Jamaican patois websites as meaning "[s]omeone who wants everything but when it's . . . [given] to them, they can't handle it," which may refer to corporate gluttony (Jamaican Proverb, 2014). Related is the phrase "crab'n choke puppy" possibly meaning that "[a] craven puppy will choke" or "[i]f you are greedy[, then] it can hurt you" (Wise Jamaican Proverbs, 2008). The implied meaning and phonology of "craven" seems to suggest "craving" (i.e. overwhelming want), and not necessarily the correct meaning of "craven" (i.e. contemptible coward). In each translation, a "puppy" may represent something desirable, which may be a unit of measurement, a goal, a lifestyle, or an object, etc., which in excess is corruptive. "Craven a-go choke puppy . . . So you want all for yourself alone, and you don't think about the other man" (Marley, 1992). The "puppy" may be a coveter, who is suffocated by excess; for example, a puppy may choke on an excessively large bone. Marley sings, "Can you dig it?" possibly asking whether the "puppy" can live frugally rather than hoard wealth (Marley, 1992). "The craven dog will lose his bone . . . [running] after something else. Can't take it for themselves alone. They don't think about the other man" (Marley, 1992). Marley symbolically may refer to devaluation of property or interpersonal relationships.

Primus' song "Too Many Puppies" seems to be about America's foreign wars, violence, and oppression (Claypool, LaLonde, & Alexander, 1990). "Too many puppies are being shot in the dark. Too many puppies are trained not to bark at the sight of blood that must be spilled so that we may maintain our oil fields . . . Too many puppies are taught to heel. Too many puppies are trained to kill on the command of men wearing money belts" (Claypool, LaLonde, & Alexander, 1990). The lyrics may be a social commentary about the role of military working dogs and veteran assistance dogs. "Too many puppies are just like me . . . afraid to see the visions of the past brought to life again" may describe PTSD flashbacks experienced by deployed military working dogs and human military (e.g. soldiers) (Claypool, LaLonde, & Alexander, 1990).

Film

Dog-themed films may differ in their depictions of dogs as heroes and victims from films in which storylines about humans are the predominant focus and dogs are jokes. In dog-centric films, humans may attempt to balance burgeoning domestic life, which includes dogs' companionship. This is discussed in detail throughout Chapter Nine. However, dogs typically must evade societal problems and endure speciesism. Through this paradigm, Walt Disney films subtly have commented on dog–human problems, such as dog abduction, breeding, pet stores, animal control, dog fur, killing and other pertinent and complex topics discussed in Chapters Five and Six. For example, in the animated film "One Hundred and One Dalmatians," Cruella De Vil, who is called "devil woman" by Dalmatian Pongo, attempts to steal and skin Pongo and Perdita's puppies in order to manufacture a fur coat (Walt Disney, 1961). The names Pongo and Perdita (i.e. Perdy) insinuate "pongo" and "perdida" meaning "I set/place/apply" and "to be lost," respectively, in Spanish, which describe the Dalmatians' toils (Walt Disney, 1961). Cruella and her goons shock the audience's conscience, and film characters are appalled by the thought of puppy fur and dog torture, discussed in Chapter Four. Two Disney characters from "Lady and the Tramp," Peg and Bull, a Pekingese and a Bulldog, respectively, briefly make cameos in a pet store window in "One Hundred and One Dalmatians" during a scene in which local dogs network to locate the stolen Dalmatian puppies; but in "Lady and the Tramp" Peg and Bull face extermination while they are imprisoned in an animal shelter (Walt Disney, 1955; Walt Disney, 1961). "One Hundred and One Dalmatians" may suggest that dogs in pet stores are the same dogs in animal shelters, who are not purchased or adopted, or in Lady's case, who are lost or stray (Walt Disney, 1961). Lady and other characters from "Lady and the Tramp" (e.g. Tramp and Jock) also appear in "One Hundred and One Dalmatians" to relay information about the whereabouts of the missing puppies (Walt Disney, 1955; Walt Disney, 1961). Their appearance in specific locations germane to the plot of "Lady and the Tramp" provides evidence that Disney purposefully illustrated Peg and Bull in a pet store in "One Hundred and One Dalmatians" (Walt Disney, 1955; Walt Disney, 1961). Jock, a Scottish Terrier, emerges from his doghouse into his fenced backyard; and Lady and Tramp, an American Cocker Spaniel and a mixed-breed, respectively, together appear to be stray outside the pet store. In "One Hundred and One Dalmatians," 84 of the 99 Dalmatian puppies had been purchased at pet stores by Cruella or her thugs (Walt Disney, 1961). The film implies that mass breeding and puppies' status as property may make them vulnerable to torture and murder. This message contrasts, and yet reinforces, Disney's commentary in "Lady and the Tramp" on extermination of dogs and puppies in animal shelters (Walt Disney, 1955).

Human-centered films tend peripherally and reductively to depict dogs and puppies. Graphic focus on dog feces is not uncommon in American comedy, but a few widely viewed films, such as "Pink Flamingos" and "American Wedding" (i.e. "American Pie III"), morbidly depict scat or coprophagia appealing to voyeurism and juvenility (Cusack, 2012; Dylan, 2003; Waters, 1972). For example, an Adam Sandler movie, "Billy Madison," depicts a human stomping on dog feces (Davis, 1995). Billy Madison's *modus operandi* is to place paper bags filled with feces onto victims' porches and set the bags on fire. When victims attempt to stomp out fires, they are smeared by dog feces. Liberally repeated dialogue from this scene includes, "He called the shit "poop!"; "Don't put it out with your boots, Ted!"; and "Don't tell me my business, devil woman!" (Davis, 1995). Later in the film, after Billy Madison attempts to earn a high school education, he humiliatingly analogizes to the industrial revolution a children's story about puppies. Madison, who has the intellectual acumen of a third grader, selects the category "Reflections of Society and Literature" during a Jeopardy-type game played against his nemesis Eric Gordon (Davis, 1995).

> Game Host: Mr. Madison, the Industrial Revolution changed the face of the modern novel forever. Discuss, citing specific examples.
> Billy Madison: Uh, Okay. The Industrial Revolution to me is just like a story I know called The Puppy Who Lost His Way. The world was changing, and the puppy was getting bigger.
> [Time lapse]

So, you see, the puppy was like industry. In that, they were both lost in the woods, and nobody, especially the little boy—"society"—knew where to find them, except that the puppy was a dog, but the industry, my friends, that was a revolution.
Game Host: Mr. Madison, what you have just said is one of the most insanely idiotic things I have ever heard. At no point in your rambling, incoherent response were you even close to anything that could be considered a rational thought. Everyone in this room is now dumber for having listened to it. I award you no points, and may God have mercy on your soul.
Billy Madison: Okay, a simple "wrong" would've done just fine (Davis, 1995).

This scene is so well-known in American culture, that is was footnoted 11 years after "Billy Madison" by a Texas judge, who denied a bankruptcy motion due to incomprehensibility (King v. King, 2006).

Or, in the words of the competition judge to Adam Sandler's title character in the movie, "Billy Madison," after Billy Madison had responded to a question with an answer that sounded superficially reasonable but lacked any substance,

Mr. Madison, what you have just said is one of the most insanely idiotic things I have ever heard. At no point in your rambling, incoherent response were you even close to anything that could be considered a rational thought. Everyone in this room is now dumber for having listened to it. I award you no points, and may God have mercy on your soul.
Deciphering motions like the one presented here wastes valuable chamber staff time, and invites this sort of footnote. (King v. King, 2006).

The scene in "Billy Madison" and the court's citation are sophomoric and acerbic, two characteristics occasionally observed to be detrimental to the American justice system and society (Davis, 1995).

Mythology

Dog myths have been used for millennia to propagate religion, reproductive rituals, and other foundations of human civilization, but American culture tends to diminish the importance and influence of ancient mythology (Cusack, 2015; Fontenrose, 1981; Johns, 2008; White, 1991). For example, Valentine's Day (i.e. Saint Valentine's

Day) celebrated in the United States as a secular holiday may have evolved from puppy sacrifice and Roman mythology about a wolf (Volo, 2015). The Feast of Lupercalia celebrated Faunus, god of agriculture; and Rome's founder Romulus and his twin Remus were honored by a fertility sacrifice of a goat. A ritual involved boys using blood soaked strips of goat flesh to slap fields and spank women; and a dog was sacrificed during a purification ritual inside a cave where the twins allegedly were suckled by a wolf. Drawing from an urn, people would choose partners' names with whom they would mate during the next year; thus, February 14 allegedly became known as the annual date on which reproduction began.

The most widespread dog myth may be the hound of hell, Cerberus, readily recognizable to Americans as the character Fluffy in *Harry Potter* (Bloomfield, 1905; Rowling, 1997). Beyond the land of dreams and gates of the sun, a dark realm called Hades was said to be inhabited by spent souls, who crossed the River of Woe without their bodies (Bloomfield, 1905). Greeks represented Cerberus using many descriptions, including some descriptions of Cerberus as passive; but many myths about the hound of hell, such as the description provided by Homer, said that the vicious dog of Hades ravaged flesh. Early in the myth's development, he was depicted as having 50 heads. Greek poetry described the hound of hell as having three heads and snakes on his back; and some Greek pottery, statues, and sarcophagi depict a single- or double-headed dog, such as a collie, with a reptile's tail. Cerberus may be depicted with snakes, who have been used to symbolize the afterlife in numerous ancient and modern civilizations, including America; and also associated with dog-faced water snakes in the *Cerberus* family. Romans also associated Cerberus with serpents and with guarding the dark kingdom. Romans consistently depicted the dog as having three forms, such as three fused bodies, necks, tongues, jaws, or heads. An explanation of three-headed Cerberus (i.e. Kerberos) is that the dog may have had two puppies, who doted on Cerberus causing the trio to appear to be a three-headed dog. This explanation may be reminiscent of the holy trinity because one entity may be the same as three entities via perception and fatherhood. Cerberus' three heads have symbolized infancy, juvenility, and old age. Tellingly, Americans are said only to be certain of death and taxes; and have joked that owning the three-headed hound of hell could save owners on a dog tax because Cerberus would only count as one dog. However, if the American government were to attempt to seize the other two dogs, then the owner would be able to claim damages from the government for the destruction of two dogs, further discussed in Chapter Six. At trial, the government's witness rigorously would be cross-examined, maintaining that Cerberus is three dogs; but then, opposing counsel would inquire as to why the witness referred to Cerberus using one name and singular pronouns. This humor suggests that America's bureaucracy and adversarial legal system could puncture the veil and deflate the aura around ancient mythology.

Puppy-shaped Art

Several famous contemporary works of art have depicted puppies through media including balloons, steel, flowers, and graffiti. Balloons pervade American culture (e.g. birthdays and holidays), and therefore, may be compatible with puppies, who are extremely popular. For example, the Macy's Thanksgiving Day Parade has included the following dogs: Frieda the Dachshund; Lucky Pup; Underdog; Snoopy; Clifford The Big Red Dog; Goofy; Beethoven; Spike from "Rugrats"; "Blue's Clues"; Scooby Doo; and Jake from "Adventure Time" (Hadge, 2014). American artist Jeff Koons' *Balloon Dog* (12 ft. x 10 ft. x 4 ft.) is a brightly colored stainless steel and reflective metallic sculpture designed in the shape of one of the most popular balloon animals, a dog. Koons made *Balloon Dog* before creating less expensive balloon animals. The use of stainless steel to reproduce a widely recognized effigy of a dog embodies Americans' view of dogs as animals, toys, and aesthetically pleasing objects. *Balloon Dog* was not Koons' exclusive foray into puppies' immense cultural resonance. Koons' second most notable work is *Puppy*. By combining a steel substructure with an overcoat of fresh flowers, Koons produced a 43-foot sculpture of a sitting puppy. Flowers, a universal medium, captured the essence of terriers' soft and scruffy coats while the steel support bolstered the sculpture to achieve terriers' stillness and unwavering assuredness. *Puppy* was displayed by the Guggenheim Museum Bilbao in Spain where terrorists attempted to disguise themselves as gardeners to transport flowerpots containing grenades and machine-guns into the museum, but their plan was foiled, and *Puppy* was unharmed (Robinson, n.d.).

The graffiti artist known as Banksy has allegedly commented on dogs by using stencils to create public murals in the United States and abroad. A sign announces that a guard is on duty in "Police Guard Pink Balloon Dog" (Ansley, 2015). In the foreground, a pink balloon dog is muzzled and leashed by a handler, who appears to be a guard or officer. The title and subject overtly refer to Koons' *Balloon Dog*. "Police Guard Pink Balloon Dog" may comment on frivolity and illusion correlating with excessively alert or hypersensitive responses to

1.1 Dirty Dawg nose art at Texas Air & Space Museum

deviance (Ansley, 2015). Another work attributed to Banksy, "Choose Your Weapon Dog," depicts a hooded human wearing a bandana to cover his or her nose and mouth; the attire hides the human's age, race, and sex (Ansley, 2015). The human is walking Keith Haring's "Barking Dog." Banksy's work comments on inauthenticity and appropriation. In "Banksy Cop Dog Graffiti Area" a leashed poodle working as a K-9 stands under a sign saying "This wall is a designated graffiti area" (Ansley, 2015). The poodle's leash is stretched to demonstrate distance from the handler. Banksy has been quoted as saying "Dogs are the original graffiti artists" (Ansley, 2015). This work may insinuate that police dogs perpetrate graffiti by urinating on objects in public. "You Complete Me, New York City" depicts a dog urinating on a fire hydrant to leave "pee-mail" for another animal—the message is "You complete me" (Ansley, 2015). The work comments on animals' emotions and communication. "Wet Dog, New York City" is a carefully splashed black background with a white dog shaking water off his or her fur in the foreground (Ansley, 2015). Like Banksy's commentary on dog urine equating to graffiti, this alleged Banksy work may suggest that mud shaken from a dog's fur acts like graffiti; perhaps the message is an insult to order. In "HMV Dog with Rocket Gramophone," Nipper, as depicted in the painting *His Master's Voice* and corporate logos, points his muzzle toward a phonograph while listening to music or spoken word (Ansley, 2015). In Banksy's portrait, the dog aims a rocket launcher at the phonograph possibly suggesting that dogs could or will use weapons. Images of dogs and the word "dog" (e.g. "Dirty Dawg") have been depicted on weapons, such as military aircraft (Texas Air & Space Museum, 2015). Symbolically, dogs have been mechanized and weaponized through pilots' nose art, which is a form of graffiti. Only some generations of military and American culture have tolerated nose art.

Literature

Some of literature's appeal is that it is transportive and timelessly reflects contemporary Americans' problems, perspectives, and attitudes. For example, Miguel de Cervantes' *Dialogue of the Dogs* memorializes his epoch by commenting on human–animal relationships in 17th century Spain (de Cervantes, 2003). Berganza and Scipio, two dogs guarding a hospital, narrate the master-servant paradox manifested in humans' debilities and dogs' physiological buoyancy. The dogs describe how wretched humans impose onto dogs subservient social status by manipulating external and internal controls. In the United States, law and culture instill appreciation and respect for working dogs, yet dogs continue to be vulnerable to maltreatment when internal and external controls fail to deter cruelty. While some imperial Spaniards may have unrepentantly mistreated dogs in ways that are currently illegal in the United States, American dogs presently seem to be torturable in new ways, such as licensed puppy mill breeding facilities, which may be relatively compatible with American capitalist society and consumerist culture (Cusack, 2015; de Cervantes, 2003; Proctor, 2014). Numerous American and European dogs have been treated as family, and sometimes, virtually like royalty, which is discussed further in Chapter Nine. For example, in 18th century Mexico "particular puppies were clearly beloved, as dressing them up in petticoats and bejewelled collars suggests. This stands in stark contrast to the treatment of dogs in . . . the portrayal of dogs' lives in Cervantes' *Dialogue*, where Berganza and Scipio, the main characters, were clearly working dogs" (Proctor, 2014, p. 22).

> [Poor dogs'] experiences were defined by work and significant abuse. If this portrayal can stand as a representation of the nature of the canine–human relationship in the early seventeenth-century Spanish world, it would seem that some Spaniards in . . . Mexico City had developed bonds with their dogs that were quite new and that appear quite familiar to the modern reader. Most importantly, these dog owners were not members of the colonial elite, but middling and plebeian Spaniards who had adopted pet-keeping practices from the Spanish aristocracy. (Proctor, 2014, p. 24)

In the Americas, immigrants may have been able to improve treatment of middle class and poor dogs due to their ability to flout traditional class roles (Proctor, 2014). Presently, working and companion dogs in Europe and the New World may be treated similarly to wealthy dogs, for example, considered to be family members. Despite some varying expectations for human–animal relationships that may have reflected class and society's needs, Americans acknowledge inheritance of human–dog relationships from Europeans, discussed further in Chapters 13 and 14. Dogs may have evolved from wolves in Europe before the existence of the land of Christendom. Thus, this human–dog legacy may be evident in areas of American art and culture relating to European history or dogs. One court synopsized the timelessness of dogs' importance to European Americans' art and culture.

> Whatever one may think of treating our dogs like people — whether it is called "humanification," "personhood," or some other means of endowing dogs with humanlike qualities — it is impossible to deny the place they have in our hearts, minds and imaginations. From Odysseus's ever-faithful dog Argo in Homer's *The Odyssey*, to the All-American collie Lassie, to the Jetsons' futuristic canine Astro, to Dorothy's little dog Toto too, they are beloved figures in literature, movies and television. And in real life, where would we be without St. Bernards and their casks of brandy in the Alps, Pavlov's conditioned-response subjects, Balto the hero sled-dog racing to the rescue in the Arctic, or, of course, the Nixon daughters' little [Cocker Spaniel] Checkers? (Travis v. Murray, 2013, p. 451)

Classic and contemporary literature may reveal and affirm that dogs are not only like humans because of mutual history, but also because of shared lives (Pickert, 2011).

CHAPTER TWO

Transportation

Automobiles

Many dogs (e.g. puppies) enjoy car rides; and Americans' fondness of riding with their dogs is evident in American culture (Crothers, 2013). For example, pets have become a new market for products made for cars, such as car seats, non-spill water bowls, seat covers, hot car detectors, and ramps (Cusack, 2015). Despite Americans' partiality for driving with dogs, each year millions of dogs may be injured and killed by cars (Braunstein, n.d.; Gaskill, 2013). A study of 259 dogs found that a history of automobile accidents increased the likelihood of dogs experiencing seizures (Friedenberg, et al., 2012). Ohio State University Veterinary Medical Center evaluated dogs, who presented with head trauma, between 1999 and 2009. The epilepsy rate for dogs at the hospital, which was one and four-tenths percent, was compared to data, physical examination records, comorbidities, and neurologic findings of dogs with head trauma. Three and one-half percent of dogs developed seizures while at the hospital; and were likelier to have been hit by cars or to have been injured during acceleration or deceleration. One tenth of dogs with traumatic brain injuries experienced seizures while in the hospital; however, nearly seven percent of dogs experienced seizures after being discharged from the hospital. Research has demonstrated that trauma and injury related to automobile accidents commonly result in neurological and physical dysfunction (Mendes & Arias, 2012). Records from animals presenting with spinal cord trauma between August 2009 and November 2010 at a veterinary hospital were analyzed for risk factors, recovery time, drug side effects, complications, and patient improvement. Forty eight dogs and nine cats were analyzed; among these, 66% had been hit by cars. Within eight hours of injury, 42% of patients had presented for care; however, 51% delayed more than one day. Animals' thoracolumbar spines were affected in 52% of cases. Fewer than half of animals (20) were euthanized; four animals did not recover; four animals died; and eight required surgery. Immobilization and rest were prescribed for 29 animals, and 72% experienced positive outcomes. Seventeen (59%) animals completely recovered; and 14% of animals partially recovered. Thus, conservative treatments were highly successful, especially in dogs with trauma to their cervical regions.

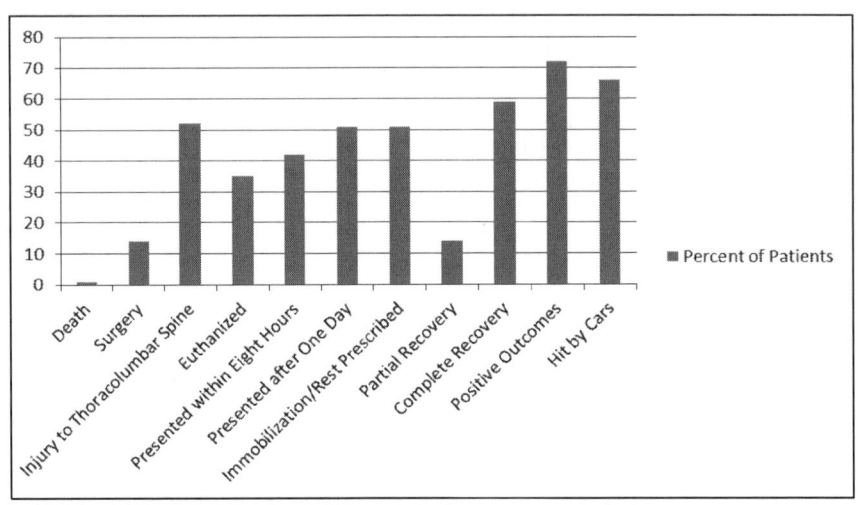

2.1 Spinal Cord Trauma (2009–2010)

Run-over rates have been studied extensively for birds, amphibians, reptiles, small mammals, and large mammals, including wolves, yet run-over rates for puppies and dogs are limited. One reason may be that detection is higher and removal may be quicker (Harro-Loit & Ugur, 2011). Another explanation may be that because dogs are not protected species their numbers are not routinely studied (Teixeira, et al., 2013).

Run-over rates may be associated with traffic density; location and geographic features, such as alligators mortally injured while crossing roads through bayous; species; and other factors (Cusack, 2015; Garcia, et al., 2012). Animals may be likelier to be killed on roads within protected areas than unprotected areas. This may be because protected areas, such as national parks, are patronized by visitors, who significantly increase certain species' exposure to traffic. Detectability and removal rates may vary according to species, body size, scavenger activity, and location where animals die after being run-over; for example, one estimate showed that mortality rates for birds was likely to be 39 times higher than detectability and removal (Teixeira, et al., 2013). Furthermore, in some regions, feral and stray dogs may actually consume roadkill or kill animals believed to have been killed by cars (Badrul, et al., 2013). Certain species are likelier to be killed in particular crossing areas or portions of the road; for example, some species of frogs may be 35% likelier to be run-over in the middle of a road than on a road's edge (Beckmann & Shine, 2015; Milla, et al., 2014; Teixeira, et al., 2013). Species may possibly influence motorists' decisions to aid animals in the roadway. One study hypothesized that decoy chicks were run-over less and aided more than decoy spiders and snakes because decoy chicks appeared to be more charismatic (Mesquita, et al., 2015). The power of infantile charisma is discussed in Chapter Nine. Another explanation may be that some motorists believed that snakes and spiders possibly were venomous (Cusack, 2015). Avoiding poisonous species is rational because contact with venomous animals and insects resulted in 348 human deaths between 1999 and 2013; and that envenomation is likelier to relate to Americans' deaths than any other kind of contact with animals or insects.

Group behavior influences puppies' road crossing and run-over rates. Domesticated puppies crossing roads alone may be likelier to be hit by automobiles than puppies crossing in packs (Griffiths & Silberberg, 1975; Jackson & Fahrig, 2011; Roger, Gilad, & Ramp, 2012). This reality may be intuitive for Americans living in dog–human families that only allow puppies accompanied by adults to cross roads; and this knowledge may also be institutionalized by the American government, which, for example, requires dogs to be leashed while walking on roads passing through Death Valley National Park, California; Grand Canyon National Park, Arizona; Guadalupe Mountains National Park, Texas; Sierra National Forrest, California; Yosemite National Park, California; and other federal lands (Cusack, 2015). Anecdotal evidence demonstrates almost no dog run-over rates in these federal parks and that road kill is uncommonly detected by motorists; however federal parks report that solitary mammals crossing roads are frequently hit by automobiles (Weaver, 2009). The "safety in numbers" theory was tested during a 29-month study of primates, which examined paved roads in the Sebitoli area of Kibale National Park, Uganda (Cibot, et al., 2015). Every hour, 89 motorized vehicles drove through the area, annually killing six species of primates. Research examined chimpanzees' behavior during 122 individual crossings. Over 90% of chimpanzees looked left and right prior to crossing the road; also looked both ways while crossing; and crossed in two or three subgroups that had approximately two individuals in each group. Healthy adult males were likeliest to be solitary crossers; but, they were likelier to lead conspecifics across roads than up trees. Approximately one-fifth of chimpanzees waited for, and made visual contact with, other chimpanzees crossing the road. Increased numbers of individuals directly correlated with increased rapidity, but young chimpanzees, females with dependents, and injured chimpanzees were less likely to cross roads. Puppies may more safely cross roads with adults and experienced dogs than with human children. One hundred and nineteen school children between the ages of seven years old and 12 years old were asked to classify 20 images according to road safety (Underwood, et al., 2007). Younger children were likelier idiosyncratically to view roads by focusing on structural characteristics and individuals depicted in the images, which may demonstrate why they are vulnerable to traffic. Some dogs expertly cross roads and may assist others to cross; for example, Patches worked as a crossing guard in Pennsylvania (Tan, 2015). In another example, a driver captured a photo of "a larger, older and wiser dog" protecting a puppy from oncoming traffic by pulling on the puppy's tail to prevent the puppy from entering a roadway (Life with Dogs, 2015).

Airplanes

American culture and changes in American society are evident in airline policies and flying procedures affecting dogs (e.g. puppies). Highly restrictive regulations were implemented after September 11, 2001 (i.e. 9/11 terrorist attack); but, they have recently been relaxed, for example, by rules permitting emotional support animals to travel outside crates while onboard planes. Arguably, as a result of 9/11, flying has become less luxurious and caused greater strain; thus, support may be reasonable for some emotionally or mentally ill passengers. Nevertheless, some evidence demonstrates backlash from cabin crews and passengers due to overcrowding (Witz, 2013).

> Classifying animals as emotional support animals has long been permitted under antidiscrimination laws, allowing owners to take them into restaurants and shops or to residential buildings that have no-pet policies. To demonstrate the need for an emotional support animal, the animal's owner needs a letter from a mental health professional. But their presence on airplanes is increasingly facing a backlash from flight attendants, passengers with allergies and owners of service animals, like [s]eeing [e]ye dogs, who say that airplane cabins have become crowded with uncaged animals who have no business being there. The Department of Transportation does not require airlines to keep data on emotional support animals. (Witz, 2013)

Despite recent accommodations for emotional support animals, civil rights complaints continue to allege violations of the Americans with

Disabilities Act (ADA) affecting service animals (104 § 327, 1990; Lou, 2015). Though American airlines must permit animal companions to fly without muzzles, some airlines reserve the right to request that muzzles be worn in certain circumstances; however, improper enforcement of this policy may violate the ADA or state laws in some cases (104 § 327, 1990). Highly disruptive or dangerous service animals may be prohibited from public places or businesses under the ADA; however well-behaved service animals cannot be prohibited from public places or businesses because they are unmuzzled (104 § 327, 1990). Thus, airlines may ask disabled individuals to choose either to muzzle dangerous or unruly service animals or fly without their service animals. Although some pilots, flight attendants, or passengers may fear or resent dogs, the ADA preempts airline polices and preferences, even when individuals aboard planes are afraid that a well-behaved dog potentially could bite or become a nuisance (104 § 327, 1990; Boortz, 2010; *The Sun*, 2015). Despite some resistance to dogs aboard airplanes, heightened security protocols have resulted in increased use of detection dogs throughout baggage and disembarkation areas. Some airports, such as Miami International Airport in Florida, employ dogs as greeters at security checkpoints to relax passengers, but not necessarily to detect contraband (Westenberg, 2014).

Typically, airlines and airports garner goodwill by accommodating dogs or publically demonstrating their appreciation for dogs. Some airlines have installed dog-friendly outdoor areas inside passenger terminals. For example, JetBlue Airways added a rooftop outdoor park at John F. Kennedy (JFK) Airport in New York that "focuses on sustainability, convenience and humanity," which also makes it beneficial to non-pet owners (Professional Services Close–Up, 2015). Several airlines offer onboard entertainment depicting live and simulated animals. For example, British Airways offers Paws and Relax channel depicting puppies, some of whom appear to be cuddled by British Airways crewmembers (*The Telegraph*, 2014). Like JFK's rooftop outdoor park, the purpose of this onboard entertainment allegedly is to "enhance the wellbeing of customers" (*The Telegraph*, 2014). British Airways said, "It might sound barking, but there's lots of research to suggest that watching pets can enhance overall wellbeing. We have sniffed out some fantastic content that is cute, comforting and sure to appeal to [travelers] of all ages" (*The Telegraph*, 2014). In addition to *America's Cutest Dog*, a television show featuring "adorable footage of dogs at play," the Paws and Relax channel also depicts recordings from hidden cameras, cartoons, and documentaries about dogs (*The Telegraph*, 2014).

Airlines publically have been remiss when puppies have been killed, injured, or lost; yet United States policymakers and enforcement agencies have been relatively uncommitted until recently to the development or enforcement of effective policies protecting animals aboard flights. For example, in 2010, 14 puppies were sent aboard American Airlines from Tulsa, Oklahoma to Chicago, Illinois during the month of August (*Chicago Tribune*, 2010). At O'Hare International Airport in Chicago, baggage handlers reported that the puppies appeared to be ill, and seven subsequently died of overheating. Overheating is a common cause of death for dogs on airplanes, especially during layovers when cargo holds are not properly ventilated (Bellandi, 1990).

American Airlines defended by claiming that they had complied with requirements for transporting animal cargo shipments during hot weather; and they supported their claim by demonstrating that ten other puppies had salubriously flown in a different shipment on the same flight (*Chicago Tribune*, 2010). The United States Department of Agriculture investigated the incident, but the results of their investigation were not publicized.

Congress has stated that consumers have a right to know rates at which airlines kill, injure, or lose animals, including dogs; animal welfarists and dog owners suggest that public knowledge of these rates would deter recklessness. In 2000, a reporting requirement bill was named after Boris, a boxer-pit bull severely injured in a cargo hold (49 U.S.C. § 41721, 2012). The Boris Bill, which essentially addressed mistreatment of dogs, required training for airline employees; and required airlines to report animal death, loss, and injury to Department of Transportation (DOT), which was to circulate the data in order to inform consumers about safety risks. The bill was weakened when DOT strictly narrowed the definition of "animal" to identify pets traveling in cargo holds while human companions simultaneously travelled in flight cabins. The narrowed definition failed to deter airlines from annually losing, injuring, or killing thousands of puppies. Animals transported by breeders, such as those flying through O'Hare International Airport in 2010 or travelling to dog shows, were excluded from reporting requirements; thus, those deaths, losses, and injuries were invisible to consumers. This was particularly problematic because animals travelling as cargo were susceptible to airline negligence resulting in animals overheating. The definition of "animal" was eventually revised to include non-pets and further distinguish baggage from animals travelling aboard passenger planes in cargo holds (49 U.S.C. § 41721, 2012). In 2012, United States Congress and DOT publically praised efforts to expand requirements for reporting animal death, injury, and loss (Menendez, 2012). Senator Robert Menendez identified why the definition of "animal" needed to be expanded. "A dog is a dog is a dog, whether he's on his way to a dog show, a pet store or vacation with the family. Consumers deserve to know just how safely airlines transport animals so they can make informed choices" (Menendez, 2012). Senator Dick Durbin articulated Americans' sense of accountability toward pets.

> No matter where they are going or who they are going with, our nation's pets deserve to be treated with care and consideration when traveling on an airplane. I commend . . . taking action to expand reporting requirements to better protect our pets and provide consumers the information they need in order to make the right choice for their pets when they travel. (Menendez, 2012)

Senator Joe Lieberman's comment resonated with Americans' sentiments about dogs, which influence policies affecting other animals.

> It is tragic that an animal would ever be treated cruelly or callously in transit . . . Too many pets have already suffered such mistreatment, and I hope that the Transportation Department's proposed rule-making will provide Americans with more information about airline animal safety efforts. (Menendez, 2012)

Propaganda for policy changes was fronted by several compelling stories about puppies, who had suffered.

> Maggie Mae, a West Highland terrier puppy, flew in the cargo hold of a 2008 . . . and was tragically crushed to death during a flight transfer at Atlanta's Hartsfield-Jackson International Airport. Since the breeder was a commercial owner and not a family household, Maggie Mae did not fit the definition of "animal" under current regulations.
>
> In another incident, Illinois resident Mr. James Hough was awaiting the arrival of a Neapolitan mastiff puppy from a breeder when he was informed that the puppy died en route aboard a . . . flight. Even though the mastiff puppy was being delivered from the breeder to its new owner, the airline did not have to report the incident because it was a commercial shipment and not technically considered an "animal" under these requirements.
>
> Thankfully, you have acted on this issue and now propose to expand the definition of the word "animal" to include dogs . . . sent

commercially via a U.S. passenger air carrier. Furthermore, we are glad that the number of U.S. air carriers that will be required to report will increase from 15 to 36 carriers. These sensible changes to current regulations better match the intent of the Boris Bill and will protect many more animals. (Menendez, 2012)

Policy changes generated positive responses from some airlines that promised to further research and better respond to dogs' transportation needs. Delta, for example, which was responsible for comparatively high numbers of deaths, eliminated passengers' option to transport dogs inside cargo holds (Bratskeir, 2015; Delta Cargo, n.d.). Small dogs may travel on board as luggage placed beneath a passenger's seat; and medium and large dogs may travel separately in climate controlled vans and aboard cargo flights. However, Delta's cargo pet shipping service costs several times more than the charge for flying dogs in the cargo hold of a passenger flight.

Trains

Puppies and dogs are associated with trains in several ways that tend to demonstrate harsher sides of American society. For example, debates have fulminated for years about admittance of dogs on passenger trains; yet, unlike airlines' recent accommodations for dogs, admittance on trains has not generally become more widespread or flexible. Another example is that train-hoppers (i.e. riders), who illegally ride freight trains, may be likelier to be ejected from freight trains when travelling with puppies than without puppies. Some train-hoppers travel with dogs for companionship, protection, and sympathy; however their dogs' may be subjected to poverty, homelessness, and malnutrition. Train-hopping dogs may be pitiable making them assets for panhandling train-hoppers.

Puppies may be killed by trains when they are tied to train tracks; are off-leash; or escape from homes. Repercussions for these events vary according to circumstance, jurisdiction, and local culture. Tragedies involving puppies and trains are not limited to the United States; and yet, localized responses in foreign jurisdictions sometimes resemble Americans' responses to lethal train accidents. For example, train officials in Hong Kong, China claimed that trains were prevented from entering a train station as workers attempted to help a dog from the tracks (Liu, 2014). This response is congruent with actions that some, but not all, American localities would take (Inquisitr, 2015). Chinese train officials also alleged that a staff member was injured in the process of assisting the dog; however officials could not locate the dog. They permitted trains to run on tracks where the dog had been seen, and consequently the dog was killed. However, protesters and the Society for Prevention of Cruelty to Animals said that photos supported witnesses' accounts that the dog attempted to climb from the tracks to a platform and that staff neglected to help and prevented passengers from assisting the dog. Protests and civil disobedience erupted in Hong Kong after it was alleged that a city train conductor knowingly struck the dog. Public tumult would be unlikely in the United States because the American public historically has been unlikely to riot or protest in response to any train collisions or public transportation accidents resulting in dogs' deaths. Furthermore, Americans may associate train tracks with lethality because of the regularity with which humans and animals are killed by trains. For example, two dogs in Texas were tied to train tracks after they had died; and one pit bull puppy was tied to train tracks after having been shot three times (Heinz, 2011; Inquisitr, 2015). Train traffic was halted so that the puppy, who survived, could be rescued. This response was similar to Hong Kong officials' initial response to a dog running loose on the tracks.

Dogs may be more vulnerable than other animals to train accidents because of their leashes, which may accidentally become tangled in tracks or intentionally may be tied to train tracks. For example, a train ran over a dog in a locality where two dogs had recently been killed, and several dogs had been tied to train tracks (Ewinger, 2012). Thus, officials at first suspected that the dog had been intentionally tied to the tracks, but investigators concluded that the dog's leash accidentally became wedged into the train tracks before the train was unable to stop. After being run-over, the dog was traumatized and defensive, but unscathed, and subsequently adopted.

Several humans have been killed by trains while chasing after their puppies; and yet, several dogs have survived these accidents. For example, a dog ran onto train tracks in Fresno, California (Lee, 2015). Although the dog's owner was able to signal to the train conductor that her dog was on the tracks, the train was unable to stop prior to striking and killing the woman. Also in California, former Del Mar Mayor Louis Terrell walked with his dog off-leash near an Amtrak train rail. Terrell's dog may have been frightened by the train's horn moments before running onto the tracks (Bacchus, Garske, & Wood, 2014). As Terrell attempted to apprehend his dog, he was killed by the train, however his dog survived. Similarly, a two-year-old boy was killed by a train that could not stop after he wandered onto train tracks with his pit bull puppy (Ghianni, 2015). The child and the puppy were taken to the hospital; however, only the puppy survived. Loss of canine life due to train collisions has not resulted in publicized policy changes in the United States.

Bicycles

Wizard of Oz begins with Dorothy Gale upset that Miss Gulch wants to destroy her Cairn terrier Toto because he chased a cat into Miss Gulch's garden and allegedly bit her. Miss Gulch appears to seize Toto by Sheriff's order so that he can be destroyed. Dorothy threatens to bite Miss Gulch before she grabs Toto and places him in her bicycle basket. Miss Gulch rides the only bicycle depicted in the film, while other characters rely on powered modes of transportation, including a horse-drawn carriage, hot air balloon, and automobiles. Along the way, Toto jumps from the bicycle basket, and runs home to Dorothy. Dorothy and Toto escape together on an adventure taking them to a dream world called Land of Oz where Miss Gulch is embodied by the Wicked Witch of the West, who rides a broomstick symbolizing a bicycle. Dorothy and Toto kill the Wicked Witch, steal her broomstick, and surrender it to the Wizard, who prepares a hot air balloon to fly them home to Kansas. As the group prepares to fly away, Toto jumps from Dorothy's arms to chase a Siamese cat thereby provoking Dorothy to exit the hot air balloon's basket and causing the hot air balloon prematurely to leave the Emerald City. Due to Toto's penchant for chasing cats and jumping from baskets, Dorothy and Toto are left behind in the Emerald City, but Glinda the Good Witch transports Dorothy and Toto home with three clicks of Dorothy's ruby red slippers. Toto's behavior and Dorothy's negligence may have been the proximate cause of problematic chains of events, yet *Wizard of Oz*'s implicit defense of Toto and Dorothy may demonstrate preference for dogs over bicyclists in spite of conflicted perspectives about liability for negligent dog owners.

Dogs and their owners may be held liable when dogs injure bicyclists. A few jurisdictions hold dog owners strictly liable for dog bites; yet typically, to determine negligence in bite or other personal injury cases, authorities consider an owner's knowledge of a dog's propensity for problematic behavior as a factor of negligence. For example, in New York, dog owners are only liable for injuries caused by vicious dogs when owners knew or should have known of their dogs' propensities. Thus, dog owners may not be liable for injuries accidentally caused by dogs to bicyclists. For example, one defendant held a dog on one side of a road in Central Park, New York while the other defen-

2.2 Mixed-breed dog in bicycle trailer

dant called their dog to cross the street just as a bicyclist was approaching (Doerr v. Goldsmith, 2013, 2015). The bicyclist crashed into the dog and sustained significant injuries. The owners were negligent in releasing their dog, who crossed the street in Central Park, but they were not liable because their dog did not bite the bicyclist. New York law only held owners strictly liable for damage caused by animals, who were known to have vicious tendencies. The decision was not without controversy. Initially in 2013, the court of appeals denied the defendant's motion for summary judgment.

[I]t is about the actions of a person that turned an animal into an instrumentality of harm. Here, the dog was in the control of defendants at all times in the split second before the accident occurred. Had [one defendant] not called the dog, and [the other defendant] not let it go, plaintiff would have ridden past them without incident. Defendants' actions can be likened to those of two people who decide to toss a ball back and forth over a trafficked road without regard to a bicyclist who is about to ride into the ball's path. If the cyclist collided with the ball and was injured, certainly the people tossing the ball would be liable in negligence. Simply put, this case is different from the cases addressing the issue of injury claims arising out of animal behavior, because it was defendants' actions, and not the dog's own instinctive, volitional behavior, that most proximately caused the accident. (Doerr v. Goldsmith, 2013, pp. 2–3)

The dissent said,

> We reversed the order denying [the] defendant['s] . . . motion for summary judgment dismissing the complaint on the ground that New York does not recognize a common-law negligence cause of action to recover damages for injuries caused by a domestic animal. Rather, the sole viable claim is for strict liability, and here there is no evidence that defendant had knowledge that her dog had a propensity to inter-fere with traffic [Internal citations omitted]. (Doerr v. Goldsmith, 2013, p. 3)

In 2015, the appellate court granted the defendant's motion.

> [Stare decisis] does not allow plaintiffs to recover based on defen-dants' purported negligence in the handling of their dogs, which were not domestic farm animals subject to an owner's duty to prevent such animals from wandering unsupervised off the farm . . . Defendants carried their initial burden on summary judgment of establishing that they did not know of any vicious propensities on the part of their dogs. In response, plaintiff failed to demonstrate the existence of a triable issue of fact as to whether defendants had notice of the animals' harmful proclivities, and consequently, defendants were entitled to summary judgment on plaintiff's strict liability claim [Internal cita-tions omitted]. (Doerr v. Goldsmith, 2015)

Thus, the dog's owners could not be held responsible under a law designed to protect the public from negligent owners of vicious dogs.

American case law discussing human liability for animals demon-strates litigiousness in American society; imperfect humaneness involved in animal ownership; animals' quasi-status as property; and Americans' willingness to shield dogs from punishment for untamed behavior. Americans may be particularly inclined to litigate deaths resulting from bicycle accidents because so few cyclists are killed annu-ally; for example, from 1999 to 2013, 24 pedal cyclists were reportedly killed by collisions with animals or humans (CDC, n.d.). Thus, the novelty and sense of unfairness present in some of these cases may catalyze lawsuits.

Space Race

In 2012, Russian President Vladimir Putin exchanged gifts with the Governor of Akita Prefecture in Japan, Norihisa Satake; President Putin gave to Governor Satake a Siberian kitten; and Governor Satake offered an Akita Inu puppy to President Putin (*Interfax*, 2012; *Interfax*, 2012). President Putin's gesture reflected a custom among Russian officials of presenting pets to foreign dignitaries. Soviet Premier (i.e. President) Nikita Khrushchev gave to President John F. Kennedy's daughter Caroline a puppy named Pushinka born from a canine cosmonaut, Strelka (Kemp, 2007).

2.3 Kennedy Family with dogs during a weekend at Hyannisport 1963. President Kennedy memorialized President Khrushchev's gift in a letter demonstrating diplomacy and gratitude for Pushinka.

President Khrushchev's diplomacy began at a state dinner when First Lady Jaqueline Kennedy asked President Khrushchev about Belka and Strelka (i.e. "Squirrel"/ "Whitey" and "Arrow" in English, respectively) (Gee, 2014; Presidential Pet Museum, 2013). Belka and Strelka were puppies when they travelled into space aboard Sputnik 2 in 1960. Soon after, President Khrushchev sent Pushinka (i.e. "Fluffy" in English) to the White House. Charlie, Caroline's Welsh Terrier, bred four puppies with Pushinka, who was mixed-breed; their puppies were named Streaker, Blackie, White Tips, and Butterfly, but President Kennedy sometimes referred to them as "pupniks" (Gee, 2014; Presidential Pet Museum, 2013). Butterfly and Streaker were given to children in the Midwest, who were chosen by the First Lady from 5,000 requests for puppies.

> Mrs. Kennedy and I were particularly pleased to receive "Pushinka." Her flight from the Soviet Union to the United States was not as dramatic as the flight of her mother, nevertheless, it was a long voyage and she stood it well. We both appreciate your remembering these matters in your busy life. (Gee, 2014)

It has been said that President Kennedy's public embrace of Pushinka symbolized his entrepreneurialism because "[e]ntrepreneurial presidents in democratic political systems are effective national leaders, a blend of the nimble lion and the shrewd fox, both carefully coated with a benign, puppy-dog-like exterior" (Walker, 1993, p. 61). Americans respond well to presidents like President Kennedy, who have been able to further Americans' foreign relations by demonstrating goodwill towards other species and cultures. "That is, we need lions that can be nimble in political maneuver who are cross-bred with foxes who shrewdly calculate the necessary ingredients for policy implementation and with lovable puppy dogs who can sustain the necessary elite and mass support to achieve their ends" (Walker, 1993, p. 70). President Kennedy's affection for Pushinka further ingratiated the Kennedy family to the American public and symbolized America's willingness to invest in long-term relations with the Soviet Union. Puppy dogs and politics are discussed further in Chapter 13.

President Khrushchev was not the only socialist during the space race to appeal to Americans by using a puppy. A puppy appeared in an interview of President Fidel Castro and Fidel Junior (i.e. "Fidelito") immediately after the triumph of the revolution (Attwood, 2002). A reporter said to Fidelito, "That's a very good-looking puppy you have there. Is he yours?" (Attwood, 2002). Fidelito replied, "No, somebody gave it to my father for a present" (Attwood, 2002). The puppy sat next to Fidelito while charmingly staring at President Castro, who briefly diverted all of his attention to his puppy and stroked his puppy's head during the interview. President Castro, who routinely appeared in military fatigues, wore pajamas while lounging on a sofa with his son and his puppy. The tone communicated President Castro's initially friendly intentions toward the United States.

Watercrafts and Ports

Mariners have reported dogs' importance for thousands of years (Galvani, 1994). In modern history, dogs' potency at sea is personified in the term "Sea Dog," most readily identified with the Virgin Queen Elizabeth, who recruited and deployed ruthless pirates during the mid1500s until the early 1600s (Dudley, 2013). The name Sea Dogs reciprocally illustrates the ferocity ascribed to dogs at sea and to Queen Elizabeth's sailors. Sea Dogs terrorized the Iberian coast, West Indies, and Pacific coast in Latin America. They were compared to "vicious curs no better than pirates and common thieves; but the Virgin Queen and her subjects knew them proudly as Elizabeth's Sea Dogs, guardians of England's shores" (Dudley, 2013). "Some of these great captains were born to wealth, some to poverty; many spent most of their lives afloat, while others came to the waves later in life; almost all were Protestant, and all were servants of a Protestant queen. They sought fame and fortune . . . while setting the stage for the rise of a British empire" (Dudley, 2013). Many recruits were poor and destitute, while some Sea Dogs became well-known, such as Sir Francis Drake, Sir John Hawkins, Sir Martin Frobisher, Sir Thomas Cavendish, Sir Richard Grenville, Sir Humphrey Gilbert, and Sir Walter Raleigh (Dudley, 2013). Just as Sea Dogs shaped England's colonies, canines continue to influence American mariners, vessels, and ports throughout the world.

Working dogs' presence on ships and at ports may reflect the climate of American military policy and culture; and the importance of dogs' reliability in the United States military. For example, the Marine Corps deploys working dogs on Marine Expeditionary Units (MEUs) (Hope, 2015). Dogs may stay aboard vessels for approximately nine months or transfer midway to kennels at ports, such as in Bahrain or Djibouti. Dogs, who may also work on aircraft deployed from vessels, may be trained to detect bombs, track people, attack, or fulfill other functions, such as boost morale. The United States Coast Guard has used working dogs since before World War II, when the Coast Guard's Beach Patrol employed 1,800 dogs to guard against

2.4 Sailor getting an early morning shave with a stray puppy dog, Umm Quasar, Iraq.

German invasion (W., 2004). Dogs help the Coast Guard to achieve maritime domain awareness (MDA) by identifying which ships, people, cargo, and nations are passing through ports. MDA ideally occurs at foreign ports where forces deploying canines are highly mobile, specialized, and rapid-response organizations. Dogs are often used to search High-Interest Vessels (HIVs), which are typically between 600 feet and 1,100 feet long. Factors such as ports of call, flag registry, nationalities, and cargo may cause authorities to label vessels as HIVs. Dogs may search cruise ships and containers for explosives and hidden persons. For example, terrorists have been found hiding inside cargo containers equipped with satellite phones, computers, airport diagrams, phony credentials, and passports. Authorities search a small percentage of cargo containers; thus, dogs efficiently optimize resources in order to detect the most serious threats, for example, explosives and hazardous waste. Cruise ship passengers have been sniffed by dogs working for local police, United States Customs and Border Protection, private security companies, Department of Homeland Security, Coast Guard, and Transportation Security Administration (TSA). Drug detection dogs may work at piers or aboard vessels, such as those throughout the Caribbean Sea and islands (Cusack, 2013; Gips, 2001). Dogs not only detect drugs, their presence also deters smugglers and encourages local governments to participate in the United States' War on Drugs. American passengers typically respond positively to drug detection dogs; and may not associate dogs' presence with a drug epidemic.

2.5 U.S. Coast Guard Coast Station Cleveland Harbor,
Ohio mascot GSXR

Numerous accounts from military members, who have hidden puppies while on deployment, attest to Americans' persistent affection for "man's best friend," even in some circumstances that breach military protocol. "Dogs were often carried aboard U.S. ships during World War II as mascots and morale builders for the men. The men would dote on the dogs and treat them as if they were crew members. [Firsthand accounts from] World War II veterans, revealed how much the dogs meant to them" (Galvani, 1994). For example, one soldier in 1958 recalled hiding a puppy while on deployment.

> With the help of a [Sergeant] and [Corporal], I got [Skoshi, my puppy] aboard [a Korean War] ship in an air cooled sea bag. We put her in a sea bag with a cardboard lining and put holes in the sea bag. We were aboard an MSTS ship [i.e. Military Sea Transportation Service ship]. We were about 3 days out and I didn't think I could hide Skoshi for the entire trip without the ship's crew knowing it, so I decided to face the music and see the Capt [i.e. Captain]. Believe me, you never saw 2 more surprised guys: the Capt laughing because he didn't know how I possibly got her aboard, and myself when the Capt called the ship's carpenter and told him to build a doghouse back aft on the quarterdeck. (*Marine Corps Gazette*, 1958)

Skoshi was examined by Army veterinarians after the ship reached the port in San Francisco, California. She was flown to Buffalo, New York where she became accustomed to life as a civilian, settled down, and had 11 puppies. This account depicts classic themes of mischief and comradery aboard military vessels; however, other evidence demonstrates varied policies affecting puppies. Presently, attitudes in the United States military may seem to be more humane towards animals because some historical accounts discuss the possibility of throwing contraband dogs overboard; yet, attitudes among some United States military members currently may be more defensive or power-thirsty than those held by past generations. In today's military, a sailor sneaking a puppy aboard a boat may be likelier to face disciplinary action than receive a doghouse. However, an account from the mid-1940s demonstrates similar risks and potential for lenience described in Skoshi's story from the late 1950s (Grandell, 2010; *Marine Corps Gazette*, 1958).

> My Mexican Chihuahua, Jeep, was indeed my buddy and friend. I acquired Jeep while stationed at Marine Corps Air Station Cherry Point, [North Carolina (N.C.)]. She was small, and except for her brown ears, she was all white. Feeding Jeep was not as difficult as I

thought it would be. Of course, there was no dog food available on the air station, but Jeep soon adjusted to Marine chow. Jeep's favorite food was SOS, or . . . [shit] on a shingle, as we called it. Our Marine Transport Squadron (VMR) deployment to El Centro, [California], was a pleasure for Jeep . . . Jeep and I were flown to Guam where we were to board USS Cowpens (CVL-25) to take us home. This again presented a challenge, because of the Navy's rules about animals, particularly pets, on board. If found, animals could be tossed overboard. I was not about to leave my Jeep behind, so I tucked her inside my shirt and boarded the ship. The first two days on board were miserable. It was difficult keeping Jeep hidden. Her big problem was having nowhere to do her business. On the third day, I took her up to the flight deck. As she was doing her business, we heard the loud voice of the ship's [C]aptain, 'Sergeant, stand with your dog in your arms.' I dreaded the worst but was relieved when the [C]aptain began talking about his Chihuahua back in Coronado[, California]. He also had a camera with him and asked me to pose with Jeep. The next day over the ship's loudspeaker, we heard, 'Sergeant Grandel! . . . [W]anted in the [S]kipper's cabin.' The [C]aptain wanted to talk more about his wife and dog back in the States. He also presented me with a couple of the pictures of Jeep and me, which I still have to this day. My buddies were waiting to find out what the "[S]kipper" wanted. Being young and cocky, I proudly told them that the [S]kipper was having difficulty navigating the ship and asked me whether we should dock [in California] at San Diego or San Francisco. We finally landed at San Francisco, and Jeep and . . . [I] spent a short time at Treasure Island before boarding a train to Bainbridge Naval Station where I was honorably discharged. (Grandell, 2010)

The former Marine snuck Jeep into a dormitory at Mount Saint Mary's College; but she was expelled by a nun after vomiting inside the dorm. Jeep lived inside a car for a few weeks, but "[t]his was neither pleasing nor fair to [a] well-deserving canine companion" (Grandell, 2010). Jeep eventually went to live with another family where she "enjoyed her civilian life with all the goodies that she was denied during the war . . . [and] Jeep remains in those heavenly scenes in the company of brave Marines" (Grandell, 2010).

Puppies' companionship has been meaningful to submariners throughout several decades and wars. Between World War II and the 1990s, little historical knowledge had been gathered about submarine mascots (Galvani, 1994). The Submarine Force Library and Museum in Groton, Connecticut inspected thousands of books, images, newspapers, bulletins, and documents to research dogs aboard United

2.6 U.S. Coast Guard Cutter Campbell mascot Sinbad. Leonard Webb shooting movies of Sinbad in the North Atlantic

States submarines. They distributed a request for information in *Polaris*, a magazine for submarine veterans from World War II. Veterans submitted letters, photographs, identification records, and newspaper clippings attesting to submarine mascots, who were the objects of rivalry among submariners. An exhibit called "Sea Dogs: Mascots of the Silent Service" depicted submariners, who purchased, bestowed, rescued, traded, and otherwise acquired puppies (Galvani, 1994). Their puppies seemed to cheerlead and amuse submariners in spite of their occasional sensitivity to depth.

> They helped relieve the tension and weariness of hours of silent running or nights of surface attacks. The men doted on their dogs. They fed them steak and bacon; they gave them ID cards and service records; they took them on liberty all over the Pacific, and more than one mascot acquired a taste for beer. Crews made their pets' leashes

and collars, complete with combat submarine insignia and service stars. Some dogs wore special coats emblazoned with their boat's war record. At least one miscreant even went to captain's mast. (Galvani, 1994)

One puppy, Garbo, lived in a forward torpedo room where she barked while standing on the bullnose as the ship got underway. As she toured the ship, crewmembers in each compartment would come to attention when she arrived. One dark night she disappeared, but the crew found her after conducting a "dogoverboard search" (Galvani, 1994). On a few nights, she drank too much beer and stumbled around hotel rooms in Pearl Harbor, Hawaii. A dog from another ship had puppies with Garbo, who were traded for cases of beer to other submarines. She eventually retired and lived a civilian life. A six week-old puppy, Sugie, wore a tiny blue sailor's jumper while joining the USS Besugo. Sugie was aboard the submarine when it sank 40,000 tons of enemy shipping during five war patrols. He allegedly detested distilled liquor made with torpedo fuel, but Sugie enjoyed beer, whiskey, and pink ladies. Sugie was spoiled by crewmembers, who spoon-fed him; but, he also ate gum, socks, and soap. Other crewmembers, from USS Halibut, picked up Skeeter from Lefty's bar in San Francisco, California. Skeeter was "charged with disturbing the peace in the forward battery compartment and with being surly and belligerent" (Galvani, 1994). Skeeter was required to appear at a captain's mast for each charge. The first case was dismissed with a warning; but after urinating on a chief petty officer's leg, Skeeter was honorably discharged in 1945. A poodle named Betty took sides during a disagreement between officers by ripping an eight-inch hole into one officer's trousers. However, after an inquiry, Betty's actions were vindicated and the officer was relieved of his duties. Some submariners' tender attitudes toward their dogs are juxtaposed by reckless behavior. For example, Potshot died after being run-over by a torpedo truck in Pearl Harbor. Luau, a dog on USS Spadefish, had not finished weaning Myrna, her puppy, when Myrna was smuggled onto USS Sawfish and fed "milk, Karo syrup, cod-liver oil, and vitamin pills" (Galvani, 1994). One night as she slept under a table, she was crushed to death when too many sailors piled onto the table causing it to collapse. Despite occasional neglect and cruelty, puppies were treated as mascots, family members, and heroes; like puppies presently working in the military, submariners' puppies between World War I and the Korean War were honored with medals, invited to walk in parades, and admired in the press and by the public.

CHAPTER THREE

Wild and Exotic Animals

Predation and Territory

Domesticated dogs are regularly attacked by wild animals, such as sharks, alligators, crocodiles, coyotes, and bears. Dogs are commonly consumed by aquatic predators; however they are not a standard portion of most sharks' diets. Some fishermen have allegedly used stray dogs as shark bait (Compagno, 2001; Mott, 2005). Alligators and crocodiles often consume dogs because they are capable of digesting almost anything; and dogs may be accessible (Animal Wire, 2013; Masson, 2013).

Though many pet owners fail actively to take measures to protect dogs (e.g. puppies) from predators, many Americans have been persuaded to care about coyote attacks on puppies because attacks often indicate that local coyotes are losing fear for humans. When coyotes attack domesticated puppies, they are likelier to attack humans, including adults and small children. Numerous studies show that coyote attacks have increased in recent years for several reasons; for example, proliferating suburban coyotes have intermingled with humans and domesticated dogs. "The safe environment provided by a wildlife-loving general public, who rarely display aggression toward coyotes, is also thought to be a major contributing factor" (Timm, et al., 2004, p. 47). Predator management programs have become contentious because they may involve cruelty and extermination. Education campaigns and grassroots community-wide behavioral changes may help to prevent puppies, humans, or coyotes from being killed; but change may be difficult consistently to institute because of lackadaisical attitudes or disbelief that humans can be victimized by coyotes. Americans may tend to perceive themselves as being capable of defending against wild animals; yet, only some dog owners have been able to rescue dogs from coyotes; for example, one man attempted to run while carrying his poodle, but coyotes ripped his dog from his arms. Education about the secondary effects, such as spread of rabies, may encourage Americans preemptively to deter some coyotes, for example, by fencing yards. Coyotes' behavioral patterns may indicate imminence of attacks on humans. Increased presence of coyotes on streets, at parks, or in yards at night will precede increased numbers of dogs being taken at night or early morning. Coyotes' increased presence during daylight hours will correlate with coyotes taking dogs during daylight hours. "Food abundance regulates coyote numbers by influencing population density as well as reproduction, survival, dispersal, and space-use patterns" (Timm, et al., 2004, p. 51). Coyotes, who eat pets in broad daylight, may view humans as prey. Occasionally, dwindling pet populations may tempt coyotes to take small children. In most cases, American children have survived, but some have been mortally injured by coyotes. As coyote populations increase in America and humans and coyotes increasingly share territories, likelihood of conflict may increase (Kenyon, Southwick, & Wynne, 2000). Large cats may prey on domesticated dogs, but they may be leery of entering human civilization as readily as coyotes. Campers, hunters, and wildlife enthusiasts may expose their dogs to danger by traveling into nature; such as one camping dachshund puppy, who survived an attacking cougar (Pelletiere, 2015). Bears are behaviorally similar to coyotes insofar as they commonly intermingle with dogs in residential areas. Black bears, for example, may travel into yards, and like coyotes, black bears may be scared by dogs. On rare occasion, bears, who attack dogs, may be thwarted by owners scaring, hitting, or shooting toward bears, such as one young woman, who protected her dog, Fudge, by punching a bear in the nose (Grass, 2011).

Though some jurisdictions enforce controversial bans on allegedly dangerous dogs, American culture generally fails to perceive dogs as being threatening to humans even though dogs allegedly kill more American humans annually than sharks, bears, coyotes, crocodiles, and alligators combined. This paradox may partially result from humans' view of dogs as defenders, who protect humans and domesticated animals from wild animals (Discovery TV, 2010; Youtube.com, 2014). "Though effective in some situations, guard dogs don't always carry out their protective role . . . Guard dogs, like any animal can become . . . overly aggressive causing harm to the [individuals, who] . . . they were trained to protect" (Kenyon, Southwick, & Wynne, 2000, p. 19). There were approximately 304 dog-related fatalities in the United States between 1979 and 1996 (Avis, 1999). Annually, dogs may be responsible for more American humans' deaths than any other single species of animal or insect (Cusack, 2015). Thus, the problem of how to analyze the significance of wild animal attacks is complex (Ingraham, 2015). For example, between 1999 and 2013, contact with rats accounted for three deaths; contact with crocodiles and alligators resulted in nine human fatalities; but contact with dogs resulted in 450 Americans' deaths (Cusack, 2015). Tilikum,

SeaWorld's renowned whale, has allegedly been held responsible for several trainers' deaths and numerous injuries. Critics have condemned SeaWorld.

> Why keep him around? Well, it's a quite simple answer; and that is, that his semen is worth a lot of money . . . In a reputable breeding program, rule number one is that you certainly would not breed an animal, who has shown a history of aggression towards humans. Imagine if you had a pit bull, who had killed. That animal would have likely been put down. (Cowperthwaite, 2013)

Americans may preserve certain species based on their recreational value to humans (Leeman, 2010).

Pups

Offspring of numerous animals are called "pups," including the following: agouti, anteater, armadillo, bat, bearcat, beaver, binturong, coyote, dolphin, fox, gerbil, guinea pig, hamster, hedgehog, mole, mouse, otter, prairie dog, rat, seal, shark, squirrel, walrus, and wolf (Enchanted Learning, n.d.; Zoo Borns, n.d.). This shared terminology may suggest common traits, such as ability to reproduce; yet it may dilute the specificity colloquially ascribed to the word "puppy" (Hammerschlag, 2015). For example, sharks' babies may be called "pups," but many of their attributes are unshared by puppies. The word "pup" fails to denote reproductive dissimilarities between viviparous dogs and sharks, and distinguish oviparous and ovoviviparous groups of sharks. The term does not indicate that puppies are man-eaters like tiger sharks; yet the term may serve as a reminder that dogs are domesticated animals, who kill more humans than all sharks combined. Tiger sharks reproduce dozens more pups than dogs; and pups gestate for seven or eight times longer than puppies (Hammerschlag, 2015; NOAA, n.d.; NOAA, n.d.). Many delay reproduction until they are several years old, unlike dogs, who may reproduce after their first year but often do not reproduce because of extensive spaying and neutering in America (ASPCA, n.d.). These lack of similarities invite comparisons between dog puppies and other species not called "pups," such as kittens, who may be socially and physiologically more similar to puppies. For example, a man believed that he owned two dogs, who were sold to him as puppies; however, he actually had raised bear cubs for two years before he realized that his puppies were actually cubs (Robertson, 2015). Dogs' individual

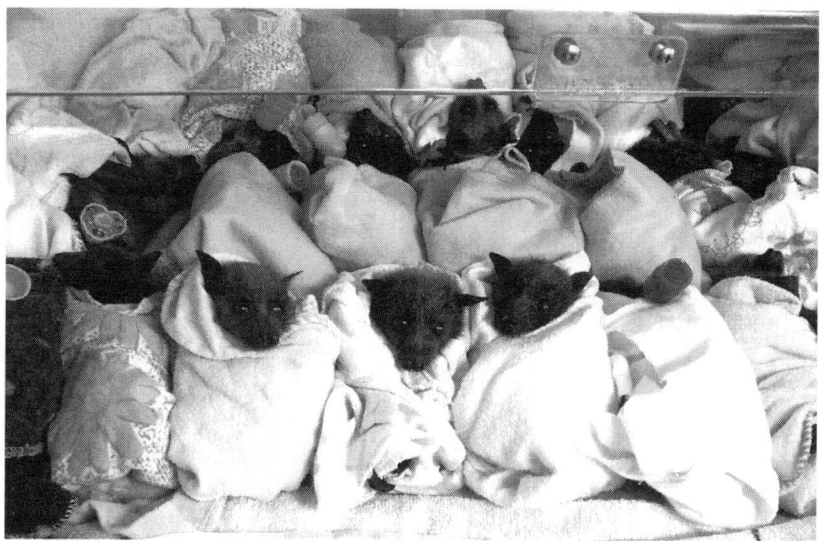

3.1 Grey-headed flying fox pups

3.2 Sleeping seal pup

names, like the word "pup," may communicate a bundle of ideas that may or may not accurately describe puppies' characteristics (Coren, 2011). A study of 291 American university students tested whether students viewed dogs' names as being indicative of their personalities and explicative of dogs' behavior. The study showed to students the same video of a dog, but used different dogs' names with each group of students. Dogs' names included Assassin, Buddy, Happy, and Killer. When a dog had a tough name, respondents described the video as depicting a hostile dog. For example, "The dog saw a man and didn't like him. The dog barked at him and tried to jump up on him to make him go away, but the man pushed him off before he could be bitten and the dog ran away" (Coren, 2012). Students perceived that dogs with gentle or positive names behaved less threateningly. For example, "The dog saw a man coming and ran out to say hello. The dog barked and jumped up to try to get the man to play. Then the dog ran ahead of him to lead him home" (Coren, 2012). Meaning associated with the word "puppy" is culturally manufactured. In effect, the word "puppy" may be as mundane or generalizable as "guys" or "people." For example, if it is directed in a command form to a group of young dogs, then all are expected similarly to respond to the command. The word is not specialized to the degree that it only refers to dogs—just like a group of dogs may be called "guys" or a group of inanimate objects may be referred to as "puppies" (Carlin, 1996). Thus the term "puppy" may be an emotional and social cue when it refers to young dogs, who are beloved in America (Bryner, 2010).

Symbiosis

Sometimes puppies and predatory exotic animals are raised together at preservations to help domesticate and pacify exotics. Symbiotic relationships may be supported by theories about the development of a protodog by humans between 3,000 and 30,000 years ago discussed in Chapter 13. Humans allegedly helped needy wolves and pups. Interspecies symbiosis and possibly mercy may be ordinary for dogs because of their interactions with humans throughout their development. Cohabitation between dogs and exotic animals may not be enigmatic while both are young or harmless; or while the dogs nurse exotic animals. Yet, these relationships may defy zero sum interpretations of the concept of survival of the fittest, and suggest that predation may be somewhat physio-social.

Dozens of symbiotic relationships between puppies and predatory exotic animals have been covered by the American press and have been used to attract visitors to wildlife areas and zoos. Relationships between dogs and tigers, cheetahs, panthers, wolves, and other animals defy Americans' typical treatment of dogs as quasi-property and family members (Good Morning America, n.d.; Karimi, 2013; National Geographic Wild, 2014). These pairings tend to portray exotics as possessing the same emotional depth as dogs; and while they also demonstrate that dogs are indeed wild animals to an extent, they may suggest that dogs are able to teach or imbue their love for humans to exotic animals (Animalist News, 2014). Dogs' status as wild animals is discussed in Chapter 14. Exotic animals may be differentiable from wild animals because they are in captivity and because they are somewhat conditioned to human presence and influence; yet some evidence demonstrates that wild animals would raise puppies without human intervention or enclosures. For example, some baboons forcibly take small puppies and raise them as members of their troops (Skylar, 2011).

Preservations, zoos, sanctuaries, and other wildlife areas are not the only locations in which predatory exotic animals cohabit with dogs; numerous humans share homes with exotic animals, dogs, and human family members. For example, a man in Brazil had approximately one dozen exotic animals, including a monkey (Barcroft TV, 2013; Brito, 2013). His animals and children, including a Chihuahua named Little, shared furniture, food, living areas, patio space, entertainment areas, etc.

3.3 Brazilian black-capped squirrel monkey (*Saimiri* boliviensis) and infant

Brazilian wildlife agents had attempted to challenge his license to raise exotics because he bred large cats. In response, he contended that because he rescued two tigers from a cruel traveling circus he had a right to breed exotic animals in a safe environment outfitted with a team of veterinarians. He characterized his participation in animal breeding as a conservation effort, but authorities requested that his large cats be sterilized. However, the man claimed that he had demonstrated his professional competence by maintaining a dog kennel at his home. Similarly, millions of Americans legally and illegally possess exotic animals (e.g. pythons and polar bears), who live with—and potentially threaten—their canine and human family members in ways that may be unreported or undetectable by authorities (Barcroft TV, 2010; Cusack, 2015). Some exotic animals are exported from the United States to other countries, where they are raised by dog surrogates or with puppies. For example, a white Bengal tiger cub and a four year old Dalmatian lived together in Germany after the tiger, who was born in the United States, was sold to a circus in Germany (Uzoo, 2009). The pair was often photographed together.

CHAPTER FOUR

Killing

Breach of Community Trust

Community leaders with ethical responsibilities have breached their duties or society's expectations by willfully or negligently torturing and killing dogs and puppies. Anecdotal evidence, current events, and criminal cases demonstrate that some police officers, soldiers, and scientists are morally chastised by the public and their communities when they illegally or legally kill puppies; however, they may not routinely suffer severe consequences. When officers kill puppies, shootings may not result in personal civil liability due to qualified immunity. Thus, law enforcement is frequently at odds with pet owners' and communities' sentiments and perceptions because many Americans would like to hold personally responsible police officers, who shoot unaggressive dogs. Under 42 U.S.C. § 1983 (2015), violative police conduct may be actionable if officers acted under the color of law; and their conduct resulted in a deprivation of rights or immunities (Orovitz, 2012). Qualified immunity is an affirmative defense that can be used to move for summary judgment when police officers acted in good faith. If a right was not clearly established, then officers will be immunized. For example, an officer, who shoots an unleashed puppy during a stop and talk with the puppy's owner may be immunized if there is no clearly established right to have an unleashed dog on a public street. The officer may claim that the puppy was threatening; however, even if the shooting amounted to an unlawful deprivation of property, the officer may be immunized. This was the case in Chicago, Illinois when a seven month-old miniature Bull Terrier bred from a world champion show dog was shot while an officer ticketed his owner for a parking violation (Yellen, 2013). Pet owners do not have a clearly established right to have puppies present during police investigations, however, friendly puppies may be present during investigations when they do not threaten or interrupt investigations (Lustig v. Mondeau, 2006). For example, Los Angeles County Sheriff's Department "and a team of 15 officers executed a search warrant . . . A pit bull puppy was tied up outside the front door, but it was friendly and did not try to bite them. After announcing that they were with the Los Angeles County Sheriff's Department and had a search warrant, they demanded entry" (Jones v. Heidi, 2014, pp. 31–32). The puppy likely was uninjured due to a friendly demeanor that police were able to differentiate from aggressiveness. Pit bulls may be likelier to be killed by police officers due to stigmatization of the breed as being dangerous. For example, a ten month-old lab-pit bull mix was shot and killed when officers entered his backyard in search of a suspect (Wagner, 2014). The dog's family claimed that their dog likely ran towards officers to greet them. The officers did not report being attacked by the dog, but claimed that the dog had charged at them. The dog's owner was placed under arrest for interfering with an investigation after he confronted officers about the death of his dog. Controversy erupted in Texas when an officer's bodycam recorded an officer making kissing noises at a pit bull and then shooting and killing the pit bull (Inquisitr, 2014). The video was used to clear the officer after investigators concluded that the dog took an aggressive stance prior to being shot. The officer had received several reports that the six month-old puppy had gotten loose and nipped at several people. The dog was loose with another pit bull, who was captured by animal control. The officer was waiting for animal control to arrive when he shot and killed the puppy. After some pit bulls have attacked officers, their owners have argued that attacks were defensible due to law enforcements' errors. However, the law does not typically support their claims. For example, in Georgia, a seven month-old pit bull puppy was shot and killed by a police after officers responding to suspicious activity accidentally released the puppy from his home's garage (Grenoble, 2015). Animal control recovered the puppy's remains and another dog from the property, and they left a note for the family. When the family returned to their home, which was covered in blood, they called for emergency help, but their call was not received. The owners eventually visited the animal shelter in possession of their dog; and later complained that the search of their home was warrantless; however, the officers' superiors claimed that the officers had acted within the scope of their duty. Police officers violate public trust, irrespective of whether they act under the color of law, when they brutally kill puppies. For example, a police officer in Baltimore, Maryland was fired and sentenced to a year in prison, which exceeded sentencing guidelines, because he unremorsefully and callously committed aggravated animal cruelty. He beat, choked, and paralyzed the terrier, who died from blood loss (Morse, 2014).

American soldiers have repeatedly been accused of harming puppies. Some of these incidents are attributed to post-traumatic stress disorder (PTSD), but this explanation is generally unacceptable when it is used to excuse harm to animals. Few soldiers experience combat; and those who do may seek therapeutic interventions, such as service dogs discussed in Chapters Two and Seven. Soldiers may be antisocial, hyper-masculine, substance-addicted, mentally ill, aggressive, or violent individuals prior to joining the service (Cusack, 2015). Military culture may justify, exacerbate, or fail to address these characteristic. Soldiers may overpower puppies to symbolize dominance and project their desire to annihilate (Herek, 1996). For example, United States Marines stationed in the Middle East recorded a video boasting about their meanness and a puppy's imminent suffering before one Marine used an overhand throw to lob the weeping puppy approximately 100 feet down a hill. Analysts discussed the effects of PTSD and trauma, but did not use these disorders to excuse the Marine's behavior.

> [P]eople who treat animals badly may act out because of their oppressive surroundings or sometimes as a result of the shock they might have suffered — be it the horrors of war or an abusive parent during their childhood[,] . . . personality variables[,] . . . context[,] . . . group situation[s,] or feeling oppressed and down and wanting to just get back at the world. . . . The Marines might tape the incident, including their laughter and indifference[,] . . . as an ego booster . . . Somehow documenting it is a way to show people 'look at what we did' and 'look at how brave we are and how strong we are'. . . . [W]hat has caused them this kind of stress so that they have to react in such a violent way . . . They're on such a power trip about what they're doing that it doesn't dawn on them how disgusting it is . . . A person can get set to such levels of psychological arousal that ordinary life can seem kind of drab, and the only way to keep yourself feeling kind of good is to do things that are dangerous or anti-social. (Friedman, 2008)

American soldiers, who commit violence against Middle Eastern people and animals, may be more threatening to American people and animals when they return from deployment. The Marine, who tossed the puppy, allegedly was discharged but was not prosecuted; thus he may continue to harm and kill animals and humans.

Unethical experimenters are rarely prosecuted for violating animal research protocols, even though they may be terminated, research programs may be suspended, and laboratories may be penalized. For example, Physicians Committee for Responsible Medicine reported that Columbia University faced serious consequences after participating in unethical research activities (PCRM, 2007).

> Columbia University is the only school to ever have its research
> program suspended by the National Institutes of Health for not
> meeting animal welfare standards. The 1986 suspension forced
> Columbia to end all animal research on vertebrates other than
> rodents, affecting several million dollars' worth of projects. Since that
> time, several Columbia research projects have sparked controversy,
> including an experiment in which an entire litter of puppies was killed
> by cardiac puncture. The school eventually paid just $2,000 in fines
> for several violations in 2004. (PCRM, 2007)

Though their research funding was suspended, financial penalties
against Columbia University were mild. The American public is often
unaware of lenient responses by enforcement agencies to cruel treatment of dogs and puppies at laboratories. Enforcement agencies and
laboratories may hide and seal disciplinary actions indicating breaches
of the public's trust.

Neighbors

Countless reported and unreported cases of neighbors killing puppies
(and dogs) with poison, guns, fire, live burial, and other means demonstrate that puppies do not appeal to all Americans; and contempt for
puppies or their owners may be great enough to risk misdemeanor and
felony charges. Some Americans opportunistically use the law in order
to execute puppies. For example, the State of California authorizes individuals to shoot dogs threatening farm animals on their property.
"No action, civil or criminal . . . [will] be maintained for the killing of
any such dog" when, "[t]he dog is found in the act of killing, wound-
ing, or persistently pursuing or worrying livestock or poultry . . . [and]
proof . . . conclusively shows that the dog [recently] has been . . . on
land or premises which are not owned or possessed by the dog's
owner" (Cal. Code § 31102, 2015). Thus, purported threat only may
need to be demonstrated by a killer, for example, who intentionally
leaves open a gate to lure a dog onto private property occupied by farm
animals. However, courts are suspicious of opportunists, and may carefully weigh evidence to determine a killer's credibility and motive; similarly, courts may scrutinize dogs' behavior history and comportment
at the time of the killing. For example, in 2004, a court in Alabama
heard testimony that the McKelvey family was bothered by dogs entering their property (McKelvey v. Alabama, 2004). Dogs killed animals, such as geese, cats, and a bull and other livestock. One cow was
beleaguered by dogs while she gave birth to a calf. When McKelvey

found his cow she was cornered by dogs, who he chased. McKelvey personally witnessed a newborn calf being eaten by two black Labrador Retrievers, which subsequently resulted in the calf's mother dying from a severe mastitis infection. One month later, McKelvey shot his neighbor's black Labrador Retriever. At trial, McKelvey alleged that he had reported the nuisance to law enforcement on several occasions and complained to his neighbors because he believed that the predatory dogs may have belonged to his neighbors. McKelvey claims that the black Labrador Retriever was stalking geese on the occasion in question when the dog became defensive and aggressive toward him. McKelvey felt threatened by the dog, who allegedly bared his teeth. McKelvey's neighbors insisted that although her dog occasionally roamed, the dog was not aggressive. His neighbors claimed that the defendant not only shot toward their house, but also fired next to their children. After hearing the gun shot, the neighbors claim to have seen McKelvey standing by their dog, who had collapsed on their flowerbed. McKelvey was charged and convicted of reckless endangerment and torturing an animal; but he appealed a charge for reckless endangerment, which the court overturned.

> The indictment does not include any facts whatsoever alleging that McKelvey recklessly engaged in conduct that created a substantial risk of serious physical injury to a person. Rather, the indictment alleged only that McKelvey intentionally tortured an animal. The crime of intentionally torturing an animal is not broad enough to include the crime of recklessly endangering a person. Absent a valid indictment encompassing the crime for which McKelvey was convicted, the trial court lacked subject-matter jurisdiction to try, to convict, and to sentence him. (McKelvey v. Alabama, 2004, p. 1027)

In the appellate court's opinion, McKelvey had tortured his neighbor's dog, but the court held that reckless endangerment of humans was not a lesser-included offense of torturing an animal.

Child Callousness

American mental health professionals may compartmentalize various characteristics of cruelty and callousness with respect to perpetrators' ages, maturity, intelligence, and motivation, including curiosity, peer pressure, mood enhancement (e.g. thrill or depression), gratification (e.g. sexual or sadistic), coercion, phobia, taking revenge, threat, trauma, stress, imitation, self-injury, attention-seeking, rehearsing violence, and emotional terror (Johnston, 2011). Psychologists' and psychiatrists' attempts to understand behavior patterns and etiological pathways may marginalize dogs when analyses explore patients' family dynamics, criminal opportunity, history, emotions, and forensic evidence, but not dogs' feelings and rights. For example, a callous child traumatized by a pedophile, who baited and groomed the child by presenting a puppy, may receive therapeutic treatment that neglects to have the patient reflect on possible mental cruelty and trauma experienced by the puppy, and only attempts to distinguish innocent puppies from the trauma experienced by the patient.

Neurological, cerebral, and mental illnesses often correlate with children torturing, mutilating, and killing dogs (U.S. v. MacDonald, 1985). Psychopathy and antisocial personality disorder (ASPD), which have been linked to various cerebral conditions, including frontal lobe impairment and pathological diseases, are likelier to cause children to harm dogs than other neurological, social, mental, or behavioral disorders (Birbaumer, et al., 2005). One study found that adolescent boys, approximately 11 years old, who demonstrated emotional callousness, suffered from impairment of the right amygdala similarly to adults suffering from lack of emotions (Jones, et al., 2009). Functional MRIs were administered to 17 boys while the subjects viewed depictions of fearful and neutral faces. Thirteen boys served as a control group. Boys with conduct problems, who also exhibited callous and unemotional traits, had less neurological activity in the right amygdala when presented with fearful faces. Children with ASPD and psychopathy lack internal controls (e.g. consciences) and fail to respond to external controls (Drislane, et al., 2013).

Callous children may kill animals by torturing them; objectifying them; or neglecting them. Children, who kill dogs, frequently use tools, such as leashes, fire, poison, guns, or knives; for example, a child in New York killed a puppy by swinging the puppy from a leash (Hanna, 2011). The puppy was struck against the side of a building and died. Though the incident could be portrayed as an accident, the child allegedly had a history of animal cruelty. The child previously used a golf club to attack a puppy, but was not prosecuted due to the owner's reticence and lack of evidence. Community members condemned the child's actions; were critical of what they imaged were negligent parents; and speculated that the child would pathologically continue to commit violent crimes throughout adolescence and adulthood. A petition of delinquency may have been filed against the child; however, the case was heard in family court, which probably resulted in rehabilitative or civil remedies, but not penological discipline or adjudication of delinquency. The fact that family court heard the case may indicate that society did not wish to harshly punish the child (Rosenthal, 2011). American law and society may demonstrate a preference for protecting children, including cruel children, more than puppies; and this case may indicate that the boy's community preferred to make his parents responsible rather than directly hold the child accountable.

Some Americans' dismissal of cruelty as childhood callousness, immaturity, or a joke may result in local divisiveness. In Alabama, an 18 year-old, Ashley Johnston, and a 17 year-old boy, tossed and decapitated puppies (Inquisitr, 2015). The teens, who used machetes to torture the puppies, recorded the events and briefly uploaded videos to social media. Sheriff Earnest Evans claimed that Johnston immediately felt remorse and removed the videos before confessing to police. Both teens were charged with misdemeanor animal cruelty. Critics complained because the charges seemingly should have been felonies. Sheriff Evans justified the misdemeanor charges because Johnston showed remorse. "It would be fair to say the 18-year-old confessed. He kind of owned it, took the photos, and he actually didn't like it. The pictures were on social media for about 15 seconds . . . From the information that I have so far, this is just two kids being stupid" (Inquisitr, 2015). Sheriff Evans' comment may seem to override Alabama's law, which requires misdemeanor charges when perpetrators kill dogs without justification and felony charges for torture.

Anecdotal evidence demonstrates that one reason that Americans may dismiss cruelty is that they are afraid to label their own children as being abnormal; and similarly, may resist labeling children in their communities; yet Americans are willing to label outsiders as being abnormal. For example, an unknown commenter posted a discussion thread about an allegedly cruel child. The post was entitled "My 7 year-old son just killed our pet puppy. Should I be concerned?" (Yahoo Answers, 2011).

> This isn't his first pet[. He] . . . killed his friend's cats when he was 5 [; we] . . . thought it was his terrible two's a bit late and dismissed it . . . [,]but it is his first dog. The dog went missing about 2 weeks ago and he said he saw our pup run out of the gate. Yesterday night I noticed a really rancid smell coming from his room. I went through his stuff to find the source and found the head of our puppy in his backpack and the puppy's paw in his underwear drawer. We sat him down to talk about punishment last night and he seemed so calm. [H]e seemed remorseless about it. My hubby and I are kind of freaked out. [H]e's had behavioral issues before—punched kids at school, beaten his sister up a few times, gotten in lots of trouble at school . . . [—]but he's just a rambunctious kid. My mother says I should put him in

counseling. [I] want this . . . [behavior to stop] . . . but I don't want to . . . [traumatize my son by placing] him in therapy. Should we be concerned or is this just a rebellious thing? What should we do? (Yahoo Answers, 2011)

The commenter seems to indicate that she would prefer not to label her son as being deviant or abnormal by traumatizing him with therapy. A few responses doubted the veracity of this post; however, every other response to this post indicated that people were willing to label this unknown commenter's child as being in need of help. Respondents identified animal cruelty as abnormal and problematic deviance requiring reform and rehabilitation. A central worry was that the child's harmful behavior would progress to harming humans, which respondents felt would be more serious. Respondents demonstrated some knowledge about correlations between early onset of psychopathy, animal cruelty, and adult criminality, but none recommend reporting animal cruelty to the police. The following is a list of discussion responses posted by unknown respondents (Yahoo Answers, 2011).

1. [O]f course there's something wrong! Go and get mental health help immediately.
2. This doesn't sound like purely rebellious behavior, and I don't blame you . . . [for] being concerned . . . Rather than just taking him to a . . . [counselor] (you will need to do this), find out information about different treatments as well. That way if you feel that one isn't . . . successful or there is something you don't like about it, you have other options there. Just remember, this isn't because of your parenting skills, some kids are like this. But the quicker you get it sorted out the better because what can start off as animals can lead into something much more sinister . . . I hope you can stop this behavior[.]
3. He needs counseling immediately. Statics show that kids . . . [,who] kill or harm pets or people . . . [at] such a young age have a tendency to become . . . troubled adult[s].
4. He needs . . . [counseling] ASAP [i.e. as soon as possible] . . . [b]efore it gets worse . . . This is not normal behavior . . . Do not be too concerned about . . . [traumatizing] him [because] . . . he needs help!! . . . I am sorry to hear that this is something you and your husband need to deal with, but this is your reality . . . [H]elp him before it gets worse . . . How can you say you don't want to . . . [traumatize] him by giving him counselling . . . [What's] wrong with you? . . . [T]his is terrible, very disturbing behavior . . . [He] showed no remorse, [which is why I'd] be locking my bedroom

door at night and have your other kid sleep in the room with you too.

5. If this is real[, then] your kid is a psychopath in the making! Get him help now and give him real punishments not just a slap on the wrist. People like him grow up to be serial killers.

6. Well if this is true, which [I] doubt it is, why the hell would you buy him a pet if you knew he had already killed a cat.

7. [I]f he was my son, I would definitely be concerned. He should be put into counseling immediately.

8. [Y]ou have a serial killer in the making . . . You may need to put him in a mental institution.

9. [Y]our son needs help . . . [because he is a] serial killer in process. (Yahoo Answers, 2011)

Respondents suggested that the boy's parents would be responsible for escalated violence if they failed presently to place their child in therapy. They were quick to label the child as behaving abnormally and condemn the commenter's hesitation to do the same. None of the respondents suggested that when children torture animals, they commit crimes. This is could be because respondents believed that it would be unreasonable to suggest that a parent should report her seven year-old son to the police. Demonstrating sensitivity to this cultural standard of reasonableness possibly may be more important to respondents than their need to punish cruel children.

Studies show that American parents may be unwilling to classify dog abuse as abnormal behavior because childhood callousness correlates with children's environments and parents' genes and behavior. Many children, who abuse dogs, have been victimized and witnessed abuse and cruelty; and parents, who abuse dogs, are likelier to abuse children (D'Oench, 2015). Callous parents may demonstrate to children that callousness is acceptable or irrelevant. Childhood callousness may be treated without family therapy or removal from the home when externalizing behavior is distinguishable from family context. An analysis of 20 measures of family context examined how fearlessness and disinhibition correlated with animal cruelty (Walters & Noon, 2015). Data was collected from 1,354 self-reports of adjudicated delinquents. Proactive externalizing and reactive externalizing significantly correlated with animal cruelty in every family context. Future violence could be predicted by a combination of parental behavior, such as serious discord, drug use, hostility, and unawareness of children's behavior; and children's interpersonal hostility, low impulse control, poor aggression suppression, and psychopathy. Interestingly, moral disengagement did not predict animal cruelty, which may explain why some remorseless youth have been willing to acknowledge that cruelty is wrong.

Self-Defense

Dog killers may claim self-defense; for example, police officers lawfully shoot and kill dogs by claiming that dogs posed a threat. An aggressive posture, growling, exposed teeth, low head position, arched back, and raised fur may indicate aggression and imminent attack (Cusack, 2015). Yet, some pet owners have complained that police killed dogs when mistakenly entering the wrong property or when animals posed no threat; for example, owners have claimed that dogs were merely sniffing, running, or barking. Police may perceive dogs, who have tough-sounding names, as being more aggressive than dogs with cute or sweet names, even though the dogs are equally harmless to officers. This is discussed in Chapter Three. Law and department policies grant deference to law enforcement officers to use of discretion in these situations, especially because criminals may use dogs as weapons to attack police officers (Cusack, 2015; Kaatz, 2014).

Members of the American public may harbor resentment toward police departments that fail to discipline police, who unjustifiably kill nipping puppies. However, the public may be accustomed to reports about police killing puppies, and to law enforcement agencies' assertions that killing aggressive puppies does not amount to wrongdoing. Thus, the public may laud law enforcement officers when they exercise discretion to abstain from killing excited puppies. For example, a woman called police to file a report (Life with Dogs, 2015). When an officer arrived at an unexpected time, her four year-old son opened the door, and his puppy defensively attacked the police officer. The puppy bit and bruised the officer's leg, but rather than shoot her, he slowly retreated and soothed the puppy. The officer was required to report the bite and verify that the puppy had been vaccinated for rabies; however, he relented to use any more severe remedies at his disposal because he believed that the puppy was simply doing what she ought to do.

Courts may be reluctant to believe that defendants, who used lethal force against puppies, acted in self-defense because puppies are relatively defenseless; and nonlethal force effectively may be used to defend against puppies. For example, in 2010, Raul Liendo was sentenced to one year in jail in Iowa after he admitted to intentionally killing his two-month old pit bull puppy by stepping on him (State v. Liendo, 2011). At first, Liendo told law enforcement that the puppy had bitten his ankles, and that he only kicked the dog to shoo the dog.

However, he also disclosed that he had been angry when he kicked his puppy. The court found that the puppy died from neglect after Liendo, who had been drinking, kicked his puppy for barking and threw his puppy against a wall. Even if the puppy had bitten Liendo, he could have defended using nonlethal force. In at least one case, a four month-old puppy acted in self-defense by pulling a trigger and shooting an owner, who had killed several of his littermates and imminently intended to kill the puppy (NBC News, 2004). The owner was given emergency care and charged with animal cruelty; and the puppy was not retributively destroyed, rather, the dog was allegedly rescued and placed for adoption.

Defendants have claimed manually to use puppies' bodies as weapons. For example, a defendant claimed that he hurled a puppy and killed a woman in self-defense (Commonwealth v. Dye, 1946).

> I arrived at my room about 3:00 A.M. and was undressing . . . [and] was pulling on my pajamas and playing with my little puppy dog when . . . [the victim] burst in the room. . . pretty well intoxicated . . . She stepped in the door—all alone—and asked me in a violent manner, [what he had to say to save himself] . . . I tried to talk nice and sweet to her to persuade her to think what she was doing . . . but she was too mad and drunk to hear what I said—I was standing in the doorway of a clothes closet pulling on these pajamas—and I said if she was aimin' to kill me—please let me die with my puppy in my arms, for I dearly loved this little dog. I picked up the dog a 3 [month-old] 15 [pound] Water Spaniel, and I threw the dog toward her so it hit her in the chest and knocked her slightly off balance . . . I then proceeded to fight for my life as I tried to take the shotgun away from her and got her turned around so she fell back on the bed. We both had a hold of the gun. I don't remember how I had held it or which end of it was in my hands but the gun was discharged the blast hitting [the victim] in the side of the head [Emphasis and internal citations omitted]. (Commonwealth v. Dye, 1946, pp. 547–548)

The lower court and appellate court were unpersuaded.

> The long affidavit to the petition does not explain how it came that the body of the deceased was found unclothed very shortly after the killing, the clothing being stuck in the mattress. Many other inconsistencies and contradictions exist between his statement read to the jury in the murder trial, his long affidavit called the "story of his life" in the habeas corpus, and his testimony in the habeas corpus [Emphasis and internal citations omitted]. (Commonwealth v. Dye, 1946, p. 548)

Within American society, this alleged response to danger would be rare and seemingly unlikely, even though criminals have used living and dead puppies as weapons to batter other people (*Los Angeles Times*, 2006; Cusack, 2015). In this case, animal cruelty, murder, and other facts seem to be consistent with interpersonal violence not self-defense (Commonwealth v. Dye, 1946).

Crush Pornography

Crush pornography is sexually sadistic obscenity depicting animal torture (Animal Crush Video Prohibition Act of 2010; Cusack, 2014; Cusack, 2015). A typical crush film may portray a woman dressed in a full body stretch jumpsuit wearing a mask and high heels. Her attitude may be nonchalant as she handles a small healthy puppy. Without much ado, she may inflict one or more of the following forms of agony: slicing, stomping, throwing, choking, wracking, mutilation, burning, cooking, drowning, incinerating, suffocation, intoxication, declawing/amputation, surgery, stabbing, punching, depilation/skinning, scalding, hanging, tail swinging, neck breaking, and bone fracturing. These horrific visuals are often accompanied by gruesome audio in which puppies' yelping is audible along with sounds of injury, such as bone snapping. Puppies may be tortured for several minutes as they stumble, fall from counter tops or tables, attempt to flee, look shocked, and lose consciousness. Audiences watching the films may become aroused by blood, carnage, and sadism. A ban on crush films was Constitutionally challenged and revised between the time of President Clinton's administration and President Obama's administration in order to narrowly tailor speech using the least restrictive means (*U.S. Const. amend. I*). Crush films, which do not generate a significant amount of revenue in comparison to other explicit genres, may also depict women raping, molesting, castrating, and otherwise sexually abusing puppies in order to appeal to audiences, who are aroused by zoophilia. The government concluded that a total ban is necessary because torturers often wear masks to frustrate investigation and prosecution. Speculation about crush films' authenticity persists, but the government believes that the films are real. In response to the films, the government has changed the landscape of the American justice system by banning the entire genre—an action that has only unilaterally been taken against one other genre of pornography (i.e. child pornography).

CHAPTER FIVE

Puppy Fur

U.S. Laws

Trading in puppy fur is prohibited by the federal government.

(b)(1)In general it . . . [is] unlawful for any person to
(A) import into, or export from, the United States any dog . . . fur product; or
(B) introduce into interstate commerce, manufacture for introduction into interstate commerce, sell, trade, or advertise in interstate commerce, offer to sell, or transport or distribute in interstate commerce in the United States, any dog . . . fur product.
(c)(1)(A) In general any person who violates any provision of this section . . . may . . . be assessed a civil penalty by the designated authority of not more than—
(i) $10,000 for each separate knowing and intentional violation;
(ii) $5,000 for each separate grossly negligent violation; or
(iii) $3,000 for each separate negligent violation.
(5) The designated authority . . . [will] pay a reward of not less than $500 to any person who . . . [provides] information that establishes or leads to a civil penalty assessment, debarment, or forfeiture of property for any violation of this section or any regulation issued under this section. (19 U.S.C. § 1308, 2015)

Strengths of the federal ban on dog fur in interstate or foreign commerce are 1) the law clearly opposes dog fur in commerce regulated by Congress; 2) the law punishes negligent violations; and 3) the government offers a $500 reward for information leading to civil penalties. One weakness may result from related enforcement issues with improper labeling; however U.S. Customs and Border Protection (CBP) feels that there is no threat of dog fur importation into the U.S. (CBP, 2012; *The Washington Post,* 2014). "In 2012, the Department of Homeland Security recommended putting an end to . . . [the] annual [Congressional] "Dog and Cat Fur report," which found only a single violation of the Dog and Cat Fur Protection Act in the five years prior" (Dowd, 2014). Nevertheless, "[r]ecognizing the special relationship between pets and their owners, Congress banned the dog and cat fur trade" (Kaatz, 2014, p. 835). Though Congress acknowledged the specialness of dogs (and cats), other species of household pets, such as rabbits and ferrets, are routinely exploited for their fur, which evidences mass cultural and societal preferences for dogs above other animals.

Only some states prohibit dog skinning or intrastate trade and sale of dog fur or skin. Lack of laws may indicate passive endorsement or an absence trade in the state. Due to federal supremacy, jurisdictional issues, and the dormant commerce clause, some states may avoid legislation that appears to reach importation, though there seems to be no market for dog skin and fur throughout the United States due to widespread taboo.

States prohibiting dog fur commerce have varying penalties, including fines and jail time; and distinct requirements for *actus reus* and *mens rea*. In Virginia, it is not unlawful to buy dog fur or skin, but, "[i]t is unlawful for any person to sell a garment containing the hide, fur, or pelt that he knows to be that of a domestic dog" (Va. Code Ann. § 3.2-6589, 2008). A violation results in a fine of not more than $10,000. In Georgia, "It . . . [is] unlawful for any person to sell the fur, hide, or pelt of any domestic dog . . . caught by a trap" (Ga. Code Ann. § 27-3-63 (a)(9), 2015). Thus, dogs' fur may be collected through other means not in violation of Georgia's anticruelty statutes. Delaware has some of the toughest laws against dog fur commerce, which are triggered if a person recklessly sells, offers, or trades dog fur (11 Del. Code § 1325A, 2015). Individuals may be prosecuted in Delaware for attempting to enter into commerce skins, pelts, byproducts, or products made from dog hair or fur. The laws are not triggered by an offer to purchase or barter, but selling, or offering to sell or bartering could result in pet forfeiture and a 15-year pet ownership ban.

> (a)(1) A person is guilty of the unlawful trade in dog . . . by-products in the 2nd degree if the person knowingly or recklessly sells, barters or offers for sale or barter, the fur or hair of a domestic dog . . . or any product made in whole or in part from the fur or hair of a domestic dog.
> (3 The unlawful trade in dog . . . by-products in the 2nd degree is a class B misdemeanor.
> (b)(1) A person is guilty of the unlawful trade in dog . . . by-products in the 1st degree if the person knowingly or recklessly sells, barters or offers for sale or barter, the flesh of a domestic dog . . . or any product made in whole or in part from the flesh of a domestic dog.

(2) The unlawful trade in dog . . . by-products in the first degree is a class A misdemeanor.

(c) Any person convicted of a violation of this section . . . [will] be:

(1) Prohibited from owning or possessing any domestic dog . . . for 15 years after said conviction, except for those grown, raised or produced within the State for resale, where the person has all necessary licenses for such sale or resale, and receives at least 25 percent of the person's annual gross income from such sale or resale;

(2) Subject to a fine in the amount of $2,500; and

(3) Required to forfeit any domestic dog . . . illegally owned. (11 Del. Code § 1325A, 2015)

Delaware's dog ownership ban would not apply to some puppy mill owners even though they routinely sell dog byproducts (i.e. puppies) and likely have access to dogs' corpses, fur, and hair (11 Del. Code § 1325A(c)(3), 2015). In Alabama, offering to sell, trade, or buy dog fur is animal cruelty (Ala. Code 1975 § 13A-11-241, 2015). "A person commits the crime of cruelty to a dog . . . in the first degree if he or she . . . skins a domestic dog . . . or offers for sale or exchange or offers to buy or exchange the fur, hide, or pelt of a domestic dog . . . Cruelty to a dog . . . in the first degree is a Class C felony" (Ala. Code 1975 § 13A-11-241(a), 2015). California's statute is somewhat inclusive, but requires specific intent (Cal. Code § 598a (a-b), 2015). "Every person is guilty of a misdemeanor who possesses, imports into this state, sells, buys, gives away or accepts any pelt of a dog . . . with the sole intent of selling or giving away the pelt of the dog" (Cal. Code § 598a (a-b), 2015). Oregon permits trade, sale, and purchase of loose dog fur or fur from animals, who died of unrelated causes (O. R. S. § 167.390(1), 2015). "A person may not take, buy, sell, barter or otherwise exchange for commerce in fur purposes the raw fur or products that include the fur of a domestic . . . dog if the fur is obtained through a process that kills or maims the . . . dog" (O. R. S. § 167.390(1), 2015). New Jersey generally prohibits dog fur or hair from entering into intrastate commerce, but makes exceptions for particular professionals (NJ Stat. 4:22-25.3, 2015).

> Any person who sells, barters, or offers for sale or barter, at wholesale or retail, the fur or hair of a domestic dog . . . or any product made in whole or in part from the fur or hair of a domestic dog . . . commits a crime of the fourth degree, provided that the person knew or reasonably should have known that the fur or hair was from a domestic dog . . . or that the product was made in whole or in part from the fur or hair of a domestic dog . . . This section . . . [will] not

apply to the sale or barter, or offering for sale or barter, of the fur or hair of a domestic dog . . . cut at a commercial grooming establishment or at a veterinary office or clinic or for scientific research purposes. (NJ Stat. 4:22-25.3, 2015)

New Jersey also prohibits the sale of dog flesh, but only when it is used for human consumption (NJ Stat. 4:22-25.4, 2015). Florida's statute requires scienter.

(1) It is unlawful for any person to knowingly sell or offer for sale, directly or indirectly, at wholesale or at retail, in this state any garment, or any item of clothing or apparel that is made, in whole or in part, from the fur of any dog . . . , or which contains or to which is attached any dog . . . fur.

(2) It is unlawful for any person to knowingly sell or offer for sale, directly or indirectly, at wholesale or at retail, or to give away, in this state the pelt of any dog . . .

(3) Any person who violates the provisions of this section commits a misdemeanor of the first degree . . . [A] second or subsequent conviction for a violation of this subsection . . . [is] a felony of the third degree.

(4) Any law enforcement agency, or humane officer . . . may seek a civil penalty of up to $5,000 for each violation. (Fla. Stat. § 828.1231, 2015)

Florida, like California, forbids individuals from giving dog fur, whereas many other states only prevent individuals from entering dog fur into commerce (Fla. Stat. § 828.1231, 2015).

Dog Fur in Asia and Europe

Thousands of stray puppies have been rounded-up to produce fur coats in China; and some puppies are bred on fur farms. These practices may mirror skinning and fur farming practices throughout Europe, Africa, Australia, and the Americas (Cusack, 2015). Yet, one difference may be that while American law may offer to dogs special consideration and heightened compassion, Chinese furriers may beat dogs to death and skin some alive (Kelch, 2014). People for the Ethical Treatment of Animals (PETA) reported that a single Chinese production plant processed 30,000 items of dog leather while 300 captive dogs were slated for slaughter (Guarino, 2015; PETA, n.d.). China farms more animals than any other nation; and their expanding production of dog byproducts may relate to emergence of dog leather and fur markets in other countries (Guarino, 2015; Kelch, 2014; PETA, n.d.).

Anti-fur campaigns in the United States highlight use of dog fur in China because of dogs' important status in the United States.

5.1 Flemish Giant and Shetland Sheepdog

Campaigns generally seek to end all fur trade of any animals' pelts, including vole, mole, mouse, rat, hare, raccoon, weasel, porcupine, squirrel, muskrat, otter, opossum, bobcat, dear, beaver, badger, boar, fox, coyote, wolf, Alaskan wolverine, leopard, bear, and others; but exposés showing dogs being beaten and crammed into wire cages are particularly powerful in the United States. Depictions of raccoon dogs being tortured and suffering are also compelling; and welfarist propaganda may focus on both kinds of dogs to highlight mass exploitation in China (FTC, 2012). Raccoon dog fur may be imported into the United States because raccoon dogs are not protected under federal laws banning domesticated dog fur importation, even though raccoon dogs are part of the same family as domesticated dogs (i.e. Canidae). Yet, businesses may intentionally mislabel raccoon dog fur as synthetic materials in order to avoid public criticism and boycott.

PETA believes that federal importation and labeling laws are insufficient because "[p]roducts made from dog leather are mislabeled, exported around the world, and sold to unsuspecting customers," in the United States and Europe (PETA, n.d.). Thus, European Union regulations against dog fur require members to create and enforce laws that are more stringent than many states' laws in the United States (Regulation (EC) No 1523/2007, 2007).

(1) In the perception of EU citizens, . . . dogs are considered to be pet animals and therefore it is not acceptable to use their fur or products containing such fur. Evidence exists of the presence in the Community of non-labelled fur from . . . dogs and of products containing such fur. As a consequence, consumers have become concerned about the possibility that they could buy . . . dog fur, and products containing such fur.

(5) As a result, certain EU fur traders introduced a voluntary code of conduct to refrain from trading in . . . dog fur, and products containing such fur. However, this code has proved insufficient to prevent the importation and sale of . . . dog fur, particularly where fur traders deal in fur whose species of origin is not indicated and not easily recognizable, or purchase products containing such fur and are confronted with the risk either that the products in question cannot legally be traded in one or more of the Member States or that trade in one or more Member States is subject to additional requirements aimed at preventing the use of . . . dog fur.

(11) Thus, in order to be more effective, the ban on intra-Community trade should be accompanied by a ban on imports of the same products into the Community. Such an import ban would also respond to concerns expressed by consumers as to the possible introduction into the Community of fur from . . . dogs, especially since there are indications that those animals may be kept and slaughtered inhumanely.

(12) A ban on exports should also ensure that . . . dog fur, and products containing such fur are not produced in the Community for export. (Regulation (EC) No 1523/2007, 2007)

In accordance with the regulation, member states' laws will penalize violations sufficiently to deter future violations. Europe's cultural partiality to dogs evident in their regulations is one origin of Americans' fondness for puppies.

Animal Fur and Hair Fibers

Hair samples, including trace evidence from animal hair and fur, are extremely valuable to the criminal justice system; and fur and hair evidence is often directly responsible for persuading juries of defendants' guilt or reasonable doubt (Cusack, 2015). Canine Combined DNA Index System (CODIS) demonstrates the power of animal fur and hair fiber evidence (ASPCA, 2010; UC Davis, n.d.; UC Davis, n.d.). DNA collected from dogfights may be entered into Canine CODIS, which shares its name with the Federal Bureau of Investigation's (FBI's) human DNA database CODIS. Several forensic tools are available to analyze dogs' DNA, however Canine CODIS is convenient because it can match DNA samples. Unidentified samples from suspected dogfighting rings and samples collected during investigations may be entered to piece together evidence about dogs' whereabouts. Humane Society of Missouri began the database with 400 samples from dogs seized during a large multi-agency operation. American Society for the Prevention of Cruelty to Animals (ASPCA), Louisiana Society for the Prevention of Cruelty to Animals, and University of California Davis Veterinary Genetics Laboratory have also participated in Canine CODIS. The laboratory may analyze hair and fur samples as well as various other organic materials collected from seized animals, who are administered buccal swabs, which are stored in CODIS and compared to other DNA samples. Hits will alert each agency that has submitted a matching sample. Hair and fur samples are more difficult to analyze when fibers lack roots or are in severe states of decomposition; however, saliva, blood, urine, or semen present on hair and fur fibers may be analyzed for DNA (Cusack, 2015). The FBI's CODIS may be used to match relatives' DNA to a sample; similarly, canine DNA analysis could be used to help track lineages thereby interrupting breeding, networking, and fighting. Lineage may be important in dogfighting because champions repeatedly may be bred and their puppies may be sold at a premium for local, national, and international dogfighting exhibitions.

CHAPTER SIX

Property

Income

Puppies are a multimillion dollar business. "Online searches for macroeconomic variables like GDP [i.e. Gross Domestic Product], unemployment rate and inflation are consistently topped altogether by online searches for puppies" (Kumar, 2015). While it's true that "in the whole history of the world there is but one thing that money cannot buy— . . . the wag of a dogs tail," "[w]hoever said 'you can't buy happiness' forgot little puppies" (Hill, 2009, p. 56; Walt Disney, 1955). Americans' participation in the puppy industry generates revenue for individuals, businesses, and the government. Income from whatever source derived is taxable under the Internal Revenue Code, including puppies given as gifts or adopted for less than their fair market value (26 U.S.C. § 61, 2015; *U.S. Const., art. I, § 8, clause 1; U.S. Const., art. I, § 10, clause 1*). However, their *de minimis* market value usually does not require reporting to the Internal Revenue Service (IRS). Though the IRS may evaluate the fair market value for breeding and training particular dog breeds, effort and expertise may vary greatly between breeders, which could change dogs' market value. Some breeders may train dogs to supplement their incomes; make dogs more desirable; or for their personal use. The purpose of breeding and training dogs also changes their value. When assessing taxable income, the IRS may require breeders to itemize their deductions and state whether dogs were bred and trained for profit or for personal use. Some reporting may seem suspicious when breeders conflate business expenses with personal use; for example, when breeders claim deductions for training dogs for personal use; or when breeders claim that dogs purchased for personal use annually depreciated. In one case, a petitioner claimed at first to have trained dogs for personal use; and then he claimed to have begun professionally training dogs (Sampson v. Commissioner of Internal Revenue, 1982). He specialized in security training for wolf dogs bred from wolves and German Shepherd dogs.

6.1 Wolf dog

He also alleged that he intended to train poodles. The petitioner had never learned to train dogs. He purchased one female and one male poodle, but, the petitioner neglected to pursue poodle training. He claimed that the male poodle, Rebel, depreciated in value over six months during year one and depreciated for 12 months during year two. He purchased Heidi, Lady, and John, who were German Shepherds; and bred them with trained wolves. His endeavor yielded 18 wolf dog pups. Several wolf dogs destroyed his dog-proof fence and had eaten cattle on an adjacent property. The petitioner sustained serious losses when his neighbors shot his wolf dogs. Shootings are discussed in detail throughout Chapter Four. The petitioner compensated his neighbors and deducted the costs from his income taxes. The IRS claimed that because the petitioner had never sold a puppy, his losses were start-up costs, which were nondeductible in 1974. The petitioner claimed that he had raised the dogs for profit; yet, the court found that he had only partially demonstrated for-profit activities. The IRS claimed that the petitioner raised wolf dogs for personal use.

> The other issue in this case is whether petitioner . . . engaged in the security-dog and dog-raising and retailing activities for profit. With respect to the latter activity, we need undertake no detailed analysis.

Even were it entered into with the intent to make a profit, no puppies were ever purchased . . . [B]usiness operations thus never commenced and any expenses incurred in 1974 were "preopening" or "start up" costs, not currently deductible . . . Although a reasonable expectation of profit is not required, the facts and circumstances must indicate that the taxpayer entered into or continued the activity with the objective of making a profit . . . It is not necessary, however, that the activity be engaged in with the exclusive intention of making a profit . . . Petitioner has the burden of proving that he engaged in the activity for profit . . . Raising vicious wolf dogs who can tear through chain-link fences and devour cattle seems to us, however, a completely different prospect than playing with Rin-Tin-Tin. Petitioner's enjoyment would have been served by raising more congenial, orthodox breeds; to create an entirely new and unpredictable canine species seems to us a step beyond personal pleasure . . . Based upon the foregoing analysis, we conclude that petitioner engaged in the security-dog activity for profit. He abandoned the poodle-raising project, however, and thus no depreciation with respect to Rebel is allowable [Internal citations omitted]. (Sampson v. Commissioner of Internal Revenue, 1982)

While the court was unpersuaded by the IRS' characterization of the petitioner's activities, it held that the petitioner could only claim some expenses, but not poodle depreciation, because he did not train poodles.

Theft

Stolen puppies make for tragic human interest news stories in the United States; and municipalities may expend resources attempting to satisfy public outcry against puppy theft. Yet, some municipalities may only investigate and prosecute pet store burglary when boutique puppies or puppy products (including medications) are valuable, or possibly dangerous to the public. Sometimes, the manner in which puppies are stolen interests the public, such as when puppies are liberated by eco-terrorists. Human interest in puppy theft, including law enforcement's interest, is particularly high when vulnerable victims are harmed. For example, a woman decided to buy a Pug puppy for a seven year-old girl, who had leukemia (Lopez, 2014). The Pug was given to a third party, who was supposed to deliver the puppy to the girl; but instead, the third party absconded with the puppy, but the puppy was recovered by police. The American public is also keen on stories in which disabled individuals receive justice, including disabled puppies. For example, two men stole a three month-old deaf pit bull puppy named Thor; and then, they attempted to sell Thor to the victim, but law enforcement intervened and returned Thor (Baltimore County Government, 2014).

Several theories of crime explain why criminals, who steal puppies, may perpetrate other crimes, such as drug dealing. Explanations include low morality, criminal environment, poor impulse control, mental illness, genetic predisposition, or callousness, discussed in Chapter Four. American police may believe that individuals, who steal puppies, could be involved in other crimes. Thus, even when police are uninterested in investigating puppy theft, they may investigate puppy theft as a pretext for gathering evidence of other crimes. In one case, a victim's puppy was stolen, but the victim's neighbor recorded the suspect's license plate number, which police traced to a vehicle that did not match the description of the vehicle given by witnesses (Howard v. Arkansas, 2004). Police located the suspect's home, and were granted consent to search the vehicle matching the description provided by witnesses. An officer smelled marijuana, and found a large plastic bag containing more than four ounces of marijuana. The suspected thief was charged with possession with intent to deliver. In another case, Jack's Pet Center was burglarized by a suspect, who was later charged with possession of drug paraphernalia (Montana v. Kelley, 2005). The burglar stole a male Chihuahua puppy, a female Doberman Pinscher puppy, and $2,700, including a collection of 36 two-dollar bills and approximately one dozen wheat pennies (Montana v. Kelley, 2005). One of the suspect's neighbors observed new Chihuahua and Doberman Pinscher puppies and cash in the suspect's possession. The neighbor later learned about the burglary while watching the local news, and alerted authorities. The police listened and looked through the suspect's window where they could see the stolen puppies and could hear whimpering. They obtained a search warrant; and although the suspect was intoxicated, he consented to a search. The suspect claimed that he had found the puppies roaming the streets following the break-in; and later changed his story to claim that he had bought the puppies at a hotel. However, police found $1,400, including 34 two-dollar bills and a wheat penny. The suspect also possessed rolling papers, burnt marijuana, and bagged marijuana. He conceded to possessing paraphernalia and was convicted of theft at trial.

In Alabama, a defendant was convicted of two counts of reckless manslaughter after he killed Chucky Morrow because Morrow had stolen his puppies (Sheffield v. State, 2010). Before Morrow's death, the defendant complained to the police about the puppy theft, and disclosed to the police that Morrow had sold drugs. The defendant threatened to incinerate Morrow's house, saying to police "I'm so mad about my dogs, I am a good mind to screw his doors and windows shut and set his house on fire with him in it" (Sheffield v. State, 2010, p. 613). Police attempted to calm the defendant by minimizing the significance of puppy theft and downplaying the value of his puppies. Police also attempted to channel the defendant's vengeance by recruiting him as a confidential informant to buy drugs from Morrow. The defendant continued to demand his puppies from Morrow; and then Morrow's house caught fire causing Morrow and his three-year-old son to die from smoke inhalation. Several witnesses testified about the defendant's insistence that Morrow had stolen his puppies. Morrow's mother testified that just before her son's house caught fire, she learned that the defendant had her son's pit bull in his possession. She testified that the defendant had wanted to buy the pit bull before her son bought the dog, so she demanded that he return the dog or pay her $60. The defendant paid $60 to the victim's mother. One witness, whose daughter was friends with Morrow's girlfriend, testified that the defendant told her that he intended to confront Morrow at his home regarding the stolen puppies. The defendant intended to administer Xanax to Morrow as a truth serum so that Morrow would divulge details about the defendant's puppies. The defendant followed through with his plan by refilling a prescription for Xanax; and a toxicology report found Xanax in Morrow's system. This evidence and other evidence resulted in the defendant being convicted of two counts of reckless manslaughter despite the fact that trained dogs failed to detect accelerant and the fact that the fire marshal was unable to indicate the cause of the fire. This case demonstrates the extent to which some Americans, such as the defendant feel attached to puppies and feel compelled to own puppies. The defendant may have believed that law enforcement failed properly to protect his property because they personally did not view his puppies as being valuable property. However, his convictions for reckless manslaughter, rather than first degree murder, may hint at this court's sympathy for the defendant's intent. At first, the defendant was convicted by a lower court for reckless murder in Marrow's death; but he was convicted of reckless manslaughter in the death of Marrow's son for reasons the trial record did not explain.

> The reckless-murder charge required proof that [the defendant] had recklessly caused the death of a person under circumstances manifesting extreme indifference to the value of human life. The

reckless-manslaughter charge required proof that [the defendant] recklessly caused the death of another person. As to the reckless-manslaughter conviction, it may be said that the jury found that the child's death did not result from circumstances manifesting extreme indifference to the value of human life or that the jury simply chose not to convict on that charge for reasons not readily apparent in the record. (Sheffield v. State, 2010, p. 621)

The defendant appealed his conviction for reckless murder claiming "that the reckless-murder conviction for the death of Chucky Morrow should be reversed because . . . the evidence was insufficient to establish universal malice" (Sheffield v. State, 2010, p. 624).

The evidence showed that the [defendant's] conduct was directed toward or aimed at Chucky Morrow and not to human life in general . . . The doctrine of universal malice, depraved heart murder, or reckless homicide manifesting extreme indifference to human life is intended to embrace those cases where a person has no deliberate intent to kill or injure any particular individual . . . When considered with the evidence in its entirety, the State's arguments that [the defendant] . . . did not have a specific intent to harm or injure any person, . . . but instead "intended to scare or send a message" and that a jury could have found that he acted recklessly with a depraved indifference to human life because he lacked knowledge of who, if anyone, was inside the residence when the fire was started . . . are not persuasive. The evidence, albeit circumstantial, demonstrated that [the defendant] burned Chucky Morrow's house, which resulted in Chucky's death. [The defendant's] act of arson was directed toward Chucky Morrow and the house where he knew Chucky lived, not toward humankind in general [Internal citations omitted]. (Sheffield v. State, 2010, p. 625)

The appellate court held that the evidence did not prove that the defendant's actions "manifested extreme indifference to human life in general" (Sheffield v. State, 2010, p. 626). The defendant did not recklessly commit arson; rather, he incinerated Marrow's house because Marrow stole his puppies.

Some criminals may use alleged puppy theft as an alibi to mislead authorities about their culpability in other crimes. For example, in New Jersey v. Bryant (2007), a pregnant woman was discovered dead inside her home. A pit bull terrier and puppies had also been inside her home when she was stabbed more than 50 times. The puppies had been sired by the defendant's male pit bull. On the night of the victim's death, the defendant told his pregnant partner that, despite her wishes, he wanted to retrieve a puppy from the victim's litter. The defendant went to the victim's apartment and returned to his home covered in blood. He admitted to his partner that he had killed the victim, but claimed that he acted in self-defense, which is discussed in Chapter Four. He claimed that the victim attacked him with a knife after mistakenly believing him to be an intruder when he snuck through the back window of her apartment. The defendant claimed that he wrestled with the victim, and she was stabbed. Investigators found that the defendant and the victim had been paramours; and that the defendant attempted to steal the victim's cocaine. A rape kit administered post-mortem detected that the defendant's sperm had been inside the victim's vagina at the time of her death. The defendant confessed that the he and the victim copulated for several hours and fought over cocaine on the night of her death. During the fight, the victim scratched the defendant and grabbed two knives. In response, he tied an electrical cord to his hand and swung a clothes iron. He beat the victim's head twice with the iron before battering and stabbing her. The defendant's crime was part of a pattern of intimate partner violence with the victim.

Family Law

The state has an interest in hearing property issues in marriage dissolutions and divorces that involve pets. Family courts have held that pets may exclusively belong to a petitioner (i.e. plaintiff) or respondent (i.e. defendant); or that parties must equally divide property, for example, by sharing physical custody of pets; yet many courts are reluctant to treat pets like children by awarding legal custody. The court in Travis v. Murray (2013) analyzed relevant issues. A couple (i.e. plaintiff and defendant) shared an apartment in Upper Manhattan, New York. While cohabiting prior to being married, the couple purchased Joey, who was ten weeks old. The couple got married, but four months after buying Joey, the defendant moved from their apartment while the plaintiff was absent on business; took possession of Joey and some property; and claimed that Joey had runaway in Central Park. Approximately two years later, the plaintiff filed for divorce and demanded that the defendant disclose Joey's true whereabouts; and asked the court to order the defendant to return Joey to the plaintiff's sole custody. The defendant answered the plaintiff's motion disclosing that Joey lived in Freeport, Maine with her mother. The plaintiff claimed that she owned Joey because she used her funds to purchase Joey prior to the marriage; and she alleged that the defendant stole her property. The plaintiff also argued that it would be in Joey's best interest to be returned to her custody because she provided Joey with care. The defendant opposed the plaintiff's claims stating that she received Joey as a gift from the plaintiff to compensate the defendant, who was forced to rehome her cat in order to cohabit with the plaintiff. She claimed financially, emotionally, and practically to have cared for Joey; for example, Joey's bed had been on her side of the marital bed. The defendant also claimed that it would be in Joey's best interest to remain at her mother's house in Maine.

> Thus, both sides invoke[d] two different approaches in determining which one should be awarded Joey. The first approach is the traditional property analysis, with plaintiff maintaining that Joey is her property by virtue of having bought him and defendant maintaining that the dog is hers as a result of plaintiff having gifted him to her. The second approach is the custody analysis, with each side calling into play such concepts as nurturing, emotional needs, happiness and, above all, best interests—concepts that are firmly rooted in child custody analyses. (Travis v. Murray, 2013, p. 451)

The court believed that it would be inappropriate to apply a strict property analysis; but weighing typical factors to determine the best interest of a child may not have been in the best interest of Joey, the litigants, or society. The court held that a "best for all concerned" standard should be applied (Travis v. Murray, 2013, p. 458).

> People who love their dogs almost always love them forever. But with divorce rates at record highs, the same cannot always be said for those who marry. All too often, onetime happy spouses end up as decidedly unhappy litigants in divorce proceedings. And when those litigants own a dog, matrimonial judges are called upon more and more to decide what happens to the pet that each of the parties still loves and each of them still wants. This case concerns one such dog, a two and a half year-old miniature dachshund named Joey. Joey finds himself in a tug-of-war between two spouses in the midst of a divorce proceeding to end their extremely short and childless marriage. In fact, the only issue in this case is what will become of the parties' beloved pet. (Travis v. Murray, 2013, pp. 447–448)

The court analyzed case law from other jurisdictions to address the parties' use of the term "custody" (Travis v. Murray, 2013). Consistent with case law in the majority of jurisdictions, the court held that the concept of legal custody did not apply to disputes involving dogs, who are legal property not children.

Courts, policies, and legislation may protect animals using civil protection orders. One policy rationale for this is that domesticated animals' safety emotionally and psychologically affects victims of intimate partner violence. Critics claim that these policies overextend legal protection to animals, which could explode into full rights leading to absurd results or unexpected changes in American culture (Pedersen, 2009). However, society has an interest in minimizing cycles of violence, which are perpetuated through animal cruelty, threats, and psychological abuse involving pets (Baxendale, et al., 2015).

The American government has an interest in intervening into domestic violence (e.g. intimate partner violence) that victimizes dogs. One reason is that research and case law demonstrate high likelihood of comorbidity between domestic violence, cruelty, and child maltreatment. A 14-year sample of 1,614 individuals, who participated in the National Youth Survey Family Study, determined that intimate partner violence perpetration by parents predicted children's history of animal cruelty (Knight, Ellis, & Simmons, 2014). Another study analyzed 307 males arrested for domestic violence (Febres, et al., 2014). Forty-one percent perpetrated animal cruelty at least once during adulthood. Yet, within the general population, only one and one-half percent of men self-reported any history of animal cruelty. Among arrestees, cruelty was significantly associated with physical intimate partner violence and serious psychological violence. Cruelty to animals during childhood may suggest a history of child maltreatment (McEwen, Moffitt, & Arseneault, 2014). Cruelty perpetration among children between the ages of five and 12 years old was analyzed using data from a longitudinal twin study of 2,232 children, whose mothers reported approximately every two years any incidents of animal cruelty perpetrated by their children. Nine percent of children reportedly committed cruelty, with approximately one-third of those persistently perpetrating cruelty. Children's history of cruelty perpetration correlated with history of maltreatment; and approximately 44% of children, who committed cruelty, had been maltreated. Sixty percent of children from disadvantaged families, who committed animal cruelty, experienced maltreatment. "The usefulness of cruelty to animals as a marker for maltreatment increases with the child's age, persistence of behavior, and poorer social background"; however, the law must protect individuals equally, thus protocols and policies are justifiable when they allow the government to intervene sooner into allegations of relatively unserious cruelty (McEwen,

Moffitt, & Arseneault, 2014). Contentions that the system irrationally may overreact to allegations of cruelty possibly may be accurate when parents' rights are challenged because they were helpless victims of abuse unable to defend their animals or children. For example, in one case, a mother challenged the sufficiency of evidence presented by Texas Department of Human Resources to terminate her parental rights after her husband abused her child and puppy (Shapley v. Texas Department of Human Resources, 1979). The mother delayed a day before presenting at a hospital with her child, who had been beaten by her husband, the child's father. Approximately three months later, the mother filed for divorce, and her husband drunkenly abused her and their puppy. Witnesses testified that they believed that the mother would allow her husband to behave abusively in the future; thus, her rights should be terminated. The court considered the evidence and sustained the mother's challenge to the sufficiency of the evidence.

> [W]e note that the mother always cared for her child. The record is to the effect that all acts of abuse were done by the child's father . . . It was only because of the mother's love for her child that the beating was ever called to the attention of the authorities in the first place. Her delay could well have been caused by her own fear of her husband. (Shapley v. Texas Department of Human Resources, 1979, pp. 253–254)

Thus, termination of rights in cases like this would not be in children's best interest and would further victimize the abused parent and puppy. However, courts may overextend opportunities for rehabilitation resulting in victimization. For example, in one case, a father was arrested for possessing drug paraphernalia; however, he admitted to social workers that he had relapsed; submitted to drug testing; and began attending Alcoholics Anonymous and Narcotics Anonymous meetings (In re O.J. v. Lynn T., 2008). A social worker noted that the father regularly failed to visit with his children although he wanted to reunify with them. He consistently tested negative for drugs; and eventually visited with his children. The father did not appear to be emotional about reunification and threw the children's puppy on the ground and broke the dog's leg. The court terminated reunification services and set a permanency hearing; but continued drug testing and visitation despite the threat to his children's puppy.

Intimate partner violence research does not suggest that only males, but never females, abuse and kill puppies in America (Cusack, 2015). Mothers killing puppies is often comorbid with domestic violence, substance abuse, mental illness, trauma, and child maltreatment

(Woodman v. Simmons, 2006). For example, children were adjudicated dependent after a six year-old child reported to Child Protective Services (CPS) in Arizona that his mother had decapitated puppies using a saw (Jessica R. v. ADES, 2008). CPS originally became involved when the boy reported his parents' fighting to police. Police and CPS discovered that the child and his siblings were living in squalor without food. They were filthy, covered in vomit, and playing with feces, which covered their house.

> The mother and the father stated that they had a dog breeding business with pit bulls and pit bull puppies on their property. There were approximately 12 pit bull dogs and approximately 10 puppies. The animals were being neglected, having no food or water and they were contained in filthy kennels. There were several dead puppies in the front yard [in] plastic grocery bags. [A] CPS investigator . . . reported that . . . [the six year-old] . . . watched his mother 'sawing heads off of some puppies' and he knew the puppies had been alive because he had heard them 'whimper.' Officers arrested . . . [the mother] for animal cruelty and the father for outstanding warrants related to drug charges and removed the children from the parents' custody. The Arizona Department of Economic Security (ADES) filed a dependency petition alleging as to . . . [the mother] that the home was filthy, she had been cruel to animals in . . . [her child's] presence, and she had been smoking marijuana and cooking methamphetamine in the home. (Jessica R. v. ADES, 2008, p. 4)

After the children's parents failed to appear, a juvenile court adjudicated the children dependent.

Personhood

Many Americans treat dogs as nonhuman members of their families with specialized social roles demonstrating dogs' identities and group membership. Dogs function as natural persons, who belong to society; receive medical treatment; own possessions; influence outcomes; work; satisfy others; and fulfill obligations; but, laws distinguish them from humans. Denial of personhood has been justified by outdated science devised to prove that dogs lack humanness.

> "Personhood" is in fact a vast and critical distinction between what humans are and what other animals are, and our evidentiary rules and our justice system work well in recognizing the gap as a legally crit-

ical one. There is no doubt that many animals are individuals in the very rough sense that they have distinct character suites; domesticated animals such as dogs and cats can act as if they were playful, or suspicious, or aggressive, or mischievous, or ridiculous in the sense that we intuitively know humans can be. But cognitive scientists recognize that our inter-specific differences go far beyond the differences in our outward appearances, our actions, or even our inner anatomical structures; humans are individuals in a fundamentally different sense. (Duckler, 2007, pp. 112–113)

Some pundits claim that dogs seem freely to participate in human families and society, but in fact, they may actually mechanistically respond to human behavior cues (Udell & Wynne, 2011). However, neuroscientific research demonstrates that dogs' possess human emotions. Dozens of dogs were trained to go in an M.R.I. scanner without restraints or sedation in order to analyze their neurological activity. The data demonstrated that "dogs are people . . . [, which] means we must reconsider their treatment as property" (Berns, 2013).

Animal welfarists in the United States have compared ownership and deprivation of legal personhood for dogs with enslavement of African Americans. A case was made by animal welfare organizations (i.e. Next Friends) under the 13ᵗʰ Amendment of the U.S. Constitution prohibiting slavery, on behalf of Tilikum, a world famous killer whale at SeaWorld (Tilikum v. SeaWorld Parks & Entertainment, 2012; *U.S. Const. amend. XIII*). The court applauded the plaintiffs, but lacked subject matter jurisdiction and dismissed the lawsuit with prejudice.

Even though Plaintiffs lack standing to bring a Thirteenth Amendment claim, that is not to say that animals have no legal rights; as there are many state and federal statutes affording redress to Plaintiffs, including, in some instances, criminal statutes that . . . punish those who violate statutory duties that protect animals . . . While the goal of Next Friends in seeking to protect the welfare of orcas is laudable, the Thirteenth Amendment affords no relief to Plaintiffs [Internal citations omitted]. (Tilikum v. SeaWorld Parks & Entertainment, 2012, pp. 1264–1265)

Congruent with the court's assertion that animals have some legal rights, pundits may argue that dogs already possess a degree of legal personhood.

Bearing in mind that legal personhood is a matter of degree depending on which rights and duties one has - one can be more or less a legal

person according to whether one is a prisoner, minor, parolee, proba-
tioner, future person, intending immigrant, corporation, animal, . . .
[et ctera]- there may be an ideal of legal personhood that creates the
continuum along which these various points fall . . . [N]ormally,
legal personhood is simply whatever particular bundle of legal rights
and duties lawmakers say we have. The law says minors cannot vote,
corporations can own property, people should not torture dogs
(dogs have legal personhood in the limited sense that humans owe the
legal duty not to torture them), . . . [et cetera]. Thus, whatever bundle
is assigned defines the different entities' degree of legal personhood.
(Dillard, 2012, pp. 4–5)

However, advocates continue to argue for increased recognition of
legal rights and formal codification of personhood for dogs, which
advocates claim is feasible in light of corporate personhood (Serafino,
2011). Yet, the problem with comparing personhood for dogs to
corporate personhood is that corporations are legally responsible for
their wrongdoings, such that they can be destroyed or punished for
committing crimes. Although allegedly vicious dogs may be destroyed,
the law cannot be used to punish dogs for perceived wrongdoings
because dogs are not legally culpable actors in the United States
(Cusack, 2015). Some animals may enjoy their privileges and immunities from persecution; and they would not trade their natural right
to be free from societal obligations in order to receive additional
protections or rights, for example, the right to vote.

Smuggling

Smuggled puppies have been bound, gagged, sedated, trapped "in
speaker boxes, screwed into the car door panels and wrapped in blan-
kets with their little legs taped to their bodies and stuffed under seats"
(Sweeney, 2010). These crimes directly relate to buyers' demand for
boutique and purebred puppies; yet, puppies supplied by smugglers
may be sick and maltreated animals, which is unanticipated by gullible
or uninformed pet owners, who may be forced to pay thousands of
dollars in veterinary bills (ABC News, n.d.). Puppy smuggling may not
result from antipathy toward puppies; but rather, it is part of the
wildlife black market, which is allegedly the largest black market after
drug trafficking (Cusack, 2015). However, puppy smuggling demonstrates particularly callous behavior because puppies are maltreated
and later sold as beloved pets. Dramatic increases "in smuggled
puppies always happens over the holidays . . . It's the American ideal:

The kids come out on Christmas morning and there's a puppy bounding out from under the tree . . . These adorable little . . . eyes" disguise maltreatment (Jung, 2009).

Smugglers violate local, state, and federal regulations and laws by falsely reporting or failing to report puppies imported from Australia, Hungary, Mexico, South Korea, and other countries (Sweeney, 2010). In California, 18 animal law enforcement agencies formed a coalition called Border Puppy Task Force (BPTF) to monitor and lessen the effects of sick puppies introduced through smuggling into the state and to reduce monetary incentives for smugglers (Mott, 2006). BPTF estimated that approximately 10,000 puppies may be imported annually from Mexico into San Diego County, California and sold for $1,000 each at shopping center parking lots. BPTF's interdiction activities, which relied on grant funding, waned since their peak last decade; however, their innovative multiagency investigations of commercial fraud continue to motivate law enforcement agencies, veterinary professionals, and policymakers to institute and enforce effective policies. For example, smugglers may falsify veterinary records to demonstrate that a dog is older than 12 weeks in order to evade vaccination and quarantine requirements; but, BPTF's efforts have raised awareness about these ploys, which increases the likelihood of detection (James, 2007). Tax evasion and regulatory breaches continue despite local, state, and federal efforts because most smugglers fail to report any importation (Winter & Gutteridge, 2015).

Homeless animals may not be owned by humans; however, they may be treated as property by the government, welfarists, and animal control agencies. Animal welfare organizations may lawfully import stray animals from other countries; for example Save a Sato (i.e. "mixed-breed" in Puerto Rican Spanish) has transported 14,000 abandoned and abused dogs from Puerto Rico to the continental United States (James, 2007). Other animal welfare organizations circumnavigate the law, which may compromise authorities' abilities to distinguish them from black market smugglers, who may claim to assist homeless animals in order to avoid taxation, regulations, and government oversight; yet, when animal welfarists violate regulations, governments may not attempt to pursue criminal or civil remedies. For example, Americans allegedly rescued dozens of stray and feral dogs from Sochi, Russia where the government purportedly culled dogs in preparation for the 2014 Winter Olympics (Edgemon, 2014; Fox News, 2014; Good Morning America, 2014; Reynolds, 2014; Vasilyeva, 2014). Some rescuers violated regulations, such as license plate registration and vaccination requirements, which complicated their attempts expeditiously to export and adopt numerous puppies; and they argued that violations amounted to harmless administrative infractions not black market smuggling. Their activities may seem elaborate, or perhaps farsighted, because hundreds of American localities and animal control organizations regularly cull stray and feral animals. Some Americans have also attempted to rescue dogs in South Korea because American culture tends to oppose dogs being shipped in crammed wire crates, tortured, and slaughtered for meat (Hodal, 2013). Koreans' multifaceted relationship with dogs is discussed in Chapter Fourteen. Many Americans' view dogmeat markets as a serious harm that should be deterred by law. In Thailand, the dogmeat business is enabled by organized crime and corrupt officials. Their operations may be open and notorious when caging dogs is legal, despite obvious connections to smuggling into China, Laos, South Korea, and Vietnam (Barcroft Media, 2012; Hodal, 2013; KARA, 2012; Shadbolt, 2013). The black market may have once related to immigration, famine and poverty, such as in Tha Rae (i.e. Butcher Village) where Catholic Vietnamese refugees began trading dogs more than one century ago (Hodal, 2013; Sattar & Reed, 2013). However, many dogmeat butcher stalls have only recently opened, which possibly undermines the idea that dogmeat has been part of traditional culture. Although prosperous smuggling operations may have transported thousands of dogs from Thailand into Vietnam through Laos, consumers should be wary of dogmeat because evidence demonstrates that more than 16% of dogs and puppies may be rabid, and many more may be ill. Asian and American animal welfare groups campaign against dogmeat markets to raise awareness; and may attempt to intervene by rescuing some animals and adopting them in the United States (Barcroft, 2012; *San Francisco Gate*, 2015).

Euthanasia

In the United States, euthanasia is a controversial practice for humans, but not for dogs. A minority of states have allowed doctors to administer medicine to assist human patients with their deaths in spite of criticism that assisted suicide is immoral. Terminally ill humans may choose medically to end their lives in California, Montana, Oregon, Vermont, and Washington (Death with Dignity Act, 1994; End of Life Act, 2015; Patient Choice and Control at End of Life Act, 2013). A Montana court record explained why physicians may assist patients to control cause of death (Baxter v. Montana, 2009).

[A] physician who aids a terminally ill patient in dying is not directly involved in the final decision or the final act. He or she only provides a means by which a terminally ill patient . . . can give effect to . . . [a] life-ending decision, or not, as the case may be. Each stage of the physician-patient interaction is private, civil, and compassionate. The physician and terminally ill patient work together to create a means by which the patient can be in control of his [or her] own mortality. The patient's subsequent private decision whether to take the medicine does not breach public peace or endanger others. (Baxter v. Montana, 2009, p. 1217)

Americans have used state and federal legislation to prevent assisted suicide and enforce traditional mores. For example, in 2006, the U.S. Supreme Court heard a case in which the federal government attempted to use the Controlled Substances Act to prevent the State of Oregon from decriminalizing physician-assisted suicide (21 U.S.C. § 801, 2006; Death with Dignity Act, 2008; Gonzales v. Oregon, 2006).

The question before [the court] . . . is whether the Controlled Substances Act allows the United States Attorney General to prohibit doctors from prescribing regulated drugs for use in physician-assisted suicide, notwithstanding a state law permitting the procedure . . . Americans are engaged in an earnest and profound debate about the morality, legality, and practicality of physician-assisted suicide . . . The dispute before us is in part a product of this political and moral debate, but its resolution requires an inquiry familiar to the courts: interpreting a federal statute to determine whether executive action is authorized by, or otherwise consistent with, the enactment [Internal citations omitted]. (Gonzales v. Oregon, 2006, pp. 248–249)

The court held that Oregonian doctors could prescribe the medication in spite of the federal government's attempted statutory interpretation.

Suicide prevention is not a primary concern for the American government (Cusack, 2013). Millions of Americans are placed on psychiatric holds each year in order to evaluate whether they are suicidal; but treatment facilities lack beds, staff, and resources to assist patients under observation. Government programs may provide low cost or free medication and emergency treatment; however, the government spends little money attempting to treat causes of social, physical, or mental illness resulting in suicide.

Although political and moral rhetoric discourages suicide because of cultural fear of eternal damnation, medically assisted suicide among humans has gained support in recent years, not only because of improved medicine, but perhaps because of decreased religious faith in divine will (Pew Research Center, 2015). Social emphasis on individual happiness and self-determinism may also play a key role in cultural shifts. American society may approve of euthanasia for family dogs, which ends prolonged suffering at the end of life, because Americans value their dogs' comfort; and because traditional beliefs do not require humans to have faith in an afterlife for dogs that is conditioned on submission to divine will.

Dogs and puppies may be euthanized without many restrictions because they are property or lack owners. One restriction is that carbon monoxide may not be used to exterminate puppies younger than 16 weeks old in several states, such as North Carolina, Oklahoma, or South Carolina (02 N.C. Admin. Code 52J .0501, 2015; 4 Okl. Stat. Ann. §501, 2015; Cal. Code § 597u-v, 2014; S.C. Code §47-3-420, 2015). Though millions of dogs are euthanized to end their suffering, millions more are euthanized because they are homeless; but some states, such as California, oppose this practice (PETA, n.d.).

> It is the policy of the state that no adoptable animal should be euthanized if it can be adopted into a suitable home. Adoptable animals include only those animals eight weeks of age or older that, at or subsequent to the time the animal is impounded or otherwise taken into possession, have manifested no sign of a behavioral or temperamental defect that could pose a health or safety risk or otherwise make the animal unsuitable for placement as a pet, and have manifested no sign of disease, injury, or congenital or hereditary condition that adversely affects the health of the animal or that is likely to adversely affect the animal's health in the future. (Cal. Code § 599d(a), 2014)

Some organizations that euthanize healthy dogs and puppies claim to compassionately prevent animals from languishing in shelters where they may be deprived or neglected.

The topic of dog suicide is somewhat undiscussed in American families, academic circles, or civic enclaves because data does not demonstrate that dogs commit suicide despite some anecdotal evidence. However, evidence does not show that dogs do not commit suicide; and so, the possibility exists that some dogs commit suicide (e.g. hanged by leash). One method may be intentionally to encounter animal control in order to be humanely euthanized. Another method may be self-destruction using roads, bridges, or other infrastructure. For example, a television commercial depicts an emotionally devastated dog attempting to commit suicide (Youtube.com, 2009). After witnessing a love interest's sexual promiscuity, the dog runs across town, passing freeways and a lawman. He heads onto a multilane tollway where the dog brokenly stares at traffic. As the dog steps into oncoming traffic a Mercedes Benz halts. Therefore, loss of life was averted. The commercial suggests that roadkill may be evidence that dogs commit suicide. Dogs' participation in society suggests that they may have intellectual capacities, practical experience, and requisite emotional states to choose violent or "humane methods" to end their lives. Roadkill is discussed in Chapter Two.

Estate and Trust

Leona Helmsley bequeathed $12 million to Trustees of Leona Helmsley July 2005 Trust (Helmsley, 2005; James, 2011). In the same clause bequeathing $12 million, Helmsley bequeathed to her brother her Maltese dog named Trouble. The provision was interpreted to leave $12 million to Trouble; however, Trouble's portion of the trust was reduced to two million dollars because a trust may not substantially exceed what will be used for a stipulated purpose— a principle that must be balanced against donor's intent (Grossman, 2007). A trust benefiting a dog could have violated the Rule Against Perpetuities because dogs are legal property, not legal persons; and the Rule Against Perpetuities limits the duration of a trust to 21 years after the designated life in being. Because Trouble was a dog, her life could not serve as a life in being; thus, Trouble's trust generally would have violated the Rule Against Perpetuities, except that New York estates, powers and trusts law § 7-8.1 allows dogs to be the beneficiaries of trusts that provide for their care for 21 years or until they are deceased (2015). Yet, Trouble's trust failed to meet basic principles of estate and trust law because $12 million substantially exceeded the amount that Trouble needed annually, including $100,000 for security, $8,000 for grooming, $1,200 for food, and $60,000 for a guardian (Abelson, 2009). Thus, $10 million were allocated to other Helmsley trusts. Millions were allegedly given to two of her grandchildren to whom she had left no money. Arguably, this decision demonstrated that various fields of law enforce dogs' status as property. By divesting Trouble of her fortune and assigning it to Helmsley's grandchildren, the court may have imposed Americans' custom of leaving money to humans, not dogs. Evidence was presented suggesting that Helmsley was mentally unfit when she chose to bequeath her money to Trouble rather than to two of her grandchildren. After Helmsley's death, nonprofit corporations, including Humane Society of the United States, American Society for the Prevention of Cruelty to Animals, and Maddie's Fund sued her estate over the amount of money granted from her trust to care for dogs (James, 2009). The nonprofit groups framed the issue as a violation of Helmsley's last wishes. However, courts cannot force trustees to breach their fiduciary duties; and the trustees demonstrated that they were acting in the trust's interest. Helmsley's Mission Statement discussed intent to care for dogs, however trustees believed that her directives allocated no money to nonprofit organizations because during her lifetime when she controlled the trust, she failed to donate any money to animal organizations.

Puppy Mills

"Puppy mills" are a business operating with excessive numbers of puppies, who are confined to cramped and unhygienic quarters. A defining characteristic of puppy mills is that the number of puppies may be statutorily excessive; or appear to be excessive relative to the amount of care paid and comfort allocated to each dog. In some jurisdictions, all breeding operations selling puppies to pet stores constitute illegal puppy mills (Henry, 2015). One reason that puppy mills are persecuted, and sometimes prosecuted, is that many puppy mills have sold sick puppies, who prematurely die. Puppy mills may sell to pet stores; do business as small family breeding operations or breed-specific rescues charging high adoption fees; or operate in a clean storefront that disguises their breeding practices. For example, owners of a puppy mill were charged with 50 misdemeanors for animal abuse and neglect for hiding inside of a home's attic 39 sick puppies, ranging from six weeks old to four months old (Alanez, 2005). The defendants also kept dead puppies in their freezer. They had not bred the dead animals, but rather, those puppies had been purchased from another breeder, and the defendants wanted credit for returning the dead puppies. They also claimed that other puppies had been purchased from the same breeder, and were sick when they assumed care of them. However, some of the puppies were sick with parasites, which could have been treated by the defendants. The puppies shared a small space, which caused diseases rapidly to spread. Several consumers complained that puppies purchased from the defendants were sick. For example, one customer paid $6,700 for a puppy, who died within ten days due to a hole in his heart. Of the 39 puppies, 35 were surrendered by the defendants for adoption.

Some puppy mills are legally operated; yet some may be owned by convicts, who have criminal histories, including drug charges, sex offenses, fraud, theft, cruelty, child maltreatment, and tax evasion. For example, in Harris v. Snelgrove (2011), a puppy mill owner had five sons from three husbands; then she was impregnated by her oldest son's roommate, who was a young adult. Her minor child's home environment caused him to be exposed to drugs and alcohol abuse; drug raids; arrests; violence; neglect; exhaustion; and truancy from kindergarten. The little boy's mother participated in several schemes, including a puppy mill that was run online to supply dogs to clients throughout the world. She placed under her sons' names her business, assets, and bank accounts in order to evade liability and legal judgments and to receive government assistance. The child's grandparents were awarded custody, and his mother was ordered to pay child support.

Animal welfarists have lobbied for federal legislation to regulate puppy mills. For example, the Puppy Uniform Protection and Safety (PUPS) Act, which is under review by a Congressional subcommittee, proposes to increase applicable protections for puppy mill dogs under the Animal Welfare Act (2009) by specifying the meaning of " "high volume retail breeder" as person who, in commerce, for compensation or profit: (1) has an ownership interest in or custody of one or more breeding female dogs; and (2) sells . . . more than 50 of the offspring . . . for use as pets in any one-year period" (PUPS Act, 2013). PUPS Act would require the Secretary of Agriculture to ensure that dogs at puppy mills receive regular access to exercise and clean living conditions; and breeders, who deal in high volumes of retail dogs, would require licensing applications and renewals to stipulate the number of dogs exempt from exercise (PUPS Act, 2013).

Although puppy mills are legal in most states, several jurisdictions effectively ban them because they are cruel. One pet shop in Phoenix, Arizona, for example, challenged such a ban. Puppies 'N Love sued after a local ordinance prohibited pet stores from selling animals obtained from breeders.

In recent years, cities such as Austin, Chicago, Los Angeles, Miami, and San Diego have passed ordinances prohibiting pet stores from selling dogs obtained from certain types of breeders. The HSUS [i.e. Humane Society of the Unites States] is a proponent of these ordinances. The HSUS believes that because many pet shops sell dogs obtained from puppy mills, governments should limit pet shops to selling dogs obtained from animal shelters. On December 18, 2013, with encouragement from the HSUS, Phoenix joined the other cities in passing a pet-store ordinance [Internal citations omitted]. (Puppies 'N Love v. City of Phoenix, 2015, pp. 4–5)

Puppies 'N Love sought injunctive relief because they mainly acquired puppies from breeders that did not operate puppy mills, such as breeders licensed by the United States Department of Agriculture (USDA) and "hobby breeders that have four or fewer breeding females" (Puppies 'N Love v. City of Phoenix, 2015, p. 9).

> If a breeder is reported to have one direct or three indirect violations of USDA standards, Puppies 'N Love states that it will not do business with that breeder. The store has a full-time employee who ensures that the breeders are "providing excellent and loving conditions in which dogs are bred and raised." (Puppies 'N Love v. City of Phoenix, 2015, p. 9)

However, evidence demonstrated that Puppies 'N Love, like many pet stores, acquired puppies from puppy mills.

> Despite these policies, Puppies 'N Love has done business with at least three breeders who have had direct violations of USDA standards. One of these breeders arguably is a prototypical puppy mill. This breeder breeds female dogs every six to twelve months, keeps dogs in small enclosures without solid flooring, and has at most six employees to take care of approximately 700 dogs. (Puppies 'N Love v. City of Phoenix, 2015, pp. 9–10)

The court ruled against Puppies 'N Love because the burden imposed on out-of-state breeders was *de minimis* and did not violate Congress' authority to regulate interstate commerce under the dormant commerce clause (Pike v. Bruce Church, Inc., 1970; Puppies 'N Love v. City of Phoenix, 2015).

> A law that does not discriminate against interstate commerce, but . . . burden[s] interstate transactions only incidentally, . . . is subject to what has come to be known as the Pike balancing test. Under this test, . . . [w]here the statute regulates even-handedly to effectuate a legitimate local public interest, and its effects on interstate commerce are only incidental, it will be upheld unless the burden imposed on such commerce is clearly excessive in relation to the putative local benefits . . . The burdens to be weighed are those that a local law imposes on the . . . interstate flow of goods, not the share of profits obtained by . . . interstate corporations . . . The benefits to be weighed are the

"putative" benefits of the law, not the actual benefits. Although the *Pike* test is deferential, courts have applied it to strike down nondiscriminatory laws . . . where such laws undermined a compelling need for national uniformity in regulation [Internal citations omitted]. (Puppies 'N Love v. City of Phoenix, 2015, pp. 49–50)

Puppies 'N Love was denied injunctive relief under Arizona's *Pike* balancing test because of society's interest in reducing puppy mills (Pike v. Bruce Church, Inc., 1970; Puppies 'N Love v. City of Phoenix, 2015).

Despite Americans' knowledge about mixed-breed dogs' strengths and the benefits of adoption, purebred and boutique dogs continue to be a multimillion dollar business. One main goal of the puppy mill industry is to create toy dogs, who continue to look like puppies throughout their lives. Generally, dogs may be more desirable to consumers when they appear to be like puppies. This is discussed in Chapter Nine. Small puppies may be likelier than larger senior dogs to be adopted; however, several factors may affect adoption, including human's gender and religion; and dog shelters' websites and marketing (Lam & Wu, 2011). A significant deterrent may be a belief that puppies living in shelters are sick, which could demonstrate that some members of the public misperceive how commonly puppies at pet stores may be ill and diseased.

Municipal and private animal control organizations may zealously attempt to shutdown unlicensed puppy mills; however, animal control organizations must act within the scope of the law. For example, Louisville Metro Animal Services (LMAS) violated the O'Neill family after they bred their two American bulldogs for the first time (O'Neill v. Louisville Jefferson County Metro Government, 2011). When the O'Neills' American bulldogs' first litter produced 11 puppies, the family placed a newspaper advertisement, and then sold four of the puppies. Two undercover LMAS officers answered the O'Neills' advertisement; and were invited into the O'Neills' home. After they investigated, they exited the O'Neills' home and alerted uniformed LMAS officers, who demanded that the O'Neills display a breeder's license. The O'Neills did not have a license, so LMAS officers seized all of their dogs, including their adult American bulldogs. LMAS stipulated that in order to return their dogs, the adult American bulldogs would need to be sterilized; the O'Neills would need to pay for a breeder's license; and all of the dogs would need to be implanted with microchips and be vaccinated. The LMAS director said that he created an ordinance that empowered him to sterilize the O'Neills' dogs; and he threatened to fine the family up to $3,000 and arrest them unless they immediately paid $1,020.95. LMAS never placed in writing any notices, allegations, or charges; however, the family paid the sum demanded by LMAS. The O'Neills' dogs were sterilized; and although their dogs had been vaccinated before being confiscated, the dogs contracted infections while in LMAS's possession. Consequently, the O'Neills had to sell the puppies for below-market value. The district court sided with LMAS; however the appellate court reinstated the O'Neills' claims that LMAS violated their right to procedural due process by conducting two separate warrantless searches and a seizure, sterilizing their dogs and implanting microchips, and demanding payment without any formal allegations. Furthermore, the appellate court found that the O'Neills were not operating an unlicensed Class A kennel; and even if LMAS could require private residences to obtain a Class A kennel designation, they had never done so previously or provided any notice that they would begin doing so. The appellate court reversed the district court on the O'Neills' procedural due process claim. Thus, private breeding was distinguishable from commercial and puppy mill breeding.

Corporations

Corporations are non-sentient legal persons, who may own sentient property, such as puppies.

> Congress provided protection for people . . . by employing a familiar legal fiction: It included corporations within [a legal] . . . definition of "persons." But it is important to keep in mind that the purpose of this fiction is to provide protection for human beings. A corporation is simply a form of organization used by human beings to achieve desired ends. An established body of law specifies the rights and obligations of the *people* (including shareholders, officers, and employees) who are associated with a corporation in one way or another. When rights, whether constitutional or statutory, are extended to corporations, the purpose is to protect the rights of these people. (Burwell v. Hobby Lobby, 2014)

Thus, the law may consider corporations' rights to own puppies as being more important than puppies' interest in possessing legal personhood.

Corporations may own puppies as mascots, including several universities, which own puppies. Despite praise bestowed on mascots, some animal welfare groups oppose corporate promotion of purebred puppy ownership due to implicit promotion of breeding and puppy mills, instead of adoption and rescue. For example, following a GoDaddy.com advertisement featuring a Labrador Retriever, People for the Ethical Treatment of Animals (PETA) "hope[d] that the puppy featured . . . will be handled with the utmost care throughout his life and that this [advertisement] . . . will not inspire people to . . . [breed] litter after litter of Labradors like him" (Bedard, 2015). PETA does not supply evidence that depictions of puppies in Super Bowl commercials correlate with increased breeding. American Super Bowl fans may overlook potential popularization of dog breeds appearing in commercials, and instead, demonstrate interest and goodwill toward corporations displaying puppies. Many corporations, like Anheuser-Busch, which also depicted a Labrador puppy in its Super Bowl advertisement, use puppy storylines for attention, but report no increase in product sales attributable to puppies appearing in advertisements (Mueller, 2015).

Breeding

Erotic manual-genital contact between humans and animals is legal in some jurisdictions; however, some jurisdictions prohibit it as bestiality or cruelty (Cusack, 2015). Customary breeding practices are normally an exception to bestiality and cruelty laws even though penetration created by breeding (e.g. artificial insemination) may reproductively coerce animals in an implicitly sexual manner that is more severe than non-penetrative external manual-genital contact (Cusack, 2011; Cusack, 2012; Cusack, 2013; Cusack, 2013; Cusack, 2014). For example, in the State of Nebraska "[a] person commits indecency with an animal when such person subjects an animal to sexual penetration . . . Indecency with an animal is a Class III misdemeanor" (Neb. Stat. Ann. § 28-1010, 2015).

> Sexual penetration means sexual intercourse in its ordinary meaning, cunnilingus, fellatio, anal intercourse, or any intrusion, however slight, of any part of the actor's or victim's body or any object manipulated by the actor into the genital or anal openings of the victim's body which can be reasonably construed as being for nonmedical or nonhealth purposes. Sexual penetration . . . [does] not require emission of semen. (Neb. Stat. Ann. § 28-318(6), 2015)

Artificial insemination may be performed "for nonmedical or nonhealth purposes," yet this law does not seem to be used to prosecute Nebraskans from artificially inseminating dogs (Neb. Stat. Ann. § 28-318(6), 2015).

Despite animals' status as property, the Animal Welfare Act (2009) requires puppies and dogs to be treated humanely, which to a limited extent, resembles a bundle of reproductive rights. For example, breeders are required to determine requisite floor space for puppies by using the following formula: "(length of dog in inches + 6) × (length of dog in inches + 6) = required floor space in square inches; required floor space in inches/ 144 = required floor space in square feet" (9 C.F.R. § 3.6(c)(1)(i), 2009). Mother dogs nursing puppies are required to have additional floor space commensurate with particular breeds' needs and behavior. A veterinarian is required to approve housing if the floor space is less than five percent of the required minimum. Primary enclosures may not be any lower than six inches above the tallest dog's head when standing; and may only enclose compatible dogs. Females in heat must be separated from sexually mature males unless they are breeding; and mothers and puppies younger than four months must be separated from adult dogs unless they are living in breeding colonies. These laws are not necessarily designed to protect dogs' and puppies' reproductive health, but the laws help to ensure their health and wellbeing during commercialized reproductive processes.

Torts

Legal and natural persons may be liable to dog owners for injuries sustained by dogs even though dogs are property; thus dogs may not have standing to file negligence claims for bodily injury, and owners may not claim tort damages for injuries to dogs' bodies' *per se,* but owners may sue for negligence, veterinary malpractice, pecuniary loss, and damage to their property (Bueckner v. Hamel, 1994; Chapman, 2009; Corso v. Crawford Dog & Cat Hospital, 1979; De Young, 2005; Fackler v. Genetzky, 1999; Gluckman v. American Airlines, 1994; Sirois, 2015). For example, five pedigree Norwegian Elkhound puppies were allegedly killed as a result of a veterinarian's negligence (Dyess v. Caraway, 1966). At approximately five weeks old, the veterinarian tested one puppy for parasites, but concluded that the tests were negative. The puppy was soon hospitalized for severe symptoms relating to tapeworms and coccidia. The mother of the litter also became infected and suffered with her puppies from serious illness for several weeks until all of the puppies died. The court applied a negligence analysis to determine whether the veterinarian failed to exercise a standard of care used by competent members of his professional community. The court found that the veterinarian met the standard of care; and that the dogs may have died even if a positive diagnosis had been given during the initial test. The court declined to apply the doctrine of *res ipsa loquitur* (i.e. "the thing speaks for itself") because it was not obvious from the evidence that the veterinarian's negligence was the proximate cause of the puppies' deaths. Damages awarded for sick and injured dogs may exceed damages for dead dogs because veterinary bills may be substantial, but most non-pedigree dogs have little monetary value.

Damages may be claimed when emotional distress is intentionally inflicted (Epstein, 2001). Reckless killing or harming of puppies may be treated by courts as negligence, breach of contract, or conversion of property; however, when conduct causes severe emotional harm, then courts may find in favor of plaintiffs. Courts may be sensitive to owners' intense emotional attachments to their pets, yet they are typically unwilling to ascribe to dogs the same emotional worth as humans despite the fact that in humans' memory causing the death of a puppy may emotionally equate with causing a human friend's death (Sun, et al., 2009). Courts may distinguish deprivation of therapeutic effects from loss of companionship. Yet, when assistance and support dogs are damaged or killed, a court may consider replacement value for working dogs' training; and a minority of courts will consider effects on eggshell (e.g. hypersensitive) plaintiffs (*Family Therapy*, 2008).

With continued introduction of puppies and dogs into the legal system, such as courthouse dogs, K-9s, and assistance dogs, courts are becoming more aware and sympathetic to dogs' emotional worth to humans. Some courts could award damages for negligent infliction of emotional distress if a defendant's conduct was extreme or outrageous; and the plaintiff's suffering was foreseeable to the defendant. However, in order to award damages, courts may need to find that dogs were victims not merely property; but most courts and legislatures do not treat dogs as victims because dogs are property, not persons. Courts may vary in the way they meet the elements, for example, some courts would also have to find that emotional closeness between dogs and their owners or handlers was the kind of close relationship described by relevant doctrines and laws, which usually apply to humans. One critic of imprecise tort law jocularly commented,

> The way society treats animals varies, so the law should not treat all animals the same according to some rigid classification system. The law should be flexible and treat certain animals according to the way

> people treat them. When an owner treats a pet like a person, the law should treat the pet like a person, too. As most dogs would agree, it all comes down to the treats. (Seps, 2010, p. 1372)

Some extreme conduct may not meet the elements when the extreme conduct is committed by defendants' dogs, but not human defendants. For example, defendants may negligently lose control of their dogs, who bite plaintiffs' dogs, however biting dogs' conduct, not defendants' conduct, would be considered extreme (Fox, Sentivan, & Grieder, 2004). Thus, plaintiffs' claims would likely fail because defendants were negligent, but not recklessly negligent. In this situation, dog's status as property, not persons may alleviate them and their owners from liability under a claim for negligent infliction of emotional distress.

Even when courts and statutes bar recovery for infliction of emotional distress, they may allow juries to award punitive damages when tortfeasors' conduct was wanton, willful, or reckless. Punitive damages, which are less commonly granted under contract law than tort law, could exceed the fair market value for a deceased puppy (Dayton, 2005). Recovery for property damage may be assessed using the dog's pedigree, age, utility, and other factors, which may also be used to demonstrate loss of companionship; however, the latter claim is far more difficult to prove (Byszewski, 2003; National Post's Financial Post & FP Investing, 2006). Each jurisdiction's case law varies in its standards for negligence and recovery (510 Ill. Comp. Stat. Ann. 70/16.3, 2014; Price, 2001; Tenn. Code Ann. § 44-17-403, 2014).

CHAPTER SEVEN

Fear and Neurosis

Puppy Training

Puppies may be trained to assist individuals, who have psychiatric disorders. Service dog companionship may be ineffective or counter-productive for some psychiatric patients. For example, a service dog handler threatening self-harm should not be admitted to a psychiatric hospital with a service dog on a leash, which could be used as a noose; yet a service dog trained to interrupt self-harm could be admitted with a patient.

The Americans with Disabilities Act (ADA) does not require service dog training to be certified; however, authorities in private businesses or public places may ask for evidence of a person's disability, such as a doctor's note; or request that a puppy demonstrate a particular task that the puppy has been trained to perform for the handler (104 § 327, 1990; Casey, 1994). For example, a person diagnosed with post-traumatic stress disorder (PTSD) may use a puppy to cover and block. A service dog does not need to have learned a particular technique from a trainer; yet, a puppy must be capable of covering or blocking on command. Although service dogs typically cannot be denied admittance, dogs may be barred if handlers cannot verify their status as service dogs.

Individuals diagnosed with anxiety disorders may use dogs to calm their anxiety. Diagnosed disabilities resulting from anxiety disorders (DSM-5 309.21, 2013), for which a puppy may be trained to assist a handler, include separation anxiety disorder (American Psychiatric Association, 2013). Criteria for a diagnosis of this disorder under American Psychiatric Association (APA) guidelines include relatively excessive fear or anxiety when an individual becomes separated from an attachment figure. Excessive stress is likely to be recurrent and worrisome; and result in reluctance to be alone or go to sleep. Children are particularly vulnerable to this illness. Physical symptoms may include headaches, cramps, nausea, vomiting, palpitations, dizziness, and faintness. To be diagnosed as a psychiatric disorder, children must likely have experienced symptoms for at least four weeks; and adolescents will likely have experienced symptoms for at least six months.

Clinically significant distress or impairment to functionality results in negative social, academic, occupational, or interpersonal consequences. Studies shows that dogs' presence increases relaxation in humans, however, puppies used as assistance dogs must be trained to assist individuals with anxiety separation, for example, by sensing anxiety and gently approaching or licking a person in distress; or they may be trained to retrieve medicine or play soothing music on an electronic device. Some of the success in using an assistance dog to treat separation anxiety lies with the patient, who must accept the puppy as a substitution for the attachment figure. Some service dogs may experience separation anxiety (Service Dogs, 2009). To some extent, a puppy experiencing separation anxiety may be an ideal companion for a child or adolescent, who cannot be alone. Yet, excessively anxious puppies may complicate a child's environment or exacerbate the child's illness by increasing panic and general anxiety. A service dog may not only assist and calm children, but a therapeutic dog may prevent future comorbidity (Mohatt, Bennett, & Walkup, 2014). Childhood anxiety is associated with future need for pharmacological and psychotherapeutic interventions, adult psychiatric illness, isolation, school failure, lack of coping skills, poor adaptation, and demoralization. Some anxiety may not qualify as a disability under the ADA when it does not limit a person's ability to perform an essential task, yet a puppy may work as an emotional support animal.

Individuals with specific phobias may be aided by service animals. Phobias may involve one or more fears of animals or insects (DSM-5 F40.218, 2013); natural or physical sites and occurrences (DSM-5 F40.228, 2013); or situations and locations (DSM-5 F40.248, 2013) (American Psychiatric Association, 2013). Puppies may be trained to aid handlers by warning them about specific humans, animals, or insects; leading handlers from certain environments (e.g. open spaces); or accompanying handlers into particular spaces (e.g. elevators). On average, individuals suffering from a specific phobia typically fear three organisms, objects, or situations. Thus, puppies simultaneously may alleviate more than one fear. For example, a person fearing heights, elevators, and airplanes may be accompanied by a service animal through an airport and aboard a flight (Grandell, 2010). Puppies regularly may assist handlers by protecting them from harm; yet handlers must rely on service dogs to be present because their reactions to phobic stimulus is debilitating, and dogs' presence helps handlers to cope with phobic stimulus. Puppies' skills may help handlers gage actual rather than feared harm in phobic stimulus (Muramatsu, et al., 2015).

Phobias of Puppies

Humans may demonstrate normal fear toward threatening and potentially aggressive puppies; but some humans are inexplicably debilitated by their fear of harmless puppies. Humans' neurotic fears of dogs or puppies have been explored for possible links to allergies, jealousy, loss, neurological disorders, parental bonding, sexual problems, and other intriguing causes.

Sigmund Freud concluded that dog phobia occurred when patients suffering from neurosis projected their sexual repressions onto dogs (Freud, 1998). Freud found that several phobias were directed at larger animals perhaps because larger animals have larger genitals, which can be problematic to young children's psyches under adverse circumstances (Cusack, 2015). In psychoanalysis, puppy phobia has been treated similarly to other animal phobias because "[i]n every case it . . . [has been] the same: the fear at bottom was of the father, if the children examined were boys, and was merely displaced upon the animal" (Freud, 1998, p. 110). Freud's analysis relied on case studies.

> For instance I mention . . . M. Wulff of Odessa, who has . . . occupied himself with the neuroses of childhood. He tells, in relating the history of an illness, that a nine year old boy suffered from a dog phobia at the age of four. "When he saw a dog running by on the street he wept and cried: 'Dear dog, don't touch me, I will be good.'" By 'being good' he meant "not to play violin any more" (to practice onanism). (Freud, 1998, p. 110)

The child's behavior involved several psychological components, including fear, repression, and projection.

Many Americans suffering from dog phobia may not overtly project sexual neuroses onto dogs. However, during therapeutic intervention or exposure to dog stimulus, they may disclose memories or traumas, such as dealing with an abusive parent or death; many recall early childhood experiences that triggered the onset of phobias (Animal Planet, 2015).

In addition to childhood traumas discussed by Freud, such as Little Hans' horse phobia caused by his observation of large horse penises during a carriage accident, Freud considered the relevance of sexual underpinnings in dog phobia as explicated by M. Wulff's analysis of a young boy (Cusack, 2015; Freud, 1998).

> "His dog phobia is really his fear of the father displaced upon the dog, for his peculiar expression: 'Dog, I will be good'—that is to say, I will

not masturbate—really refers to the father, who has forbidden masturbation." . . . [M. Wulff] then adds something in a note which fully agrees with my experience and at the same time bears witness to the abundance of such experiences: "such bias (of horses, dogs, cats, chickens and other domestic animals) are, I think at least as prevalent as *pavor noctumus* [i.e. night terror] in childhood, and usually reveal themselves in the analysis as a displacement of fear from one of the parents to animals. I am not prepared to assert that the widespread mouse and rat phobia has the same mechanism." (Freud, 1998, pp. 110–111)

Thus, some prevalent animal phobias may have different etiologies, which possibly relate to immediate fear of contact rather than sexual repression.

Puppy phobia (i.e. dog phobia) is a kind of anxiety disorder that has been studied in depth, but is not fully understood (May, et al., 2013). It is a specific phobia that often affects children, who typically respond well to cognitive behavioral therapy. Yet, in some cases, therapy is impractical; and patients may not seek treatment until adulthood. A study of 12 female dog-phobic university students measured therapeutic interventions using an eight-month follow-up (Hoffmann & Human, 2003). Participants first experienced dog phobia during early childhood and adolescence with approximately two-thirds recalling a traumatic event that correlated with the onset of dog phobia. However, 17% reported that they vicariously learned dog phobia. Fear Survey Schedules and observational assessments of students exposed to dog stimulus (e.g. eye contact with a dog) demonstrated students' need for therapeutic intervention, such as desensitization and learning. At the eight-month mark, respondents followed-up with 75% reporting that therapeutic intervention had significantly improved their lives. Thus, while it is possible for some minors and adults independently to overcome dog phobia, therapeutic interventions may have a high degree of success in a brief amount of time.

Neurotic Puppies

Dogs may suffer from neurosis as a result of neurological, social, environmental, or trauma-related factors. Neurotic conditions may manifest as social and non-social fear, separation problems, anxiety, and destructiveness (Temesi, Turcsan, & Miklosi, 2014). Some puppies vicariously may assume neurotic behavior patterns after being raised in neurotic environments. Approximately one-fifth of American adults suffer from anxiety neurosis, which may meet diagnostic criteria established by American Psychiatric Association (APA) (DSM-5, 300.02, 2013) (ADAA, 2014; American Psychiatric Association, 2013). Excessive and reoccurring worry or apprehension, which cannot be controlled and causes distress or impairment for at least six months may be diagnosable in adults if a person experiences at least three of six main symptoms: 1) restlessness or edginess; 2) fatigue; 3) loss of concentration or mental continuity; 4) irritability; 5) muscle tension; and 6) sleep irregularity, including excessive or unsatisfying sleep (American Psychiatric Association, 2013). Americans, who suffer from neurosis, may feel anxious in response to their dogs' apparent anxieties or neurosis. Some may feel that irritating relationships are normal or congruent, yet some others may respond to their dogs using therapeutic interventions, medicine, or other modalities. Psychological and clinical treatment for dogs is lacking in comparison to modalities available for humans. Ostensibly, one reason may be the variety of psychological differences between purebred and mixed-breed puppies. Questionnaires and behavioral testing may better help to measure and treat breed-specific canine anxiety (Tiira & Lohi, 2014). Objective data may be collected through observation, but it limits professional interventions to defined situations and sequences. Questionnaires facilitate long-term analyses, but they suffer from owners' subjectivity. One study used questionnaires to classify different dog typologies according to their levels of fear; and the information was used to map genes relating to neuroses, such as separation anxiety, fear of strangers, and noise phobia (e.g. thunder) (Tiira & Lohi, 2014). Subjectivity was low among 36 dog owners, whose questionnaire responses were consistent with behavioral tests repeated over an eight-month period. Another questionnaire administered to 833 dog owners examined pet neuroses by matching factors with characteristics. "For example, toy dogs had a higher risk to show neuroticism and dog-directed fear. Female owners . . . more frequently report[ed] human-directed fear in their dogs. Female dogs showed higher level of dog-directed fear. Older dogs score was higher on neuroticism and neuroticism correlated with the time of acquisition" (Temesi, Turcsan, & Miklosi, 2014).

Some neurotic behavior has been described as a control tactic used by dogs environmentally to maintain homeostasis (Toolsidass, 2008). This could explain some older dogs' increased neurosis because as dogs age they become more adept at controlling their environments. Yet, young puppies may exhibit specific kinds of neuroses relating to deprivations; for example, puppies whose movement is excessively restricted may experience tics; and puppies deprived of appropriate suckling early-on may excessively suckle later, like children, who suck their thumbs (Bennett, 2013). Some dog trainers may believe that neurosis is caused by owners' failure to control dogs, and that training may change dogs' behaviors and environment (Basso, n.d.). While training may resolve some dogs' neuroses, others may require neurological or therapeutic treatment.

CHAPTER EIGHT

Drugs

Intoxication

Cruel dog owners often consume or abuse intoxicants. For example, a domestic dispute involving a drunken woman resulted in her being charged with animal cruelty (ABC 7, 2012). Police had ordered the woman to leave her residence; but she insisted on taking her puppy with her. The puppy, who was days old, was abused but unharmed by the woman when she shoved the puppy down her pants; and then shook the puppy down her pant leg after police ordered her to remove the puppy from her pants. The puppy plopped on the floor, so police ordered the woman to pick-up the puppy; however, when she grabbed the puppy, she flung the puppy into a stroller. In that case, the puppy was unharmed, but when puppies are harmed, charges may not be more severe than when they are not harmed. For example, a drunken teen was arrested for suspicion of first degree cruelty when a neighbor alleged that the teen threw his puppy at a tree and punched his puppy in the eye (Lawson, 2012). The puppy's eye was injured, but the puppy recovered. In many jurisdictions, willfully intoxicated perpetrators may only face misdemeanor cruelty charges.

Puppies are commonly drugged and plied with alcohol. In cases where puppies have voluntarily become intoxicated, courts have had little tolerance for human companions' negligence. Juries tend to become prejudiced against a "'dog poisoner' and a 'poisoner of puppies at that'" (State v. James, 1961, p. 216). Negligence has been equated with cruelty even when drunken owners were unaware that puppies became intoxicated; or owners did not intend for their puppies to overdose (Cusack, 2015). For example, one puppy patronized a bar with a human companion (Show, 2012). The puppy was served and drank several shots of hard liquor. He repeatedly fell because his blood alcohol level was almost .035%. The legal limit for adult motorists was .008%; and a human could have been killed by the puppy's blood alcohol saturation. The puppy's human companion was charged with cruelty and felony drug charges because he was found to be in constructive possession of hydrocodone pills; and his bail was set at $30,000 because he was on probation for other drug charges.

Legalization of medicinal marijuana correlates with increased harm to puppies. A study 76 dogs analyzed exposure to marijuana after medical marijuana licenses in Colorado increased by 146% over a five-year period beginning in 2005 (Meola, et al., 2012). During that time frame, marijuana toxicosis in dogs had quadrupled; and foods made with marijuana, such as medical grade tetrahydrocannabinol (THC) butter, were increasingly associated with dogs' deaths. Direct relationships between prevalence of intoxicants and toxicosis may result whenever particular substances' availability increases. For example, anecdotal evidence suggests that miniscule amounts liquid nicotine contained in electronic cigarettes have caused convulsions and death in growing numbers of children and puppies (Radnedge, 2014). In response, the United States Food and Drug Administration will likely require warning labels (Goldschmidt, 2015).

Smuggling Drugs

Drug traffickers have attempted to use puppies, who may be rescued through America's War on Drugs. For example, puppies introduced into penological environments may be used to facilitate drug dealing. Sometimes, puppies are trained surreptitiously to enter prisons to transport contraband. Puppies are used to smuggle drugs on airplanes, in cars, and in other locations because they distract law enforcement and give an innocent veneer. However, law enforcement is trained to observe the totality of the circumstances and detect distractions. Puppies used to smuggle drugs may be confiscated and adopted.

Some cartels have used puppies' stomachs to transport drugs. Cartels operating in Latin America and Western Europe have allegedly fed drugs to puppies or sewn drugs inside their abdomens (*Animal People News*, 2006). Puppies subjected to either method are typically cut open; and their corpses are discarded after the drugs have been transported. For example, a cartel abandoned 15 dogs in trash bags at a music festival after a cartel cut open the puppies' bellies. Authorities suspected that the puppies had been stolen from their families. Puppy theft is discussed in Chapters Six, Ten, and 11. In Columbia, puppies were surgically implanted with soft plastic packs of brown liquid heroin, which were stitched under loose abdominal skin (Baker & Rashbaum, 2006). Ten puppies, including many Labrador Retrievers, were rescued through United States Drug Enforcement Administration intervention before they were killed by the cartel. Three puppies died from infections, but the remaining dogs survived despite having been implanted with a pound of heroin. Some puppies may be implanted with more than one pound; for example, a cartel poured two and eight-tenths pounds of contraband into each puppy (Morán, 2013). Puppies entering the United States have been detected with contraband in their stomachs. For example, a sheepdog puppy was transported to New York from Columbia with a belly full of cocaine packaged inside ten condoms (Roberts, 2013). Agents at New York's John F. Kennedy (JFK) Airport suspected that the dog appeared to be sick due to drugs, which led agents to order an X-ray. Spanish police arrested a Venezuelan cartel member, who implanted six and six-tenths pounds of heroin into three puppies in Columbia (AP, 2015). Europeans have become overwhelmed by this sort of cruelty over the past ten years. In 2008, the United Kingdom undertook an antidrug campaign that depicted a dog being used as a drug carrier (Roberts, 2013). The campaign against cocaine cost one million pounds. Aggressive responses throughout Europe also included an Italian court ordering 49 cartel members from Ecuador, Peru, and El Salvador to stand trial for butchering puppies.

Animal Testing

Pharmaceutical companies in the United States test on dogs despite having access to records of previous research and highly accurate computer models; inherent cruelty; and limitations of studying human physiology and biology using dogs. Due to methodological barriers and cruelty, pharmaceutical testing on animals is at the center of numerous high profile controversies and campaigns waged by animal welfare organizations, such as Humane Society of the United States (HSUS). Animal enterprises, such as pharmaceutical laboratories, have described animal welfare advocacy as "terrorism" (Yates, 2011). Animal enterprises have lobbied for legislation, such as the Animal Enterprise Terrorism Act, which occasionally may be used to construe demonstrations similarly to animal liberation (i.e. terrorism) (18 U.S.C. § 43, 2006).

> Supporters of the Animal Enterprise Terrorism Act (2006) label as "terrorists" mainstream animal welfare corporations such as the Humane Society of the United States (HSUS) and People for the Ethical Treatment of Animals (PeTA). Animal advocates fear that conventional forms of protest, such as boycotts and street demonstrations, are being redefined within such legislation as potential "acts of terror." (Yates, 2011, p. 469)

Even though this problem has manifested throughout the world, the conflict is particularly salient in the United States due to abundant pharmaceutical companies, active animal advocacy groups, free speech, and weak enforcement of animal experimentation protocols.

The Humane League of Philadelphia v. Berman and Company (2010, 2013) publically identified conflicts between animal enterprises and animal welfarists. In 2008, Center for Consumer Freedom (CCF) circulated an advertisement in *New York Times* and on CCF's website allegedly defaming HSUS and The Humane League of Philadelphia (The League). The advertisement was placed by Rick Berman, who campaigns against HSUS. Berman claimed that The League was originally named Hugs for Puppies; and was established for the purpose of terrorizing animal enterprises. He claimed that the group was affiliated with violent convicted terrorists incarcerated in federal prison. Several of Berman's allegations possessed tinges of truth, but were mostly false. He claimed that in 2006, The League's president had threatened a pharmaceutical company employee, specifically alleging that The League's president threatened to kill a pharmaceutical company employee's children. The president had been convicted of making terrorist threats, but the charge related to holding a protest sign on private property, not terrorist threats. Allegations of terrorist threats were reported by the media, but remained unsubstantiated. Although The League was subject to restraining orders, there was no judicial determination of fact; the group had not been established in connection with any terrorist organizations; and their activities mainly involved public awareness campaigns and advocacy. The League sued Berman's lobbying company for defamation; and their case survived the summary judgment stage in county court; but the defendant's motion for summary judgment was granted on appeal because Berman provided documentation showing that he believed the veracity of his advertisement. Although he made misleading or unsubstantiated claims, Berman did not maliciously circulate lies that he knew were false (The Humane League of Philadelphia v. Berman and Company, 2013).

> In support, the moving defendants offer a compilation of different documents that indicate that: (1) [Stop Huntington Animal Cruelty] SHAC has had a Philadelphia address and that a 2002 group e-mail introduced SHAC Philly as a chapter of SHAC USA . . . ; (2) SHAC USA 'has launched a relentless campaign of terror' . . . against, and was convicted for its 'campaign to terrorize,' a laboratory which tests products on animals . . . ; (3) . . . [T]he League's president . . . was found guilty by a Pennsylvania court of, among other charges, making

"Terroristic Threats [With Intent] To Terrorize Another" . . . ; (4) in 2006, 2007, and 2008, Pennsylvania and New Jersey courts issued temporary restraining orders and permanent injunctions enjoining [The League's president], . . . Hugs for Puppies, SHAC USA, and other non-parties from, among other things, protesting on the property of, and harassing individuals associated with, the animal testing laboratory, a pharmaceutical company, an accounting firm, and a Philadelphia restaurant . . . [T]he League posted legal notices of those orders on its website [Internal citations omitted]. (The Humane League of Philadelphia v. Berman and Company, 2010, pp. 8–9)

The facts relied on by the defendant did not demonstrate that The League conspired to violate the Animal Enterprise Protection Act; however, documentation corroborated the fact that Berman actually believed the contents of his advertisement (18 U.S.C. § 43, 2006; The Humane League of Philadelphia v. Berman and Company, 2010). Because The League was a public figure, The League would have needed to prove that Berman maliciously lied. Berman's motion for summary judgment was granted because he demonstrated deficiencies in the record that would prevent The League from pleading all of the elements (e.g. actual malice) (The Humane League of Philadelphia v. Berman and Company, 2013). The record could not be used by The League to show that Berman had serious doubts about the veracity of his advertisement; or was aware that his advertisement was probably false.

Drug Dealing

Organized crime links drugs to gang culture, unreported revenue, gambling, and dogfighting. Drug dealers may sell large-breed puppies to increase the visibility of the membership in a gang. Thus, they may entice customers to gamble in dogfights; however, connections between gambling and dogs may also be nonviolent, for example, in craps "puppy paws" is a ten rolled with two fives; a club flush may be described as "puppy feet"; and an ace of clubs may be called a "puppy foot" (Dalzell, 2008).

Drug dealers may have a variety of motives for selling pit bull puppies; for example, disguising drug clients as puppy buyers (Housing Authority of the City of Norwalk v. Ross, 1993). The court heard evidence of this ruse in U.S. v. Washington (2014).

It is true, as defendant contends, that the observation of frequent visitors to the residence who stayed for only a brief period of time was consistent with innocent activities such as people responding to an advertisement offering puppies for sale. However, the visitors also may have been illegally purchasing drugs as the concerned citizens, and the narcotics unit officers performing surveillance, clearly suspected. (U.S. v. Washington, 2014, p. 9)

In People v. Peterson (2007), the Sacramento County Sheriff observed numerous people visiting the defendant throughout the day during a brief time period. The sheriff obtained a warrant to search the defendant's house; and they noticed barking dogs in the backyard. The defendant attempted to flee, but was apprehended. The sheriff seized contraband, including a gallon container filled with powder, crystals, and rocks; a bag of white powder; methamphetamines; an unregistered loaded shotgun; shotgun shells; scales; $2,000 cash; and marijuana buds. "While the deputies were conducting their search, the telephone rang many times. One of the deputies answered four of the calls. Each time the caller asked, 'Is it clear to come through?' After receiving a positive response, each caller hung up. Within about ten minutes of the calls, three people appeared at the house" (People v. Peterson, 2007, p. 3). While incarcerated, the defendant married Robyn Byrnes, who testified that she legitimately had earned the cash while working as a food server. She also testified that "a lot of people visited their house to see their pit bull puppies" (People v. Peterson, 2007, p. 4). The court failed to find her testimony to be credible particularly because she claimed never to have seen the defendant sell drugs; and because "[t]here were no women's clothes in the master bedroom or anywhere else in the house. All the clothing in the house appeared to be male clothing of one size" (People v. Peterson, 2007, p. 3). Another defendant also attempted to use puppy sales to explain large quantities of cash. The dealer possessed more than $36,000 in cash, most of which was found inside a strongbox hidden under a one-pound bag of marijuana (State v. $36,560.00, 1996). She attempted to claim that she sold candles and puppies, but that she mainly subsisted from government aid. The court held that her evidence lacked credibility; and the state was entitled to forfeiture of her cash, which was found to be drug proceeds.

Dealers may use puppies as pretexts for completing drug transactions. The court record in Self v. State (1981) described an example of this scenario. The drug dealer "insisted that he never participated in a drug transaction at [David] Koon's home. He testified that he went there . . . to look at Koon's Doberman [Pinscher] puppies. He averred that while en route to the rear bedroom where the puppies were kept

[William] Gates stopped him . . . and asked appellant to sell him Dilaudid, which appellant refused" (Self v. State, 1981, p. 793). Another defendant charged with aiding and abetting a drug sale claimed that he was too engrossed with a drug buyer's puppy to notice that the drug dealer handed drugs to the buyer (State v. Thurman, 2015). The drug buyer was a confidential informant, who wore an electronic listening device. A recording of the men's conversation demonstrated that they never used the word "drugs," but did discuss a puppy; "and at one point, the informant suggested that [the defendant] could obtain a puppy in exchange for 'a ball,' which is a slang term referring to a quantity of cocaine" (State v. Thurman, 2015, p. 2). A jury was unpersuaded by his defense; and he was sentenced to 60 months incarceration. Another defendant, Jason Miller, was convicted of murder; but, he claimed that he acted in self-defense when he went to check on a puppy and collect a drug debt from the victim, but was attacked with a sword, which cut his torso, hand, and forehead (Ohio v. Miller, 2008). The court failed to believe Miller's explanation for why he shot the victim approximately nine times. Self-defense is discussed further in Chapter Four.

Despite actual correlations, law enforcement and courts generally do not consider puppies to be evidence of crimes, like cash or drugs, unless they can demonstrate additional evidence of crimes. For example, in one case, a drug dealer offered testimony that he sold pit bull puppies and drugs. The central issue in that case was whether the drug dealer's knowledge of pit bull breeding and sales demonstrated that he was sufficiently intelligent and familiar with basic math to have been more forthcoming with the court about his drug sales, which he appeared to be unable to calculate during a sentencing hearing.

On June 30, 2004, a search warrant was executed at [Antoric] Wilson's residence in Chattanooga, Tennessee. Approximately 1,100 grams of powder cocaine, forty grams of crack cocaine, 750 grams of marijuana, $7,500 in cash, and an SKS semiautomatic assault rifle were seized from Wilson's bedroom . . . .Wilson further testified that he had been using cocaine daily for two years. He also stated that he had not been employed since 2000, and that he supported his drug habit by selling CDs, shirts, and by breeding pit bull dogs and selling their puppies. Wilson stated that he sold pit bulls for $200 to $400 per puppy and that he usually had three or four litters per year. Wilson also stated that the $7,500 found in his dresser came from selling CDs, puppies, and shirts . . . Wilson's attorney then set forth mitigating factors—citing to Wilson's youth, lack of education, and the fact that he grew up in a fatherless household. Wilson's attorney also argued that Wilson did not purposely make false statements during his sentencing testimony, but was probably confused. Wilson's attorney asserted that Wilson was a slow learner and pointed out that while he received an attendance certificate from high school, he did not graduate . . . The district court also compared Wilson's testimony regarding his drug distribution to his testimony about his dog breeding activities. The district court noted that while Wilson was able to discuss in depth the breeding and selling of pit bulls and even drew distinctions between the selling prices of puppies bred from several different combinations of dogs, he had trouble testifying to his selling of cocaine despite the fact that he was referring to $100 or $250 sales, which involve little aggregation or math skills. (U.S. v. Wilson, 2007, pp. 261–265)

Because of his alleged attempt to lie, he was charged with perjury, which contributed to his 240-month sentence.

Drug dealers, users, and law enforcement may substitute terminology with "puppy"; for example, in State v. Carrethers "puppy" implied "gun" (2002).

Randall Bowen, a homeless man, saw the defendant searching for something in the alley behind the victim's home. The defendant told Mr. Bowen that he was looking for a puppy and asked Bowen to help. Mr. Bowen declined and walked up the street, but a few minutes later he returned and assisted the defendant in his search when the defendant offered Bowen drugs to help him find a blue bandanna. They found the bandanna in the alley half a block from the victim's house. It was wrapped around a handgun. (State v. Carrethers, 2002, p. 4)

"Puppies" may be used to describe drug addicts; for example, during an investigation, police told a drug dealer that one of his clients had purchased drugs from another seller (U.S. v. Skinner, 2005). The drug dealer assured police that his client, an addict, would not permanently switch dealers. "[T]hat's one of my puppies and your puppies don't turn on you if you take care of them. If you give your puppies milk, you give them a place to sleep, you give your puppies food and your puppies don't turn on you. They don't go into somebody else's yard unless somebody else offers them something else better" (State v. Graham, 2013, p. 5). Police may also use the term "puppy" to describe drug abusers; for example, the court record in Soffar v. Johnson (2000) referred to a "puppy dog."

Most of the officers at the Friendswood Police Department described Soffar as a "puppy dog" who was always around and under foot. Universally, they regarded him as being brain damaged from drug abuse and unable to think much farther ahead than the present day. Soffar was described as eager to please and eager to get along with the police. (Soffar v. Johnson, 2000, p. 427)

"Puppy" may be used literally in official records discussing history of drug abuse; for example, an appellant pointed to injection marks on her arms and said, "I've got a new puppy. These are scratch marks" (Smith v. Texas, 2007, p. 7). However, later she admitted to using methamphetamine. In another case, a heavy drug user was accused of improperly possessing Cocaine, a puppy dog whose name was memorialized by court records (Druery v. Texas, 2007).

Some drug dealers actually refer to young dogs when using the term "puppy" during drug deals, and these conversations are entered into evidence. For example, in U.S. v. Mark (2012), drugs dealers working from Saint Thomas and British Virgin Islands were running drugs to North Carolina. Drug deals were discussed on the phone and in person at a farm in Saint Thomas. The farm was used to raise dogs for fighting. Gelean Mark wanted to send a champion fighting dog and ten kilos of cocaine to North Carolina. He solicited services from various couriers to make his delivery; and organized a deal through brokers, some of whom had met at a dogfight in North Carolina. A special agent with Drug Enforcement Administration, Michael Goldfinger, conducted surveillance.

Goldfinger saw [Vernon] Fagan park . . . in a white [M]azda, and get out holding a small black puppy and talking on a cell phone . . . The government also introduced several wiretap phone conversations from Fagan's phone . . . Fagan was recorded having a conversation with an unidentified female about the price of "it" and "bricks" and the profits he could make off of "it" . . . .Later that day . . . Fagan and Mark spoke on the phone. Mark referred to a puppy, and told Fagan to leave it at a particular cage. The jury could have inferred that that puppy was the one Fagan was carrying when he was observed by Goldfinger . . . [and was recorded asking Mark] 'What to do with the dog?' (U.S. v. Mark, 2012, pp. 41–45)

The jury was able to infer the co-occurrence of the recorded conversation about the drug deal and the puppy with the events observed by Goldfinger when he saw Fagan carrying the puppy.

Some drug dealers may carefully prevent their puppies from

accessing drugs. In one case, a drug dealer attempted to proffer evidence that he routinely hid his drugs from his puppy, in order to demonstrate that his drugs were not in plain view when police searched his home, which would have constituted an exception to the warrant requirement. The defendant had sold drugs to an undercover officer during a controlled buy. The defendant, Fernando Ribeiro, was arrested outside his apartment. Police entered his apartment with a documentary warrant, but claimed that they saw drugs in plain view; thus, they did not require a warrant to search and seize those drugs.

> Ribeiro owned a large tower-type speaker cabinet, which sat unplugged on the floor of his bedroom. Inside the cabinet were two speaker units, stacked one on top of the other, with the lower unit approximately six inches from the ground. Each unit was supposed to be covered by a metal grill, which required a screwdriver to remove. Once a grill had been unscrewed and taken off, however, the speaker units were attached to the cabinet by simple clips and could thus be easily removed and quickly replaced. Ribeiro admitted that he unscrewed the bottom grill for easier access to the inside of the cabinet. A police officer entering the bedroom saw the lower speaker unclipped from the cabinet and hanging off to the side, thus exposing the cabinet's insides to plain view. In the space where the speaker normally belonged, the officer saw a large clear plastic bag filled with white powder, which later proved to be 200 grams of cocaine. The police seized the cocaine, as well as other bags also inside that contained 140 grams of heroin, seven grams of crack, and 6,000 ecstasy tablets. Elsewhere in the apartment, police found and seized scales, a laptop computer, plastic baggies, $65,000 in cash, and some identifying documents. (U.S. v. Ribeiro, 2005, p. 47)

The defendant explained that he had a five month-old toy poodle, who he protected from drugs, which proved that his drugs were hidden and not in plain sight; and thus, the search violated the Fourth Amendment and the evidence should be suppressed. "Ribeiro claims that it simply 'defies belief' that he would have left the drugs in plain view because (1) he wanted to keep his girlfriend ignorant of his dealing and (2) more importantly, he had a 'young puppy in the apartment known for chewing up everything in sight.' If he had left the speaker open, 'the result would likely be a dead puppy and ruined drugs' (U.S. v. Ribeiro, 2005, p. 53). The court failed to accept Ribeiro's argument that he consistently hid drugs to protect his "young puppy"; and instead held that "[t]he reality is that people can be careless" (U.S. v. Ribeiro, 2005, p. 53). Thus, the evidence was admissible.

A defendant seemed to have hidden his drugs in locations that were inaccessible to his puppy (State v. Loper, 2003).

[The defendant had] two smaller bags of crack cocaine, one containing crumbs weighing .55 grams and the other containing rocks weighing 8.42 grams, and a vial containing 9.80 grams of PCP[;] . . . a rock of crack cocaine lying on the sink[; and] . . . a 'phenomenal' amount of crack cocaine on the kitchen sink next to a razor blade with residue on it . . . The crack cocaine on the sink was determined to weigh 120.93 grams. In addition to the drugs already mentioned, a search of the premises uncovered the following: a vial of 17.74 grams of PCP in the freezer; two empty vials with PCP residue inside a shoe in the kitchen; two more vials of PCP weighing a total of 20.53 grams in a refrigerator drawer; a large bag containing several smaller bags with huge pieces of crack cocaine weighing a total of 96.55 grams in a vegetable bin; seven MDMA (ecstacy) pills and a bag of 3.22 grams of crack cocaine, including crumbs and one larger rock, inside an oven mitt hanging on the kitchen wall; and an electronic scale and a second razor on a saucer, both with cocaine residue, on top of a kitchen cupboard. Also, two vials of PCP, one weighing 16.40 grams and the other weighing 16.94 grams, were found under a headboard in a bedroom. (State v. Loper, 2003, pp. 10–14)

Despite his efforts to stow his drugs, a small puppy potentially could have been poisoned by residue on the vials inside the shoe, falling drugs, or drugs behind the headboard; and a large puppy may have been able to eat drugs on the sink, cupboard, or other locations.

Drug dealers often openly sell drugs around their children and puppies, a fact that may help law enforcement to identify drug dealers and explain the basis for probable cause on search warrants. For example, witnesses in a drug case told police that "they had purchased drugs from a black male and he had his black female daughter and a pit bull puppy at the residence" (Mendoza v. Whitehouse, 2008, p. 17). Police entered a residence, which they believed matched the description; however, they realized that they had entered the wrong house, so they obtained a new warrant accurately identifying an address that belonged to the suspect matching witnesses' description.

Some drug dealers blatantly may expose puppies to drugs. For example, one defendant kept 107 grams of cocaine and one-half gram of heroin inside a puppy food bag (Illinois v. Fair, 2014). The defendant claimed that he did not know anything about a puppy living in his home; however, he owned a dog, who he claimed only ate adult dog food stored in another area of his kitchen. In one case, police accidentally exposed a puppy to drugs inside a drug dealer's home; however their error resulted in the discovery of drugs and a drug conviction (State v. Rivera, 2012). Police responded to a home invasion during which an occupant was shot in the face. After the victim had been transported to the hospital, a detective at the house investigated and almost cleared the scene; but before doing so, the detective noticed a puppy. "[T]he detectives placed the puppy in a bedroom, but realized it could not stay there since there 'was stuff [in the bedroom that the puppy] could eat.' The detectives then decided to go to the basement to see if there was a cage . . . or if it would be suitable to leave the puppy . . . with some food and water until the victim's family could come" (State v. Rivera, 2012, p. 4). The detectives were not conducting an illegal search; but instead, they demonstrated concern for the puppy's well-being.

> [T]he detectives had a reasonable belief that the puppy's life was in danger, and therefore were justified in taking the action they did. Because the animal in question was a puppy, the detectives acted reasonably in trying to find a secure location within the residence where the puppy could be left. The detectives were aware that [the victim] . . . , who the detectives reasonably presumed to be the puppy's owner, had been taken to the hospital with a serious wound, and there was no indication when someone would come to the residence to care for the puppy . . . [T]here is nothing in the record to indicate that the detectives were using their concern about the puppy's welfare simply as a pretext to search for drugs or other contraband at the residence. (State v. Rivera, 2012, pp. 25–26)

Despite feces and other indications of the puppy having been in the basement, detectives believed that the puppy could not stay in the basement. As they were in the basement deciding what to do, they observed in plain view drugs inside a package wrapped in cellophane that had been cut open with a cross shape. Detectives obtained a search warrant and found 850 pounds (i.e. 20,000 grams) of marijuana worth approximately $1,000 per pound (State v. Rivera, 2012). The evidence was admissible because police only entered the basement to care for the puppy, not to search without a warrant. Thus, consistent with their duty to serve and protect, police cared for the puppy and seized the drugs.

CHAPTER NINE

Babies and Puppies

Development

Studies and anecdotal evidence show that babies bond with puppies and may learn tasks from them, such as climbing stairs, crawling, or using toys. A baby may learn to communicate by interacting with a dog, who sings, pronounces human words, barks, or indicates; for example, one baby was depicted in a video competing with an Alaskan husky dog to pronounce the word "mama" (Lynch, 2015). Roo is an example of a dog whose presence may assist small children with language and math skill acquisition (Read to Roo, n.d.). Roo works as a therapy dog visiting elementary schools and libraries with his handler. His positive demeanor encourages young children to read, practice spelling, and work on math problems. Human babies do not universally rely on dogs to develop or refine basic skills, such as crawling; but some human babies learn from dogs (Stevens-Scott, 2014). Similarly, puppies do not always require role models to learn to crawl, climb stairs, or howl; however human and canine role models may instill confidence and facilitate skillset formulation (Doucette, 2012). This is discussed in Chapter Two. Puppies learning from humans may additionally benefit from learning behavioral patterns and thought processes resembling human thinking. It may be possible that babies, who learn from dogs, have an advantage over babies exclusively learning from young siblings because dogs are more intelligent than young children; and many young children have not refined their interpersonal and social skills as much as dogs, who may have experience as family members (Boya, Dotson, & Hyatt, 2012). Despite the benefits of babies learning from dogs, parents may be criticized for treating children like puppies, for example, by leashing children or allowing them to urinate in public (Morán, 2015). One criticism is that children may become confused about human socialization; however, research shows that young children are likely to demonstrate their understanding of species origin and heredity irrespective of their upbringing unless they are feral (Cusack, 2015; Johnson & Solomon, 1997).

Estrus

Humans and canines may share sexual homologies, such as estrus (i.e. oestrus) (Gangestad & Thornhill, 2008). Some research demonstrates that humans may detect estrus similarly to how puppies and dogs detect estrus that "perfumes" the air (Nature, 2013). Relationships between seduction, male detection of female fertility, and females' earnings were researched in a 2007 study analyzing the effect of ovulation on the amount of tips earned by erotic dancers (Miller, Tybur, & Jordan, 2007). Female dancers working in Albuquerque, New Mexico at typical adult clubs were included in the study. Clients were usually White or Hispanic men between the ages of 20 and 60 years old, who consumed intoxicants. Dancers performed topless, but they covered their pubic areas and typically snipped tampon strings to prevent them from being seen by clients. Though dancers enhanced their appearances using lotion, makeup, hair dye, and hair removal, they atypically wore perfume. Approximately ten percent of dancers' total daily earnings were derived from stage dances. The majority of their income was earned by charging ten dollars for lap dances during which they sat on customers' laps and gyrated in the main area of the club for the duration of one song. For $20, dancers would provide lap dances in a partitioned area. Dance prices were paid as tips rather than as fees, but minimum prices were enforced by bouncers. Approximately one-third of dancers' income was earned in the private area of the club, with the remainder of their income earned in the general area; thus, an average lap dance earned $14. Dancers attempted to offer as many lap dances as possible to new and repeat clients; and sometimes, clients agreed to a three-song minimum. Completed 14-page questionnaires were collected from 18 dancers, who were primarily heterosexual. They reported data about their menstrual cycles for 60 days. All had regular menstrual cycles; seven used hormonal contraception; and 11 had not used any hormonal contraception within the previous three months. The dancers were on average 27 years old, and had danced for approximately six years. Actuarial data suggested that fertility peaks between the ninth and 15th day of a 28 day cycle; but drops during the first week which includes menstruation. The study used actuarial data to divide early and late menstruation. Dancers' menstrual cycle data was divided and analyzed in three stages: days one through five (menstrual), days nine through 15 (fertile), and days 18 through 28 (luteal). Dancers earned fewer tips during menstruation irrespective of hormonal birth control use. During estrus, tips peaked to approximately $354 per shift ($70 per hour); during the luteal phase dancers earned $264 ($50 per hour); and tips decreased to approximately $184 during the menstrual phase ($35 per hour). Dancers, who used hormonal contraception, which creates hormonal pseudopregnancy, did not experience a peak in their earnings. Hormonal contraception users earned $193, which is an $80 difference per shift. Unspoken cues, such as fatigue, bloating, pain, and irritability, rather than estrus, could have signaled ovulation to increase male spending. This possibility does not negate the role of estrus, but complements.

A study examined possible relationships between male Beagle puppies' testosterone level and their attraction to estrus (Beach, Buehler, & Dunbar, 1983). On a few occasions, Beagles were allowed to visit females at their cages. One of two categories of females could be selected by males: 1) female in estrus or 2) spayed female. Males were given the choice as young puppies (one to three months) and mature puppies (22 to 24 months). The study examined males with unaltered testicles; sterilized males; and males altered as young puppies, who had been injected with testosterone for three months. All males preferred visiting females in estrus. Intact males first exhibited a preference when they were between four and six months old. Their attraction increased between four and 18 months; and their testosterone levels peaked at ten to 12 months old, but then decreased. Males, who were administered testosterone, precociously preferred to visit estrus females during the first through third months. Even when they did not receive testosterone, their desire to visit females increased until 21 months. Altered males began preferring to visit females in estrus at ten to twelve months. These males did not experience an increase in attraction until they were administered testosterone at 24 months, at which point, they were attracted to females in estrus similarly to intact males.

Fertile phase females may be attracted to testosterone. Findings from one study contradicted rhetoric claiming that fertile phase human females are attracted to wealth because fertile phase human females were only as likely as infertile females to be attracted to wealth; but, the study found that females appeared to be attracted to male aggression (Gangestad & Thornhill, 2008). Males appearing to be arrogant, strong, and attractive, who confronted their own sexualities, were most appealing to fertile phase women. Fertile phase women were less attracted to sexually monogamous men, who may have been viewed as lacking virility or desirability.

Female and male hormones and sexual cues may similarly motivate humans and puppies. Anecdotal evidence and studies repeatedly show that humans and animals respond to similar stimulus. For example, a randomized study of young adult American males and females assigned to participants a red condition or a white condition (Elliot & Niesta, 2008). A photo appearing to be from a yearbook reportedly depicted an attractive, young, blonde woman pleasantly smiling. Photos of the woman wearing red resulted in the woman being rated as more attractive. Studies repeatedly show that women wearing red are more sexually desirable to men. Overall attraction based on virtue, personality, or intelligence is unaffected positively or negatively by the color red. Red has been used by humans to symbolize aggression, passion, and lust for thousands of years; and arguably it may be a sexual cue. Red may be used to symbolize sex and fertility because it actually correlates with sex and fertility (e.g. menstrual blood and afterbirth). For example, many primates' perinea and vulvae may be ruddy similarly to dogs' genitals or humans' genitals during arousal and intercourse, perhaps demonstrating physiosexual similarities between humans and dogs (Gangestad & Thornhill, 2008).

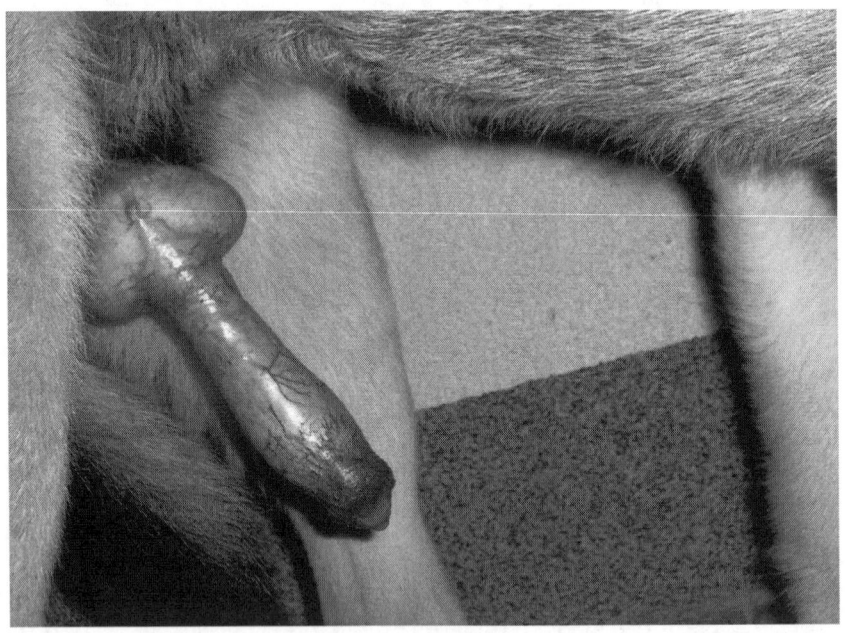

9.1 German Shepherd's penis

Puppies Not Babies

Social analysis suggests that childless couples, known as "dual-income-no-kids" (DINKs), have flourished recently with some DINKs diverting their parental instincts toward puppies (i.e. "dual-income-no-kids-with-a-dog" or DINKWAD). In cases where DINKWADs are not redirecting parental instincts, they may be highly involved with pet puppies, who they view as peers. DINKWADs may challenge traditional family structure, yet continue to promote social stability.

> 'Dogs are for people who can't have kids,' a gay newspaper columnist . . . [said] recently. It's true that homosexual (and straight) couples who can't or don't want children of their own often migrate towards dogs as child substitutes and view the arrangement as a different kind of family, but a family nonetheless. Such dog-based "families" may [be] . . . beneficial [because] . . . people with a family mentality are more likely to form stable, safe neighborhoods and have a vested interest in the community. Those without children may benefit from nurturing a living creature and learning to be less self-centered. (Pedersen, 2009)

DINKWADs families may be structured, but also value pampering.

> Canines, with their pack instincts and trainability, are by far the most likely pet to be anthropomorphized as a family member, a best friend, or a "fur baby," treated accordingly with gourmet meals, designer apparel, orthopedic beds, expensive therapy, and catered birthday parties . . . The "my-dogs-are-my-kids" crowd isn't being tongue-in-cheek, either. They act on their beliefs, buying Christmas presents, photos with Santa, cosmetic surgery, and whatever-it-takes medical care for their animal. In fact having a puppy, claimed one "mother," is 'exactly the same in all ways as having a baby.' And while pushing a dog around in a stroller would have gotten you directions to a mental health facility twenty years ago, today it's de rigeur to see a canine in a stroller (or a papoose). (Pedersen, 2009)

DINKWADs may spend more for functional bonding and convenient pampering because they are committed to their families (Boya, Dotson, & Hyatt, 2012; Brant & Bonaldi, 2011; Defabritiis, 2012; Sutherland, 2015).

Research on DINKWADs demonstrated similarities in their daily routines and social status with "highly involved" dog owners (Boya, Dotson, & Hyatt, 2012). Similarities included morning walks and shared breakfast time. In the evening "pet parents" fed their dogs before preparing dinner for themselves or other humans in the home (Boya, Dotson, & Hyatt, 2012). After dinner, dogs socialized with families on beds, floors, and sofas, and while watching television; some humans read while socializing with dogs. Many "fur babies" shared their "pet parents'" beds; or they slept next to them on the floor or in a dog bed (Boya, Dotson, & Hyatt, 2012). Dogs were assigned several anthropomorphic roles, including "peer" or "child" (Boya, Dotson, & Hyatt, 2012). More than half of "highly involved" pet owners were married, had above average income, and at least one quarter held graduate or professional degrees (Boya, Dotson, & Hyatt, 2012). They vacationed with their dogs, made sacrifices for their dogs, and believed that their dogs acted like panaceas. "Strongly attached" dog owners ascribe human characteristics to animals, which may change DINKWADs' perceptions of physical and social boundaries (Boya, Dotson, & Hyatt, 2012). Gender differences among contemporary DINKWADs may not be as relevant as in traditional marriages (Boya, Dotson, & Hyatt, 2012). Some research has found that in 73% of American households with dogs, women are the primary caregivers (Dotson & Hyatt, 2008). "Highly involved" pet owners may equally provide care (Boya, Dotson, & Hyatt, 2012). As dog owners, DINKWADs may benefit from marital partnerships because only 22% of American singles own dogs (Dotson & Hyatt, 2008). For DINKWADs, "dogs play an . . . important role in meeting human needs for companionship, friendship, unconditional love and affection. The more disconnected . . . [DINKWADs are] from each other, the deeper . . . the bonds . . . with . . . pets" (Boya, Dotson, & Hyatt, 2012). Thus, DINKWADs may substitute partnership and dogs for traditional marriage, including gender roles, intimacy, and children. Yet, they may not have children because nothing can take the place of their dogs in their hearts (Walt Disney, 1955).

Puppy Pregnancy

"Puppy pregnancy" is a type of pseudopregnancy (i.e. pseudocyesis). Generally, patients with pseudocyesis believe that they may be pregnant despite impossibility (e.g. male patient) or extreme unlikeliness (e.g. infertile). Pregnancy may be suspected due to false positives, postpartum illness, tumors, gender dysphoria, sexual abuse, delusions, and other causes (Cusack, 2015). The term "puppy pregnancy" is derived from an Indian superstition that a dog bite or contact with an aroused dog may cause human males and females to become pregnant with puppies. Mass hysteria allegedly convinces individuals to experience pregnancy, but the superstition may not be totally baseless because individuals may experience hypersexual arousal after being bitten by rabid puppies. In one case, a 28 year-old woman presented with inexplicable heightened sexual arousal; her diagnosis was that she had contracted rabies (Senthilkumaran, et al., 2011). Her symptoms were that she became unusually interested in having sex with her husband and experienced multiple orgasms for several days. For two or three weeks, she was bothered by persistent arousal until she presented for medical treatment. After discovering that an unvaccinated puppy had bitten her two months prior, her doctor ordered an MRI scan and other tests to confirm a cases of rabies.

Indian males living in rural villages may be convinced by superstition and mass hysteria that they have been impregnated by contact with or proximity to puppies. A case study of puppy pregnancy in six males and one female in India found that patients' communities endorsed puppy bites as an etiological pathway for spontaneous pregnancy (Chowdhury, et al., 2003). Mental illness (e.g. obsessive-compulsive disorder or anxiety-phobia) was present in approximately half of the cases. One prepubescent child was so disbursed by his belief that he alleged to have vomited a dog embryo. Most modern American adults may be unlikely to experience puppy pregnancy because they understand that humans cannot be impregnated by dogs; however, some American children could fear or experience puppy pregnancy after being sexually abused by humans and trained dogs (Cusack, 2015; Johnson & Solomon, 1997). American males may believe that they are carrying a human pregnancy; and they may be likelier to seek treatment sooner than females suffering from pseudopregnancy. American culture emphasizes particular old wives' tales and superstitions; thus, strong responses to cultural pressures are relatable. For example, many Americans, including some obstetricians, erroneously believe that fetuses should not gestate after nine months, which results in induced labor for millions of healthy pregnancies despite fallibility of sonography sometimes resulting in inaccurate due date estimation (Declercq, et al., 2014).

American culture has generally resisted deviations from the traditional family structure, even though American laws have facilitated progressive reforms. Thus, in the case that medically-assisted puppy pregnancy was to become possible, American society may respond to it like miscegenation or same-sex marriage (Loving v. Virginia, 1967; Obergefell v. Hodges, 2015). First, traditionalists would claim that interspecies breeding is a crime against nature. Second, the U.S. Supreme Court may hold that the U.S. Constitution protects individuals' private decisions to have children and families. One unique issue would arise because puppies presently do not have human rights in the United States; thus, third, rights for human–animal hybrids would need to be analyzed under a new paradigm. Medical hybridization could open the door to problems involving zoophilia and attempts sexually to reproduce with hybrids. Thus, fourth, these issues would need to be decided using legal, ethical, and historical frameworks consistent with American tradition and contemporary society's attitudes.

Parental Instincts

Dogs and humans may be born with the potential to become parents (Mauritso, 2014). "Cultures around the world have long assumed that women are hardwired to be mothers. [Research] suggests that caring for children awakens a parenting network in the . . . same circuits in men;" thus, humans are "born with the circuitry to . . . be sensitive caregivers, and the network can be turned up through parenting" (Norton, 2014). Neither humans nor dogs appear to be born with activated parental abilities, even though both seem to be able to identify caretakers. One neurological characteristic of puppies and babies making them incapable of parenting is that they developed sensorimotor skills in stages (Gagnon & Doré, 1994). Object permanence is developed once they realize that objects, which have left their view, continue to exist but are hidden. Infants' cognition in early stages (i.e. stages one and two) is limited. Infants do not follow objects using their heads or bodies once objects have left their visual fields; however, they eventually learn to track objects and can recover partially hidden objects (i.e. stage three). Later (i.e. stage four), infants search for disappearing objects and objects that have disappeared from particular places; but they do not search for objects that have disappeared from unsuspected locations. Finally, infants learn to search for hidden objects at any given location (i.e. stage five); and infants are able to infer that objects inside containers have disappeared (i.e. stage six). This series of tests was administered to 70 puppies between the ages of four weeks to nine months. At two weeks old, wolf and dog pups detect scents; and wolf pups may also begin socializing (*U.S. News & World Report*, 2013). Wolf and dog pups may develop hearing when they are four weeks-old, which is when dog pups may begin socializing.

Data showed that five week-old puppies were able to locate visibly hidden objects (Gagnon & Doré, 1994). Their skills improved through their eighth week, but then stalled throughout the next nine months. Thus, the study suggested that during their first years, humans may be better than puppies at solving problems in which objects are invisibly hidden, even though some research suggests that puppies develop skills to locate hidden objects at rates similar to human infants. Puppies

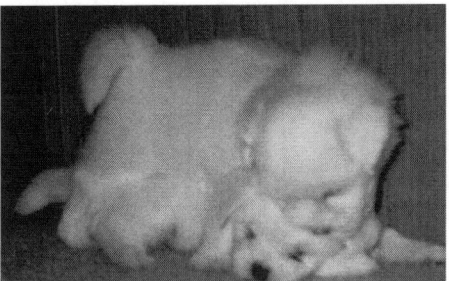

9.2 Maltese-Havanese puppies beginning to socialize

become fertile during their second years, thus puppies may transform neurologically from infants into adult dogs after their first year. Some dogs are more adroit than children or adults at finding hidden objects. Another study examined development of object permanence in 69 purebred puppies representing five breeds. Three month-old puppies could locate an object hidden in the same place; and nine month-old puppies could locate objects that had been invisibly hidden. Unlike human babies, who consistently perform similarly on object permanence tests, these puppies individually varied and were less predictable according to weeks and months.

American culture and subcultures may encourage parenting, even when it contravenes individual or group norms. For example, thieves may more considerate of babies' parents more than other adults. A field study discarded onto local streets 240 wallets, most of which contained photos. The return rate was almost half (Wiseman, 2014). Approximately 14% of wallets without photos were returned; yet, more than three-quarters (88%) of wallets containing a baby's photo were returned. A little more than one-quarter (28%) of wallets containing a photo of a senior couple were returned, but almost half (48%) of wallets with family photos were sent to the address inside the wallet; and more than half (53%) of wallets exhibiting a photo of a puppy were returned to the owner. Thus, wallet finders and would-be thieves may have been most compelled by babies, who were perceived as being more like puppies than young children, adults, or seniors, despite that old age "[i]s second childishness and mere oblivion, [s]ans teeth, sans eyes, sans taste, sans everything" (Shakespeare, 2004). A likely explanation may be that puppies and babies share fresh facial structures and similar proportions, such as large cartoonish eyes (Gould, 1980).

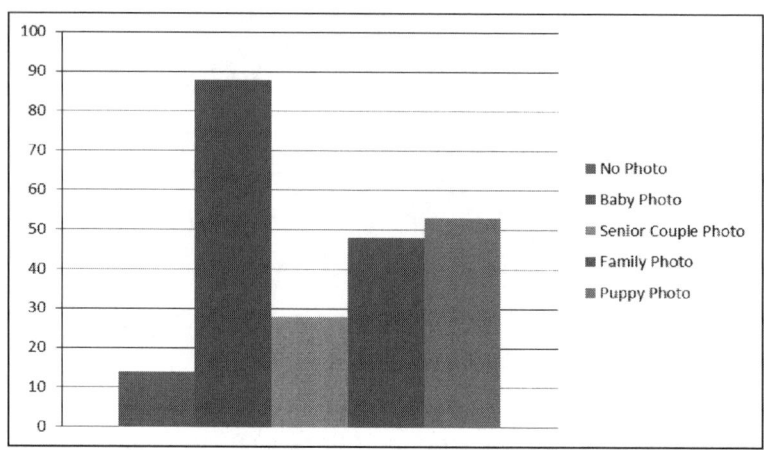

9.3 Percentage of Wallets Returned

Data shows that the human brain rapidly may respond to unfamiliar infants' and puppies' faces, but not unfamiliar adults' faces, due to the proportions and structures of babies' and puppies' faces (Glocker, 2009; Kringelbach, 2008). "When we see a living creature with babyish features, we feel an automatic surge of disarming tenderness. The adaptive value of this response can scarcely be questioned, for we must nurture our babies" (Gould, 1980).

Adult humans' brains innately may be hardwired to respond to their children, and perhaps to care for dogs. One study of mothers demonstrated that mothers' brains distinctly respond to images of their own infants in pain (Parker-Pope, 2008). First, mothers were required to leave their 18 month-old infants in a room causing their infants to cry. Then, mothers watched videos of other infants and their own infants crying. MRI brain scans demonstrated significant differences between how mothers neurologically responded to their own children and other children. This hardwiring may be used to care for dogs. Brain scans were administered to 14 mothers, who had children between the ages of two and ten years old, and each owned a dog for at least two years. Research demonstrated that when mothers saw depictions of their children or dogs, a common neural network crucial to formation and maintenance of pair-bonding was activated (Perry, 2014). Research also shows that oxytocin secretion increases when humans cuddle or interact with dogs, which further validates some Americans' treatment of dogs as children.

CHAPTER TEN

Food

Chocolate

Americans may believe that chocolate is a heavenly aphrodisiac that improves mood by stimulating release of phenylethylamine and serotonin (Afoakwa, 2008; Hospodar, 2004). This belief has been widespread throughout the Western hemisphere for millennia. Between AD 250 and 900, some pre-Columbian societies, such as Mayans, may have believed that chocolate possessed divine and healing power (Lippi, 2009). Aztecs used cocoa pods to symbolize life and fertility. Like Mayans, Aztecs allegedly believed that cocoa plants could imbue them with supremacy and wisdom. Despite extensive historical faith in cocoa, data shows that chocolate's effects may be environmental and psychosomatic rather than physiological and physical. For example, a study of 163 women examined whether daily consumption of chocolate correlated with mood and sexual behavior (Salonia, et al., 2006). Participants' mean age was 35 years old within a range of nine years. One hundred and twenty women ate chocolate daily. Their average age was 34 years old. Women, who did not eat chocolate daily, were approximately 40 years old. The two groups did not have significant differences in depression, sexual arousal, sexual satisfaction, or sexual distress.

Americans may associate chocolate with privilege; and relative to dogs, Americans may view chocolate as an organismic privilege because dogs are seriously allergic to chocolate. For example, research does not show that American dog owners avoid buying chocolate due to its toxic effects.

> Chocolate poisoning is one of the most common toxicological emergencies in dogs. The degree of toxicity highly depends on the oral dose and the metabolism. The reason for the high prevalence of this intoxication is due to the fact that dogs often have access to a wide range of chocolate-containing foods with toxic ingredients . . . [D]ogs are mainly affected because of their appetite for sweet foods, and smaller dogs appear to be more susceptible to intoxication than larger dogs. (Agudelo, Filipejova, & Schanilec, 2013)

Thus, puppies may be most susceptible to chocolate overdose, yet puppy owners are not known to abstain from eating chocolate in their homes.

Chocolate's distinct effect on humans, large dogs, and puppies call attention to physical, sexual, and social differences between canines, children, and adults. For example, during Easter, American children search for hidden baskets filled with chocolate bunnies and eggs symbolizing fertility; however, dogs and puppies must be monitored (Waggin Tales, 2013). Easter chocolate mainly is eaten by adults, many of whom claim to experience aphrodisiacal effects. Adults purchase most chocolate (92%) with the intention of consuming half of their purchases; and more than half (58%) of chocolate purchases are made at Easter (NCA, n.d.). Average adults ate 113 pieces of chocolate in 2010, but children only ate 107. Adults' chocolate consumption represented 81% of all chocolate consumption. Perhaps alleged benefits for mood and libido are myths justifying why adults feed themselves a food that poisons their dogs and may corrode their children's teeth and health.

Demographic data may support an inference that privileged American adults enjoy chocolate. Europeans consume 49% of the world's chocolate, while North Americans consume 24%, with the United States consuming 20% of the world's chocolate (CNN, 2012; NCA, n.d.). Europe imports approximately 59% of the world's cocoa; and the United States imports 21%. Typically, only 2% of children independently purchase chocolate for their own consumption. Chocolate is mostly consumed by married (53%) White non-Hispanic adults (70%), who are employed (53%), have minor children (43%), are educated (28%), and have an average annual household income above $100,000 (24%). Myths may allow privileged Americans to justify chocolate consumption. Demonstrating that perhaps new generations are questioning myths, consumption recently has decreased among children between the ages of two and five years old

Breastfeeding

The euphemism "puppies," used to connote "breasts," may insinuate relationships between puppies and breasts, such as interspecies wet nursing (Cusack, 2015). Lactation occurs to many females mammals during and after pregnancy; and it may be detectable to fetuses and newborns offspring (Breastmilk, 2014). Newborn mammals exhibit a sucking reflex, but newborn puppies and humans suckle differently. Puppies are capable of writhing toward and locating their mothers' nipples; however human infants are powerless to maneuver their bodies toward nipples; thus, without human or animal intervention, babies are incapable of surviving. Though human infants may latch to nipples, they are passive participants. Therefore, society's promotion of lactating women's active participation may be congruent with survival of the species as well as purported physiological benefits to wet nurses and mothers despite occasional political opposition to insinuations about biological determinism.

Females, who are more willing publically to breastfeed, possibly better compensate for infants' incapacities. However, lactating nipples may lack physical continence, which may be perceived as sexual incontinence in violation of traditional Christian norms for public decorum. Some critics may claim that breastfeeding ought to be private due to physiological and hormonal links between orgasm, breasts, oxytocin, and lactation. Complaints about sexual overtones allegedly apparent in public breastfeeding have resulted in vociferous campaigns in support of public breastfeeding and legislation separating public life from religious morals (Cusack, 2012). While shaming has attempted to perpetuate age-old paradigms about the importance of females appearing to be chased, some Americans may believe that public breastfeeding is consistent with societal institutionalization of females' physiological roles. Rather than believing that indecent exposure defines public breastfeeding, some Americans think of milk as being food; thus, public breastfeeding, at a restaurant, for example, would not be distinct from dining, but analogous to it, allowing breastfeeding women to fulfill society's expectations.

Despite alleged benefits of breastmilk for newborns, species and race may be factors that impede wet nursing because some families prefer for wet nurses to be the same species and race as their children. While a few studies may conclude that humans and animals have detrimentally dissimilar milk composition, breast milk will be virtually identical between two women if those women had similar lifestyles. One study found that nutritional content, such as fat, enzymes, lactose, and proteins, did not vary with women's race, age, or diet (Jenness, 1979). Milk composition was also found to be consistent between both breasts. One study examined breast milk from 51 mothers of Malaysian, Chinese, and Indian heritage (Kneebone, Kneebone, & Gibson, 1985). Fatty acids were examined to determine whether differences would manifest despite the fact that the three groups of women lived in close proximity in Malaysia. Dietary intake was associated with culture, which altered fatty acid composition. Chinese mothers' breast milk had a lower saturation of fatty acid than Malay or Indian mothers. Each groups' fatty acid levels were consistent with Western mothers, who subsisted on well-balanced diets. Thus, compositional differences were not related to racial differences, but rather to cultural or lifestyle differences. A study of Black Americans and White Americans found that Black infants lacked vitamin D, which is consistent with findings generally showing vitamin D deficiencies among Black Americans (Taylor, et al., 2006). Yet, vitamin D deficient breast milk may not have adverse effects on preterm infants. Vitamin D status among Black and White children is significant during the first two weeks after birth; however infants receiving vitamin D rich formula may have the same vitamin D status as infants predominantly consuming breast milk, which undermines the importance of wet nursing.

Cultural, biological, and nutritional considerations suggest that human wet nurses may be unideal for several reasons. First, it may be viewed as an affront to norms and American culture (Cusack, 2015). Second, human breast milk may not be more suitable for puppies than formula designed to meet puppies' nutritional needs. Third, puppies are capable of actively participating in feeding; thus, human intervention generally is unnecessary. Fourth, American women's desire to breastfeed puppies may relate to American preoccupation with food or pressure to breastfeed (Srinath, 2012). Lactating women may justify wet nursing in order to share mealtimes with puppies or not to waste breast milk; however, breast milk may be unhealthy for puppies, for example, if it has been at room temperature for too long.

Depictions of women breastfeeding puppies increasingly have come to the public's attention through social media. Images posted on the internet may blur lines between private and public breastfeeding; and cause interspecies wet nursing to be correlated with public spectacle. For example, a Colorado woman was publicly harangued after she used social media to share a photo of a puppy suckling her nipple. A report said that despite "the backlash she fears from the "taboo" action . . . [t]hat dog is alive because [she] . . . took that initiative" (KRDO, 2014). Puppies are unlikely to require human wet nursing particularly because most puppies wean early in their development when they are still with their mothers; however, under rare circumstances breastfeeding may be lifesaving for orphans or estranged pups. Despite disadvantages and controversy, lifesaving interspecies wet nursing may be acceptable to mainstream Americans. For example, consistent with other similar anecdotal evidence, Americans seemed to respond with pity when police "rescued a malnourished 2-year-old boy found being breastfed by a neighbor's dog" (*The Huffington Post*, 2015). Americans' pity may indicate that if interspecies wet nursing aids survival, then perhaps lifesaving symbiosis is tolerable even when depictions of it are exploited by social media.

Breastfeeding puppies may be irresponsible because human breast milk may be an unideal source of nutrition; for example, puppies may be lactose intolerant. Puppies should not necessarily be fed human breast milk or infant formula when puppy formula is available.

All animal species have a specific composition of their 'mother's milk'. Human is very different from dog, and although none of the formulas available for human or dog do a perfect job imitating the correct balance of nutrients for their specific species, dog formula will be much closer to dog milk than human formula would be. In the absence of dog formula, human formula might be better than regular cow milk, but it would still not be as good as the dog formula. (Banfield Hospital, 2015)

Even though ingredients present in human formula, such as polyunsaturated fatty acids, are found in dog milk replacer formula, "[a] mother dog's milk provides everything the pups need during their first four weeks of life . . . The babies will need to be fed a commercial canine milk replacer . . . specifically formulated for puppies, as cow's milk and other milk replacer can cause diarrhea" (ASPCA, n.d.). Because puppy formula composition varies significantly, any nutritional overlap between human and puppy formulas may be brand specific.

Findings suggesting nutritional deficiencies in dog replacer formula may support arguments in favor of interspecies wet nursing. One study analyzed five dog milk samples and 15 dog formula samples (Heinze, et al., 2014). Each of the dogs ate an appropriately supplemented diet. Dog milk and milk replacers were analyzed for concentrations of total protein, essential amino acids, sugars, total fat, essential fatty acids, calcium, and phosphorus; and energy density was calculated. Results from milk replacers were compared to milk samples from mature dogs as well as recommendations made by the National Research Council. Calories, fat, calcium, protein, phosphorus, and acids varied between brands. In approximately 93% of the formulas, there was less calcium than in dog milk. At least one acid present in dog milk was undetectable in 80% of formulas. Generally, dog milk replacer formula lacked several kinds of essential nutrients in comparison to dog milk; however, dog milk was also found to be deficient in comparison to National Research Council's recommend allowances for puppies. This final finding could potentially be used to undermine conclusions about nutritional deficiencies in human milk.

Commercial milk replacers for puppies have been available for decades and are commonly used for rearing orphans, for ill or weakened neonates, to supplement dog milk for large litters, and to mix with commercial puppy diets during the weaning process. Numerous products are available, but unlike other pet foods, the nutritional adequacy standards these products are expected to meet are not clearly defined. These factors make it difficult for pet owners and veterinarians to select appropriate milk replacers for their needs. Indeed, there is evidence that dog milk replacers may be quite variable in essential macronutrient and mineral concentrations among specific products and in comparison to dog milk. (Heinze, et al., 2014)

Furthermore, research supported by a grant from Nestlé Purina PetCare concluded that dog replacer formula nutritionally may be inadequate for puppies.

Results of this study suggested that currently available puppy milk replacers contained variable nutrient concentrations and were not close matches to dog milk. Many products had potentially serious problems such as inadequate calcium, insufficient calcium-to-phosphorus ratio, low caloric density, inappropriate feeding directions, and excessive lactose concentrations. All of these concerns could contribute to poor puppy growth and viability. (Heinze, et al., 2014)

Although these conclusions may support some women's claims that human breast milk could nourish some puppies equally or better than replacer formulas, data consistently demonstrates compositional differences in breast milk across species.

In mammals, milk provides a source of key nutrients that act individually and jointly to insure optimal growth, development and protection of the neonate during its initiation and adaptation to the extra-uterine life. These nutrients include proteins, lipids, carbohydrates, minerals and vitamins. The precise composition of milk varies between different mammalian species and over the course of lactation representing a likely evolutionary adaptation to the respective species' life history and ecological niche. (Rostami, et al., 2014)

Thus, like milk from women of different races, milk from different species may vary due to environmental differences. Different species' milk may also share significant nutritional similarities. A study designed to analyze milk oligosaccharides (OS) throughout lactation in a Labrador Retriever, a Schnauzer, and three Alaskan husky mixes discussed comparability of other species' lactations.

> Generally, early dog milk showed highest concentration of OS similar to observations done with other mammals such as rat, mouse, cow, and humans. Yet [fluctuations] regarding specific OS [levels] exist [throughout lactation] . . . It is likely that the varying amounts of OS in milk point to specific needs of the suckling newborn over the course of lactation. When comparing the gross composition of canine milk with milk from other species, there appears to be a striking similarity to rat milk . . . [Although puppies'] specific reproductive and developmental needs . . . are addressed by the unique composition of canine milk . . . [,] environment influence[s] the variation in milk composition. (Rostami, et al., 2014)

Thus, benefits of human breast milk may vary as women's milk ages and puppies develop; yet generally, puppies may be better aided by rats because of the composition of rats' milk.

10.1 Dam nursing her pups

Another possible advantage for puppies wet nursed by rats instead of humans is that rats have multiple nipples. In a study of ten puppy dog litters, 47 individual puppies typically alternated nipples during a single feeding session and demonstrated no preferences for particular nipples (Arteaga, 2013). Rats' anatomies may better fit with puppy dogs' feeding styles; however, human wet nurses could allow puppies to alternate nipples during a session according to puppies' preferences (Mothering, 2011).

Peanuts

Vulgar enclaves of American culture perpetuate an urban legend that dogs perform oral sex on humans, who smatter their genitals with peanut butter. Essentially, this rumor suggests that dogs would voluntarily perform oral sex on humans if they were bribed; and this jocular myth minimizes the seriousness of animal sexual abuse by suggesting that dogs could benefit from sexual contact by receiving a treat. Though the urban legend does not seem to be well-founded, it has been depicted in American movies and television shows, including an episode of "Orange is the New Black," which portrays a female inmate using peanut butter to induce cunnilingus from a dog participating in a prison dog program, discussed in Chapter Twelve (Gennis, 2014).

> In the episode, Big Boo [a butch lesbian inmate] once again proves that she can turn anything into a tool for sexual pleasure. Though this time, she might have definitely gone a bit too far. While feeding Lil Boo, Big Boo marvels at the excited way the dog licks up the peanut butter . . . [Big Boo says to Lil Boo] 'You like to lick that, don't you? Just lick, lick, lick,' Boo muses, until a light bulb flashes and she decides to try putting the peanut butter . . . somewhere else. (Gennis, 2014)

Americans, who perpetuate the peanut butter rumor, may acknowledge exploitation. For example, the actress, who performed the scene in "Orange is the New Black," said "Well, of course, . . . [t]hat's abusive to animals" (Gennis, 2014). On the television show, Lil Boo is unable to continue the prison dog program because Big Boo believes that their relationship has gotten "weird" (Gennis, 2014). Thus, the dog directly suffered consequences, which could have involved returning to an animal shelter without having received training to become a more adoptable candidate.

Some dogs have been trained to detect peanut particles to prevent allergic reactions. Peanut allergies can include anaphylactic shock and lethal responses to peanut residue. Peanut detector dogs, who may cost approximately $10,000 to train and maintain, may learn to detect peanut particles in their handlers' food and in the nearby vicinity (Chitale, 2009; Story, 2014). Only one in 300 dogs may have an appropriate temperament for training because dogs constantly work due to the prevalence of peanut particles in American foods and products. Over the course of six months, peanut dogs use object permanence skills, discussed in Chapter Nine, to learn to search for traces of peanuts (Dog Trainers Workshop, n.d.). Some dog breeds may be prone to working as peanut detector dogs because they are experts in agriculture; for example, Border collies use their "hypnotic eye" to control livestock and may excel as trufflers (Armao, 2013).

Children's lack of tolerance to food allergies and increased tendency to make mistakes causes them to be especially vulnerable to severe allergic reactions. Youth belonging to "Generation Rx" may be more likely to use peanut detector dogs, even when their allergies are not life threatening, because of that generations' propensity for medicalization. Children from higher income families have been found to be likeliest to experience peanut allergies possibly correlating with immunities being stunted by excessively sanitized environments (ACAAI, 2012). Affluent families may be able to afford peanut detector dogs not paid by health insurance.

CHAPTER ELEVEN

Technology

Tools and Entertainment

Modern puppies may learn to use remote controls, touchscreens, lights, automatic doors, mechanical gates, game consoles, the internet, and other electronic and technologic implementations (Raiford, 2015). Although many may learn in order to assist humans; others learn for their own benefit and entertainment. Technologically adept puppies represent a new demographic for app developers. "The increasing demand for highly automated and flexible tasks capable of assessing visual learning and memory in nonhuman animals has led to the exciting development of a wide array of prefabricated touchscreen-equipped systems" (Friskies, n.d.; Klee, 2013; Meade, 2014; Wolf, et al., 2014). Some puppies' owners pay approximately $50 per hour to train puppies to use apps and other technology. Puppies' use of technologic devices may elucidate the criticality of technologic training in the Digital Age. Most puppies, like humans, learn to perform specific functions through reward-based training systems (e.g. smearing peanut butter on touchscreens). After puppies are trained to use technology and play games, they may learn to enjoy the objects of the games (Wolf, et al., 2014). As greater numbers of apps are designed to entertain puppies, humans may believe that puppies' use of technology grants them greater control over puppies; for example, some humans may be better able to control puppies' energy when they use tablet computers (AOL, 2015). However, some puppies generally may be bothered by apps designed to entertain them; and demonstratively reject app training resulting in increased conflicts with owners. Well-designed technology gives trained puppies sufficient control to demonstrate various skill-levels and proficiency (Gray, 2013). Thus, technology may allocate greater control, and possibly, autonomy to puppies. Usable features, such as switches, pulls, levers, and buttons that are suited to dogs' physical capabilities and physiologies are as important as user-friendly programming. For example, several dogs have been trained to drive cars devised for canine drivers (Driving Dogs, 2012). They are able to brake, steer, honk, and operate other features. Although few studies have measured dogs' abilities independently to use technology, and benefits, if any, to humanity, innovative technology and ergonomic machinery could change the extent of dogs' participation in domestic and public life.

Medical Devices

Prostheses, such as wheel-legs or blade-legs, are becoming rather common while digitized body parts, such as pacemakers, increasingly help more dogs to live longer. Expensive prostheses and medical devices highlight evolving social status, value, and significance of dogs in human society. The cost of prostheses and devices also raises implications about divides between medical care for financially prosperous families and disadvantaged families because sophisticated treatment for pets may be relatively expensive.

A prosthesis clinic employee discussed escalating use of prostheses and shifts in philosophical paradigms.

> We have seen a dramatic increase in how many patients we get to help . . . Over the last decade, experiencing the movement . . . [to] do some pretty cool things . . . as a society; we're not just looking at animals as discardable; we're looking at . . . [ways] . . . to help . . . through prosthetics or adaptive devices . . . When a dog is very defensive, and it cowers, and it doesn't want to do a lot that it use to; and then you apply a prosthesis so that they can go back to normal life; and you see them back to eating; they're very social; they want to go out and greet the other dogs; well, you can tell there's a definite behavior shift; and that happened after they had their prosthesis applied and they learned how to use it . . . [T]hat's happiness! (PBS, 2014)

His comment correlates increased numbers of patients with greater compassion in society; and suggests that prostheses and medical treatment provides opportunities for altruism and happiness. People assisting animals in need of artificial limbs and organs acknowledge that "it's not like there's anything seriously wrong. [They] just need a little help" (PBS, 2014). Some human companions, who are missing limbs, adopt amputees for companionship and to amplify symbolic speech created by their use of prostheses. Humans and dogs using prostheses may demonstrate competence and completeness in spite of physical challenges.

> [People will think,] 'That dog has will and perseverance and courage. He's a great dog . . . [not] disabled or impaired' . . . [He's] missing a

paw, but that's just part of his physicality. One of the things . . . that [a courageous dog] . . . does show . . . is that it doesn't really matter if you're wearing a prosthetic or born missing a paw. It's kind of 'What soul do you bring into the world?' . . . It's true of people too. . . . You should judge people more on the soul they bring to the world, and not the physical appearance. (PBS, 2014)

Pet owners and clinics that can afford to provide prosthetic limbs may feel that it is a matter of conscience rather than emotional enrichment or sociality (Castillo, 2013). For example, a prosthesis clinic employee discussed ethics (PBS, 2014).

> I think if we can save an animal and make that animal have a higher quality of life by giving them a prosthetic . . . limb, then we are obligated to do it because . . . it sends the message that animals aren't just sort of there for our own entertainment and amusement, that these animals aren't things, or property like couches, it sends a message that they are sentient beings, who have a right to a full and rich life. (PBS, 2014)

However, these ideals expose disparities between those, who have the means to achieve "a full and rich life," and others, who do not (PBS, 2014). For example, most dogs in need of pacemakers do very well after surgery, but only a small percentage receive pacemakers to improve their hearts and extend their lives (Johnson, Martin, & Henley, 2007). An examination of pacemaker implantation in 104 mature dogs and puppies found that 103 dogs survived implantation; but major complications resulted in merely three fatalities; while only six dogs died from sudden death months or years after the procedure. After one year, dogs had an 86% chance of survival; after three years, dogs had a 65% chance of survival; and after five years, dogs had a 39% chance of survival. However, most animals in need of pacemakers will not receive them because they can cost several thousands of dollars (Malakoff, n.d.; Mott, n.d.). Many persons in the United States similarly are disadvantaged because their health insurance is inadequate or requires them to pay a portion of the cost (Christensen, 2013; League of Women Voters, n.d.). Arguably, dogs belonging to families that can afford pacemakers may have higher economic statuses than humans incapable of affording them.

Loss and Abduction

Subcutaneous microchips may be used to identify found pets, and electronic dog tags and GPS may be used to locate missing dogs. Technology routinely used to train animals may be used to locate missing animals, for example, a smartphone may be configured to track pointer dogs (Bianchi & Holland, 2014). Wearable technology transmits system positions, which can help locate a missing animal within a given area. This concept is not new—for decades hunting dogs have worn electronic collars, which could be used to track lost or dead dogs, for example, inside alligators' bellies (Kaczor, 1995). Certain technologies may work against dog owners' interests, such as apps or GPS that lack sufficient accuracy or devices that may be hacked. Homes' Wi-Fi networks make it possible for hackers to access connected devices, such as electronic gates, computers, security cameras, dog monitors, or home alarm systems (Fowler, 2015; Yahoo, 2015).

Wearables are becoming increasingly specialized, for example, some may detect dogs' pain (Pet Pace, 2014). Dog owners victimized by pet abduction (e.g. domestic violence) may be able to ascertain whether abducted pets have been maltreated and are experiencing pain, seizures, or erratic movement. These innovations may psychologically empower dog owners. Wearables and other technology may help to quell property disputes about stray animals. Abducted dogs may be abandoned; and later rediscovered through the use of tracking devices; however, original owners may not have sufficient rights in property law to claim abducted dogs, who have been rescued by innocent parties. Original owners and finders may be tempted to ask courts to award custody of puppies using a best interest standard, however, courts may be bound to strict or quasi-property analyses. For example, in Morgan v. Kroupa (1997), a finder took home a stray dog; but, she posted notices and contacted the humane society before adopting the dog into her family. The original owner located the dog a few miles away and drove to the finder's house to request custody of his dog; however, the original owner was denied by the finder. As the original owner was leaving, the dog jumped into his truck and left with him. The finder sued the original owner to recover the dog. A Vermont court considered whether the matter should be decided according to property law, as a child custody case, or based on the parties' emotional attachments to the dog. The court favored a property analysis, and ruled that the finder had substantially complied with the statute. In Vermont, finders of lost property and animals were required to make two descriptive notices and post them in two public places near where the property or animal was found within six days. Property worth more than ten dollars was required to be announced in a local flyer for three consecutive weeks. The notice was first to be recorded by the local clerk of courts after which the original owner had 90 days to reply. The statute required extensive notification because it addressed lost farm animals, who may be significantly more valuable than stray dogs; thus, it likely did not apply to lost pets, and an absence of case law about stray dogs supported the court's conclusion that the extensive reporting requirements only applied when finders wished to claim lost farm animals.

> Here . . . we are dealing with a mixed-breed dog that was given away as a puppy and was five or six years old when it became lost. Like most pets, its worth is not primarily financial, but emotional; its value derives from the animal's relationship with its human companions . . . [A dog] may have a lot of emotional value but there's nothing in the record to suggest that the dog has a fair market value of any significance . . . Ordinary common law or statutory rules governing lost personal property therefore do not provide a useful framework for resolving disputes over lost pets. Instead, courts must fashion and apply rules that recognize their unique status, and protect the interests of both owner and finder, as well as the public. (Morgan v. Kroupa, 1997, p. 103)

Finders are encouraged by society and law to make reasonable effort notify a dog's original owner, for example, communicating with a humane society or police department and posting notices or advertisements; and similarly, original owners may contact local animal shelters and place notices in order to locate missing dogs. Taking each party's actions into consideration, the court balanced whether reasonable efforts were made. In this case, the finder acted reasonably and substantially complied with a law applying to valuable animals. The finder also acted in the public interest by caring for a stray dog for one year. Noticeably, the court neglected to evaluate whether the dog indicated a preference for the original owner by jumping into the original owner's truck.

Finders of property, who are required by law to post notices before claiming property, may use social media to make general announcements to the public and blast pertinent networks. Individuals have notably relied on social media to locate and recover puppies. For example, a Jack Russell terrier named Patch was lost while riding a train; however, Twitter users helped locate and reunite Patch with his owner (Dogs with Jobs, 2000). Tracking missing animals on social media occasionally results in success stories, but often results in comments that do not contribute to reunification. For example, Bruno, a young Bernese mountain dog, accidentally was flown to Cuba after an airline failed to unload him (*The Canadian Press*, 2015). His human companion live-tweeted and updated followers about his frustrations with the airports and airline officials. Although Bruno received a large show of support, and some of his owner's messages were retweeted, social media likely had little impact on Bruno's return. A Facebook campaign led to international press coverage of a puppy named Caramel (Kirby, 2015; MSN, 2015). Social media users from Asia, Australia, Europe, and North America expressed concern and helped to locate Caramel, who had been abducted from her home during a burglary. Caramel's Facebook page generated more than 12 million comments. After local news reports identified the victim and the public's response on Facebook, an unsuspecting buyer returned Caramel to her original owner. Caramel's reunification represents an exception, not a rule for lost or stolen dog webpages.

CHAPTER TWELVE

Pups in Criminal Justice

Prison Programs

Puppies raised in jails may serve several purposes, including dog training apprenticeship programs; service training; companionship; and rehabilitation. Prison dog programs work well because inmates relate to dogs. Inmates may view themselves as training for new lives after reentry; and they may also view themselves as being in need of a second chance (Cunningham & Seirup, 2014). These inmates "took something from the world . . . Now their time has meaning and they're giving something back" (*Corrections Today,* 2014). One inmate said, "The very first dog that I had . . . was very afraid . . . and he wouldn't even come out of his cage . . . [Now,] [h]e's happy. I think in a sense, he forgot his past" (Cunningham & Seirup, 2014).

In the Don't Throw Us Away Program, homeless dogs are rescued from streets, abandoned properties, remote areas, and other locales. They are introduced into the program to avoid euthanasia at animal shelters and to find adoptive families, who visit prisons at the end of eight-week training modules. Thus, prison pet programs not only entice adopters and alleviate overflow from shelters, they also aid homeless dogs.

Many programs initiate training modules by allowing dogs to choose inmates rather than assigning dogs to inmates. Female or male dogs may be handled by male or female inmates; and occasionally, female dogs may have puppies, who are trained with them or following their mothers. Inmates and dogs bond and trust one another throughout training because "it's a privilege for . . . [inmates] to have this unconditional love from the dogs[, who] . . . become a lifeline [of] . . . oxygen" for inmates (Cunningham & Seirup, 2014). Puppies' presence in prison may encourage trainers to put aside gang identities, obsession with addiction, and other negative thought patterns and focus on constructive tasks that benefit others and the community. Training programs may condition inmates to consider how their rehabilitation benefits the community, for example, adoptive families and shelters; and teach them the value of animal welfare. "'The minute we start thinking of other people or other animals as being dispensable or disposable, we suffer that indignity . . . , we lose parts of ourselves' . . . [So,] 'until one has had a relationship with an animal, part of one's soul remains unawakened'" (Cunningham & Seirup, 2014). Inmates gain self-esteem by being chosen by the program, dogs, and adoptive families, and by participating in a progressive penological movement that nurtures reform. Together, dogs and inmates build confidence and experience physiological benefits (Barker, et al., 2010; *Corrections Today,* 2014).

12.1 Ruth, a prisoner-trained service dog placed with a wounded servicemember

Doggone Express (n.d.) operates several programs, including Big House to Your House, an animal training program utilizing inmates; Companions for Life, which teaches veterans to train their service animals; and Paws for Change, a program for at-risk and delinquent teens. Big House to Your House creates organizational culture by using jargon, such as C.A.T.S., meaning Canine Assessment Training Staff. A Master Canine Assistant Trainer (C.A.T.) will participate for six months; train three new C.A.T.S.; and train at least three dogs. Like other typical training programs, each dog receives approximately six weeks of training accumulating approximately 1,000 contact hours with a C.A.T., who keeps logs similar to K-9 training logs recording canine performance, hours, environment, and behavior. Some dogs excel in training, and learn more complex skillsets, such as responding to cue cards and performing tasks in compliance with American with

Disabilities Act (ADA) requirements (104 § 327, 1990). Veterans with post-traumatic stress disorder (PTSD) may train dogs to cover and block when handlers feel intimidated or threatened by an individual in their environment; dogs may learn a distress response to soothe handlers experiencing stressful stimulus; and they may be trained to perform a task, such as retrieving medication. Training programs may be customized to achieve various goals while training dogs inside or outside prisons with C.A.T.S.

Doggone Express (n.d.) efficiently combines several programs and goals. In addition to psychological, spiritual, emotional, and physical aspects of a holistic outlook, Doggone Express is a 501(c)(3) that views shelter dogs as salvageable materials and inmates as tax users, who are an inexpensive labor force. Veterans working with the Companions for Life program may train with C.A.T.S. in prison in order to practice training skills and bond with dogs. Veterans are at greater risk for criminality and incarceration than non-Veterans, thus, exposure to prison environments may deter criminality by demonstrating serious consequences of deviant behaviors likelier among veteran populations, such as driving while intoxicated, pornography crimes, sexual assault, domestic violence, and drug addiction (Cusack, 2015). Under the rational choice theory, veterans may be less likely to commit crimes if they witness penological environments. Inmates are viewed as "good people, who make bad decisions," and interconnected pet programs not only allow veterans to witness serious consequences of poor decision-making, inmates socializing with veterans may be positively influenced or inspired (The Big House to Your House, n.d.). Similarly, at-risk youth and juvenile delinquents are likelier to commit crimes and become incarcerated. Juvenile participants, who experience accomplishment and responsibility, may learn to help, care, work, and avoid drifting into deviance.

Juveniles, veterans, and inmates participating in programs rely on successive approximation, operant conditioning, and transference to train dogs (Doggone Express, n.d.). Successive approximation identifies a goal and then breaks apart the goal into achievable components, which can successively be learned through a reward based system. After a dog and handler learn to complete several components, the cumulative effect is the accomplishment of a larger complex task. Behavioral transference reinforces the importance of consistently repeating a learned skillset while in the training environment and new settings. Inmates may apply B.F. Skinner's operant conditioning by supplying dogs with positive reinforcement for performance; and Ivan Pavlov's classical conditioning by associating precedent conditions with stimuli. Using these techniques may teach participants intellectually to metabolize negative and positive effects of institutionalization and regimentation.

Prison Hunting Dogs

Institutions and departments of corrections may house and train dogs to track escapees; and local, state, and interstate agencies and officials occasionally may request to borrow tracking dogs. Tracking dogs have few weaknesses, which include overheating and years of training. Young puppies are not sufficiently trained to participate in field work, but some may begin working after training three-quarters of a year (Cusack, 2015; Lillich, 2013; Younger, 2010). The dogs are often hounds from bloodlines of tracking dogs with "high success rate in tracking" (Younger, 2010). Refining complicated training skills may require several years, yet dogs may work in less specialized roles in the interim while they train.

Numerous states train, maintain, and lend tracking dogs, whose reputation proceeds them due to their effectiveness and friendliness. Texas Department of Criminal Justice not only pays inmates to make harnesses and badges for working dogs, they allegedly have also used inmates for more than a century to train tracking dogs (Brown, 2002; Lillich, 2013).

> The bloodhounds used by the Texas prison system have been considered possibly the best in the world for at least a century. Some of the bloodlines run back nearly that far. Texas prison bloodhounds are not just used in tracking escaped inmates, their services are requested by the FBI [Federal Bureau of Investigation], DEA [Drug Enforcement Administration], state law enforcement agencies inside and outside Texas, and by search and rescue squads throughout America. (Brown, 2002, p. 175)

Texas prisons continue to convey a tough reputation, but their department has allegedly developed jargon suggesting that institutional respect for inmate handlers has increased.

> During a . . . prison escape, a newscaster referred to the fact that Texas prison dogs, accompanied by inmate kennel men, had been dispatched to assist in the search. The expression "inmate kennel men" probably brought chuckles to a few older guards and even a few ex-convicts who might have watched the newscast. That particular term did not exist until recently, after the reorganization of the "new" Texas

Department of Criminal Justice. The "old" Texas Department of Corrections, or TDC, was far less complimentary in the classification of inmates who handled the bloodhounds . . . [I]nmates who handled the dogs in the field were simply known as "dog boys." Even earlier, convicts working in the lease camps during the 1800s probably wouldn't have known how to respond to the expression "inmate kennel men." But inmates did handle the dogs back then, only they were known commonly as "dawg boys." (Brown, 2002, pp. 175–176)

The anecdote suggests that inmates, guards, and departmental culture have developed more politically correct jargon perhaps reflecting new reformative approaches to corrections. This shift may relate to policy changes protecting inmates from torture and murder by dogs (Schoales, 1995).

Various departments' use of inmate handlers demonstrates the benefits of tracking dog training programs to society, dogs, prisons, and inmates. Florida's Department of Corrections posted a copy of a letter from 1927 that offers a glimpse into the value of prison tracking dogs.

There is one feature of the prison management that, in my judgment, can be improved. I refer to the large number of escapes that are made from the various road camps about the State. I think that this can be greatly improved by the State Road Department maintaining a pack of well trained track dogs at each camp. I have observed that no dogs are kept at any of the camps at present except in instances where the wardens in some few camps have dogs that they privately purchase and keep at their own personal expense, whereas if the State Road Department or some department of the State would keep dogs at every camp the percentage of escapes would be reduced promptly, and would save a great cost to the State both in labor saving of escapes and in the recapture and return of these escapes to the prison. (Florida Department of Corrections, n.d.)

Florida's department explained that "Today, most prisons have tracking dogs or access to them in cases of escape. In fact, these dogs are often requested by local law enforcement to help track criminals, lost children and elderly missing adults" (Florida Department of Corrections, n.d.). Inmates in Florida have been used to train some tracking dogs. Inmate volunteers are tracked by dogs following a fresh scent or using of an article of clothing belonging to the inmate. Handlers are shielded from harm because dogs are leashed throughout training exercises. "But even if the dogs were let loose, the inmate would not be in danger. . . . They would lick him to death" (*Gainesville Sun*, 1990). Many programs permit qualifying inmates to care for dogs, which "breaks the dull prison routine for the volunteers" as does exercise around thousands of acres of property surrounding some correctional institutions (*Gainesville Sun*, 1990). Dogs trained in Florida, such as Jimmy Ryce Center bloodhounds, not only track escapees, they may also be used to track missing children, which increases their demand (*Gainesville Sun*, 1990). Some dogs trained in Florida may work in other states, such as Arizona (Younger, 2010). Dozens of bloodhounds have worked in the Arizona Department of Corrections, where they may live in kennels at prison complexes (Allen-Bell, 2014). Each week they are deployed to work with other agencies; however, searches typically conclude when dogs require rest (Burnside, 2013; Giles, 2013). Nevertheless, tracking dogs are able to hunt targets for long periods until a search is terminated. Bloodhounds often rigorously train and work for several years before retiring.

Courthouse Dogs

Some members of American courts train dogs and puppies to be soothing workers, who facilitate justice. Inside some judges' chambers, courtrooms, courthouse hallways, and interview rooms, dogs work to comfort traumatized or troubled witnesses. Many courthouse dogs are employed to comfort anyone in distress, for example defendants. Witnesses' exchanges with dogs may give a veneer of reliability to witnesses and to their testimony. Though courts, program propaganda, and handlers claim that neutral comforting does not endorse a defendant's testimony, arguably, it may cause a defendant to appear to be more likable or innocent. In court, a jury is empaneled to observe a defendant and all witnesses' demeanors. An interactive dog may change a defendant's demeanor and jurors' perceptions. However, dogs may neutralize jurors' tensions and make them feel more relaxed, which could help safeguard Constitutional guarantees for fair trials.

Some state's attorney offices employ dogs exclusively to comfort alleged child victims. The prosecution may create subtle advantages for particular witnesses, who appear to be endorsed by dogs. Potential unfairness may be more substantial when courthouse dogs are referred to as "trained advocates" (Hampton, 2011). Dog lovers empaneled on the jury or sitting on the bench may be persuaded to believe alleged victims' testimony when dogs' are portrayed as victim advocates. Advocate dogs' presence at trials may complicate the appellate process because biases may be too subtle for defense counsel to articulate

(Bowers, 2013). In order to raise an issue on appeal, the issue must be raised at trial; however, it may be difficult to memorialize on the record when exactly a dog has demonstrated a preference for a victim or bias against a defendant. Technically, most dogs are not members of the court; thus, judges typically instruct juries not to consider dogs' behavior whatsoever. Although a dog's presence may generally be raised by defendants on appeal as a potential source of bias, on appeal the prosecution could argue that "[t]he record demonstrates that the presence of the dog did not interfere with cross-examination, which was lengthy and thorough. The record also demonstrates that the jury followed the trial court's instruction not to consider the dog in any way" (Bowers, 2013, p. 1309). To demonstrate bias, defense counsel may need electronically to record dogs' behavior and court members' responses; however, courthouse dogs are trained and examined for appropriate personalities to reduce biasing behavior. Furthermore, jurors' thoughts cannot be controlled, and they may believe that other members of the court, such as a court reporter or bailiff prefer one party or another, and consequently formulate opinions about the veracity of witnesses' testimony based on these beliefs. Thus, inappropriate behavior would likely need to be obvious in order to raise a genuine issue.

Some dogs' skills and their personalities are refined over the course of four to six weeks of training, which sufficiently instils professional behavior (Gilliam, 2015). Other dogs are trained for more than a year. For example, Assistance Dogs trains dogs to respond to over 90 voice commands; thus training may take between 18 and 24 months. One black Labrador Retriever named Lydia, who was trained by Assistance Dogs, gave birth to six puppies when she was two years old. After eight weeks, she ended maternity leave and resumed working for the Fifth Judicial District Court in Carlsbad, New Mexico. "Lydia is the mother of the next generation of courthouse dogs . . . [a]nd just as Lydia was identified as good mother material when she was very small, her pups were born and bred to enter their mom's profession, to be helping dogs" (Mauritso, 2014). Lydia's puppies were trained to be helping dogs beginning with school children, and then graduating to alleged child victims in courthouses or working for government agencies. For approximately ten years, dogs may work at courthouses and alternate positions, such as in the civilian sector, military, and law enforcement.

Grooming

Grooming is an essential part of many prison dog training programs in which dogs are bathed and brushed; their nails are clipped; and their ears are cleaned (Maynard, 2013; State of North Carolina, 2010). In addition to routine grooming, some prisons offer to inmates grooming training and certification; and a few prison kennels specialize in boarding and grooming for local dogs in the community. For example, Washington Corrections Center for Women in Gig Harbor, which trains rescued animals, sustains their program by offering boarding and grooming (PPP, n.d.). They have 28 indoor dog kennel runs for large and small dogs, which provide access to exercise areas, and are outfitted with beds and toys. Sterile dogs may be boarded for $19 and fertile dogs may be boarded daily for $21. Animals boarded at the prison may be groomed for a fee, and local animals may visit by appointment for "day grooms" (PPP, n.d.). Burnaby Corrections Centre for Women (BCCW) in British Columbia, Canada trained women through a business program to perform dog grooming services (Werb, n.d.). Female inmates earned training certificates by working at Freedom Kennels, which was located at the prison. That kennel maintained a ten-run boarding and grooming training facility where inmates earned weekly wages and aquired skills that led to employment after reentry in grooming and pet industries.

> Most of the women . . . in the program have never had a job before . . . They don't know how to dress appropriately, [have never had the] the opportunity to work with co-workers or deal with the general public . . . [At BCCW] they learn all of those things, and the clients phone down to the kennels and speak to them, and . . . they are polite and deal with them professionally . . . All of [these] are important skills for them to learn. (Werb, n.d.)

Inmates at Pitchess Detention Center in California are trained to groom adoptable dogs (CSC, 2013). Jail employees may pay inmates ten dollars to have their pets groomed at the prison, which helps to cover inmate training costs. Inmates may earn "good behavior" for working in the grooming unit. The ratio of work-to-sentence reduction is approximately four-to-one days; and inmates earn an adult education certificate after 120 hours of work. Some programs require inmates to acquire clerical skills and experience over several years (Washington State Correctional Center for Women, n.d.).

Decatur Correctional Center in Illinois is a minimum security female prison housing approximately 790 inmates at a cost of $28,944 per inmate, which funds numerous rehabilitative programs, including dog grooming certification (Illinois Department of Corrections, 2013; Illinois Department of Corrections, 2015). Decatur offers dog grooming and boarding as well as Groom Elite Certification for inmates at the Correctional Ladies Improving Pets (CLIP) salon. Inmates groom shelter dogs while learning breed recognition and grooming styles. The dog grooming program, which emphasizes inter-species respect and compassion, reflects Decatur's rehabilitative ethos and programming. One anonymous internet user described on Illinois Prison Talk (2008) Decatur's programs.

> They offered . . . [General Education Diplomas (i.e. GED)] classes, a janitorial maintenance certificate class, math classes, culinary classes and a type of computer programming class . . . [They have] had horti-culture classes . . . They offer low security inmates work release or OPD (outer [perimeter] duty) where they leave Decatur and go to Springfield to clean offices. They have a mother/baby unit where preg-nant mothers can raise [their] child while in prison (but there are qualifications for that) . . . [T]hey also have a program for mothers to live in that unit if they have outside relatives that will bring [their] children to the facility at least 2 weekends a month and the children stay. When the children are there those inmates eat [their] meals [in] the unit with the children. They have a drug unit that you can get good time credit for the contracts you complete. They have a program where the inmate can read books to . . . [her] child . . . and have them videotaped and mailed to the child. They have a theatre for movies, a gym, beauty shop, and a library. They also have a dog grooming program. They also have industries where women can work but there are guidelines for that also. They offer a . . . [women's] closet that inmates can use to take home clothes if they have none. Inmates will work somewhere in the facility such as the kitchen, laundry, commis-sary, unit porter, etc. plus they have daily duties . . . as assigned by the officer. (Illinois Prison Talk, 2008)

Dog grooming training is likely offered because it benefits inmates similarly to exercise, education, work, and active parenting (Illinois Prison Talk, 2008). Women's prisons are particularly suitable for rehabilitative and reformative opportunities, such as grooming training programs, because of lower incidence of violence in minimum, medium, and maximum security prisons. At any level of security, inmates with histories of animal abuse may be excluded; some programs will exclude inmates with any history of violence against vulnerable victims (e.g. children or seniors).

CHAPTER THIRTEEN

Civilization and Society

Antiquity

Americans' anthropomorphic treatment of puppies, for example in art, work, or family, may be similar to ancient practices glorifying or deifying puppies and dogs. Some ancient cultures may have viewed dogs as magical creatures, ascribed spiritual roles, or given special rites, such as burial. For example, the Eirene cult may have prepared for theatrical battle simulations by sacrificing a puppy (Cebrián, 2010; Jia & Betts, 2010). Demons, deities, and spirits, such as Erinyes, Hecate, and Keres, were associated with wolves and dogs, some of whom were considered to be like warriors; thus, bloody rituals and sacrifices commonly involved dogs. Some Germanic and Greek warriors used words referring to wolves in their names; and some Irish warriors' names referred to dogs, for example, in the name "Cú Chulainn," "Cú" meant "hound" or "dog" (Cebrián, 2010; Jia & Betts, 2010). Research may demonstrate that Tarascan and Mayan cultures, which relied on working dogs, promoted a belief that dogs ushered souls through an afterlife; and yet, these cultures may also have bred dogs for food (Mark, 2014). Protestant Americans may be dissimilar from numerous ancient groups, including Roman Catholics, who have associated dogs with saints, death, spirits, and the afterlife. For example, Greco-Roman myths about the hound of hell, discussed in Chapter One, resemble Hindu rituals in which dogs are harbingers for the god of death (Cebrián, 2010; Jia & Betts, 2010; Poladian, 2015). Some mesoamerican gods have been depicted as dogs, and some Aztec and Mayan dogs were buried with their human counterparts. Aztecs, Mayans, and Tarascans may have circulated a myth about a great flood destroying humanity. The only two humans to survive were decapitated by a god, who sewed the humans' heads to their buttocks in order to create modern dogs. Ancient myths in Mesopotamia, Egypt, Greece, and Rome may have described dogs as accompanying gods and serving in familial roles.

Present-day puppies literally and symbolically serve as leaders and employees; for example, archeology dogs and conservation dogs may work to identify distinct environments (Fiegl, 2012). Conservation dogs are able to detect species by identifying their whereabouts, habitats, or excrement on land and in water. Archeology dogs locate bones and artifacts, and like cadaver dogs, who detect decomposition, archeology dogs trace bones. Dogs are capable of detecting odors transferred onto objects (e.g. rocks and logs). Migaloo, the first archeology dog, was used to detect Aborigines' bones in Australia, which were important finds for land conservation and protection. Aboriginal elders granted archeologists permission to train Migaloo using bones and fragments contained in the South Australian Museum. Some ancient cultures, such as the Israelites, may have despised puppies; and possibly would have resented the idea of dogs coming into future contact with their bones (Miller, 2008). Israelites depicted in the Bible described dogs as villainous and vile; and compared dogs to enemies and fools (Psalms 22:16). However, they also valued dogs, who worked as guards, shepherds, and travel companions (Miller, 2008). Duplicitous attitudes are discussed further in Chapter One.

Utilization of working dogs has been scrutinized by critics abiding by ancient beliefs; for example, press in England, France, Scotland, Spain, Norway, and other countries have reported that some Orthodox Muslims have complained about working dogs, including bomb detection dogs sniffing suspected terrorists (Kern, 2012). Policy changes have been considered, for example in London, England where bomb detection dogs may only sniff passengers' luggage in order to avoid physical contact with passengers (Kern, 2012; Whitehead, 2008). Yet, contact with certain artifacts or items, such as a Koran, may be offensive to Orthodox Muslims (Lanting, n.d.). Some Europeans may be perplexed by Orthodox Muslims' belief that dogs are spiritually unclean.

> The call to ban [dogs may] represent . . . an attempted encroachment in Europe of Islamic Sharia law . . . Muslim assertiveness with such attempts to impose Islamic legal and religious norms on European society in Europe is growing . . . Americans, usually noted for fierce independence, might put up stronger defenses. (Lanting, n.d.)

The American government may attempt to capitalize on Islamists' prohibition against dogs (Cusack, 2014; Rasul v. Myers, 2008). "[G]overnment studies indicate that the dogs' security usefulness is increased significantly when an enemy's religious beliefs hold that canines are unholy and unclean. In such cases, the mere knowledge that the [government] employs canines might dissuade would-be attackers of ships and critical facilities" (W. 2004). This response is not particular to Orthodox Muslims. Some Americans similarly may be deterred by an encounter with a working rat because in the United States, unlike in other countries (e.g. India or China), rats may be considered unclean.

Archeologists relying on dogs may be frustrated by Orthodox Muslim leaders or policymakers prohibiting dogs at some sites. Perhaps if dogs buried next to humans were to be discovered at sites related to Islam, then low opinions of archeology dogs may improve. "The universal human propensity to bury dogs either on their own or within human burials . . . has significantly enhanced the archeological visibility of dogs" (Larson, et al., 2012). Thus, evidence of past human–dog relationships could possibly alter perceptions of working dogs.

Civilization and Human Society

Data shows that dogs and puppies evolved within the past 20,000 years (Lobell & Powell, 2010). However, canine bones dating back to more than 31,000 years ago were discovered in Goyet Cave in Belgium. Generally, in the 19th century research demonstrated that puppies had descended from jackals, but that hypothesis was abandoned when evidence pointed to gray wolves, foxes, and coyotes as predecessors for modern puppies. The bones in Goyet Cave had a short snout in comparison to contemporary and prehistoric wolves. This finding may be evidence that Aurignacians, who first occupied Europe, began the evolutionary transformation. Ten thousand year-old dog skeletons have been discovered throughout the world, and a 14,000 year-old skeleton was found in Russia. Some research suggests that nearly all dog domestication began in China 16,300 years ago. DNA testing on 1,500 dogs allegedly traced all dog domestication to south of the Yangtze River in China where more than 50 female wolves may have been domesticated over several generations. Yet, research also points to several simultaneous loci of evolution throughout the world, including in India beginning with Indian Pariah Dogs (Lobell & Powell, 2010; Mark, 2014).

Some research suggests that human civilization developed with prehistoric human–wolf relationships, such that dogs and humans simultaneously became civilized. While other data may demonstrate that wolves evolved into dogs after humans had become civilized, but their utility to human societies advanced human civilization.

It has been previously thought that fields and crops attracted wolves to villages, leading to interactions with humans that eventually resulted in a cooperative or symbiotic relationship. Human intervention in canine evolution thus produced the variety of modern dog breeds commonly seen today in homes and dog parks throughout the world. (*Popular Archaeology*, 2013)

These hypotheses suggest that present-day puppies may continue past work to build a symbiotic survival system.

13.1 Chihuahua

Genetic studies suggest that most dogs breeds were developed in the Old World (e.g. Europe and China); and, for the most part, contemporary dog–human relationships in the New World have been inherited (Larson, et al., 2012). Some ancient dog breeds serve as a touchstone for dogs' development in the New World. A study of DNA collected from 19 wolves and 1,375 dogs representing 35 breeds found that persistent genes connecting contemporary dogs to ancient dogs may have survived due to geographic isolation (e.g. Alaskan Malamutes).

> [T]his is despite the fact that dogs were an integral part of the human occupation of the New World and that several modern breeds, including the Chihuahua, are thought to have been at least partly derived from domestic dogs native to the New World. The general lack of . . . lineages in the Americas is likely because of the fact that European breeds, initially introduced only 500 [years] ago, have over-whelmed the native lineages. (Larson, et al., 2012)

In the United States, humans may share a similar pattern whereby members of ancient cultures (e.g. Greek, Indian, and Chinese) emigrate from their native regions and mix with other cultures and genes to form the American melting pot (Goldberg, 2013).

Politics

Puppies symbolically have been besmirched and panned in American politics. A recent example occurred when President George W. Bush explained that the consequence of losing the war in Iraq would be that terrorists would act like a "puppy dog," who would follow Americans home to the United States (Clarke, 2007). President Bush's anthropo-morphic description juxtaposes Orthodox interpretations of Sharia law that consider dogs spiritually to be unclean. Islamists' judgment of dogs is insinuated in a video produced by Islamic State of Iraq and Syria (ISIS) depicting a child holding a rocket launcher while allegedly saying that President Barack Obama is a "dog of Rome," who will be decapitated (Stanton, 2015). The video may imply that Obama's master is the Roman Catholic Church, and suggest that Christians and dogs are unholy to Islamists.

President Bush's "puppy dog" comment not only confronted Is-lamists, it misrepresented puppies (Clarke, 2007). Though one public health issue resulting from stray puppies is that puppies follow humans; a challenge for animal control is that many stray puppies avoid hu-mans. Thus, while President Bush's comparison may have been apt and compelling in some regards, it was somewhat inaccurate. Nevertheless, many combatants may be like puppies because they are young. This comparison is discussed in Chapter One. Combatants likely achieve a sense of maturity by participating in warfare, and without militaristic structure, some young combatants prone to aggression would become violent deviants and recidivists (Cusack, 2015). Participation in organized militias and militaries may help combatants to channel aggression; and yet, they intrinsically mature (Mondak, et al., 2010). "Indeed, anyone familiar with puppies and old dogs can understand how the human decline in [e]xcitement [s]eeking might be biologically based" (Mondak, et al., 2010). Thus, bellicose youth may become more peaceful and stable as they outgrow combat roles.

Russia's First Deputy Prime Minister used an image of a puppy to mock America on social media. He uploaded online two side-by-side photos of President Vladimir Putin caressing a cheetah in one picture and a second picture of President Barrack Obama holding a poodle named Baby, who lost one leg after surviving years of torture at a puppy mill (Clarke, 2007; Popkin, 2008; Rogozin, 2014). The photos were captioned by the Russian official with the phrase "We have different values and allies" (Popkin, 2008; Rogozin, 2014). Americans may view amputee dogs as possessing courage and charisma. This is discussed in Chapter 11; and charisma is highlighted in Chapter Nine. However, the likely meaning of his internet post may have insinuated that Russians are tough and formidable, while Americans are delicate and imbalanced.

In political parlance, the term "puppy federalism" denotes shallow infatuation with the idea of federalism that ignores alleged flaws present in contemporary abandonment of framers' intent as recorded in the U.S. Constitution, The Federalist Papers, and other documents (Rubin, 2001). "Thus we can enjoy the idea of federalism because we have forgotten the grave problems associated with its actuality. What we have instead is puppy federalism, a thin patina of rights talk draped across the areas where we have opted for decentralization as an administrative strategy" (Rubin, 2001, p. 47).

> [P]uppy federalism . . . like puppy love . . . looks somewhat authentic but does not reflect the intense desires that give the real thing its inherent meaning. The main purpose of puppy federalism is to convince ourselves that we have not altered the conception of the government that the Framers maintained, when, of course, we have; that we are not a bureaucratized administrative state, when, of course, we are. (Rubin, 2001, p. 38)

"Puppy federalism" implies that federalism has evaporated into nostalgic rhetoric (Rubin, 2001). Thus, use in this context is consistent with other insulting references in American politics that condescendingly defy American culture's approbation for puppies.

CHAPTER FOURTEEN

Comparative

Europe

Europeans may uniquely remedy or fail to respond to crises according to their economic resources, culture, and attitudes toward dogs in particular circumstances. For example, approximately one million dogs in Greece may be homeless after the collapse of Greece's housing market (BBC, 2015; Kottasova, 2015). Italy suffered a housing crisis during the same decade, but their homeless dog population allegedly did not drastically increase; and although Serbia did not experience a severe housing crisis, like Greece and Italy, they have "huge problems with stray dogs" associated with "notoriously low standards in animal welfare" (Gec, 2015). In the United States, financial and housing crises caused disproportionately more dogs to be abandoned at animal shelters and euthanized (Diamond, 2007).

Americans and Europeans may share similar philosophies about compassionately treating dogs, yet possess distinct sensibilities and implement divergent policies (Cusack, 2013). For example, animal testing on puppies may be denounced by some European politicians, while a lack of policies and laws in the United States may indicate low opposition (European Commission, 2015). One reason may be that laboratory and testing services in the United States are growing industries, which are subsidized by state and the federal governments, universities, private grants, parent companies, and other funders despite availability of computer models, safe formulas, and data from past studies which have been relied on more in recent years by some Europeans cosmetic companies.

Africa and Australia

Wild dogs in Australia, Africa, and the United States may be distinguishable from domesticated and feral dogs (CITES, 1963). In the United States, wild dogs bite fewer humans than domesticated or feral dogs; yet, their status as wild animals potentially could lead some people to perceive them as being more threatening due to highly publicized human deaths caused by African and Australian wild dogs; for example Lindy Chamberlain-Creighton was crucified by the media after her baby was taken from a campsite by an Australian dingo (Whiteman, 2012). She was convicted in the murder of her baby, but her conviction was quashed after she wrongfully had been sentenced to a life term in prison and had served several years.

Some wild dogs may be killed without due process because they are not private property or protected by law. They may be excluded from local dog bite ordinances and laws requiring vicious domesticated dogs to be humanely destroyed; yet, wild dogs held in captivity may be shielded from cruelty by treaties, policies, and laws designed to preserve protected and exotic species (Corbett, 2008). They may be spared from a 'death sentence' due to public interests (Cusack, 2014). For example, a mother accidentally dropped her toddler into a zoo's African painted dog exhibit in Pittsburg, Pennsylvania where her toddler was mutilated and killed (Golgowski, 2013). The African painted dogs were relocated from the zoo but not destroyed. Rather than blame the wild dogs, some critics blamed the child's mother for leaning over the exhibit; while other critics blamed the zoo for failing to secure its exhibit's viewing area.

Carolina dogs (i.e. American dingoes) may be feared because of their status as wild; however, they have not been known to cause human deaths in the United States (Heimbuch, 2015). In the United States between 1999 and 2013, dogs caused approximately 14% of animal-related fatalities, including deaths caused by livestock and poisonous animals and insects (Cusack, 2015; Forrester, Holstege, & Forrester, 2012; Langley, 2005; Langley & Morrow, 1997). Between 1999 and 2013, 197 dog-related fatalities among White males represented approximately 44% of all dog-related fatalities during those years. Approximately 49% of dog-related fatalities transpired in Southern United States. White Southern male Americans may be the likeliest demographic to participate in dogfighting, which possibly could explain their disproportionately high exposure to vicious dogs (Evans, Gauthier, & Forsyth, 1998; Wells & Hepper, 2012). Despite North and South Carolinas' location in Southern United States, Carolina dogs have not been reported to cause human fatalities.

Wild dogs in Australia, Africa, and the United States may be similar to or distinguished from feral dogs by society, culture, and law. For example, in some American jurisdictions, homeless or feral dogs may be protected from hunting or trapping under anticruelty statutes applying to dogs; in other jurisdictions, feral and stray dogs may be viewed as wild animals resulting in vulnerability to humans. However, "[f]eral dogs fit somewhere between wild and domestic animals. Classified by sub-species (Canis lupus familiaris), feral dogs are domestic animals. Classified by behavior (having ferae naturae), feral dogs [may] act like wild animals" (Nowicki, 2014, p. 13). Some American jurisdictions may treat wild, feral, and stray domesticated dogs as wild animals or as nuisances because, unlike domesticated animal companions, they are neither owned nor sheltered, which is discussed further in Chapter Six. Some feral dogs are socialized and may work as guard dogs; thus, they may be distinguishable from wild dogs due to their participation in human society and socialization (McConnell, 2009). The problem of distinguishing classes of dogs based on factors, such as status, habitat, roles, and DNA, has become more salient as dingoes increasingly continue to breed with domesticated dogs, share habitats with humans, and populations of pure dingoes dwindle worldwide (Corbett, 2008). Thus, legal definitions of "dog" and "puppy" may need to be reconsidered by policymakers and societies.

Asia

Treatment of puppies in Asia varies in context depending on country, culture, custom, generation, topography, and other factors. For example, some buyers and vendors in Thailand, Vietnam, South Korea, and other countries participate in the dogmeat industry, discussed in Chapter Ten. Throughout Japan, cafes atypically serve dogmeat. Some evidence demonstrates that a few Japanese restaurants may offer dogmeat to cater to Korean immigrants and tourists in Korea Town (Boundless, 2011; Say No to Dog Meat, 2013). Yet, some reports suggest that pet dogs are a part of 15% of Korean households and may be treated like family members (Chay, 2010). Like Japanese dog cafes, some Korean dog cafes shelter dogs and provide human–dog companionship. For example, since opening in 2001, Bau House Dog Café has offered a variety of dogs and puppies (Choi, 2015; Dining Addiction, 2013).

This miscellany of attitudes and processes shaping dogs' lives is generally reflective of Asian and American societies insofar as no singular philosophy unifies all values or policies. In the Unites States, volunteers may play with puppies at local animal shelters or visit dog-friendly outdoor cafes with their puppies, however, dog cafes have not been established. Cat cafes have slowly gained momentum in the United States because cafes may function as adoption and boarding centers; somewhat similarly, an American dog adoption company rented and delivered puppies in ten cities to corporate customers

14.1 Bau House Dog Café

during lunchbreaks for 30 minutes of companionship (Glenza, 2015; Rainey, 2015). Dog Café planned to open in conjunction with a coffee company and charity (Rainey, 2015). Reversing the roles that dogs and humans normally assume at food cafes, Dog Café may serve food outside the restaurant to humans while dogs and humans occupy indoor seating.

Latin America

Pope Francis discussed sexual abuse and trafficking in Latin America by condemning gendered violence in his hometown, Buenos Aires, Argentina. "In this city, women and young girls are abducted and . . . subjected to the use and abuse of their bodies. In this city, there are men, who make profits with their brothers' flesh. The flesh of all those slaves . . . [is] worth less than the flesh of a pet . . . A dog receives better care than our slaves, who are kicked, who are torn apart (Pope Francis, 2013). Pope Francis' comment possibly insinuates cultural differences between America, Asia, and Latin America because in Buenos Aires, one pet's flesh is worth more than all of the slaves' flesh. His strong message is meant to help human victims, yet he overlooked the problem with maltreated and abandoned dogs in Buenos Aires, who may not be used for their flesh, but may receive inadequate care (McComb, 2010; Plowden, 2015). However, his comment also hinted at Argentina's progressive animal welfare movement; for example, they have allegedly granted basic rights to a nonhuman primate (Chappell, 2014). Argentinians may use grassroots campaigns to advocate for compassionate treatment of homeless dogs.

> The abandonment of pets is increasing in Buenos Aires, professionals and activists say. They blame nationwide economic problems . . . and insensitivity to animals. Over the past five years, more than 40 citizens groups have formed to attend to homeless dogs . . . , according to official figures. The activism has spurred the Buenos Aires city government to create its own program. The city aims to extend the free spaying, neutering and primary care services it provides. (Laens, 2015)

Though the plan has been implemented, lack of economic resources has allegedly slowed follow-up with allegations of maltreatment perpetrated against homeless dogs (Wander Argentina, n.d.). Altruistic and self-serving motives may inspire welfarists and community members to improve for homeless dogs. In at least one case, a pack of stray dogs deterred an attacker, who abducted and attempted to rape a girl (Moon, 2013). Thus, even if some citizens of Buenos Aires do not adopt homeless dogs, they may share protective relationships with homeless guard dogs.

Conclusion

Society's needs, values, and attitudes demonstrate that puppies (i.e. dogs) are the subjects of elevation and degradation; reverence and profanity; attention and neglect. Some human–dog relationships cultivate, inform, discipline, and protect humans; and have caused domesticated wolves and dogs to create work for themselves and maintain unique roles. However, human–dog relationships beneficially and harmfully distinguish dogs from humans and other animals. *Laws, Policies, Attitudes, and Processes That Shape the Lives of Puppies in America: Assessing Society's Needs, Desires, Values, and Morals* contemplates effects on American society of connate and inherited relationships as they have evolved and entangled for hundreds of years. This book presented several chapters and sections that introduced and delved into the processes by which American customs, culture, and government have pioneered new routes for improving dogs' lives and meeting society's need to acknowledge dogs. These include technological, familial, and legal strategies to transform tradition, improve care, and provide remedies. Yet, Americentrism, corporatism, and self-centeredness may correlate with destructive policies and attitudes, for example militarism, which intentionally or negligently threaten dogs' safety and ignore homologies between dogs and humans.

Dog–human relationships are part of many families' lives in America. Dogs may seem to express genuine desires to be part of human families and contribute to their homes, and their wholesome appeal and influence on American families may sometimes motivate societal and legal institutionalization of morality or ethics. For the most part, American norms demand decency and enforce sexual exploitation taboos; however, society distinguishes commercial breeding from cruelty, therefore, dogs may participate in or be subjected to reproductive coercion. Criticism and activism have contributed to some law and policy changes, but many Americans continue to ignore or demand mass commercial breeding. Deterrence of puppy mills and puppy smuggling may be low because of deficient law enforcement and customers' willingness to pay high prices. Yet, costs may increase after some customers discover that their new puppies are sick or had been maltreated. Not all Americans buy dogs from breeders or pet stores; many Americans adopt and rescue dogs. They may feel that it is a matter of personal and social conscience to help dogs; and a few may feel obligated to wet nurse orphan dogs (Cusack, 2013). Interspecies wet nursing is not necessarily taboo, but public breastfeeding diverges from norms in America; thus, public interspecies wet nursing may excessively flout norms thereby incurring public wrath. This social value relates to mores about sexual continence more than expectations for dogs in public. Other than foundational prohibitions against injurious biting, American society imposes weak parameters on dogs' public behavior, even when dogs are treated as children by their "parents." Dogs may urinate, sound-off, sit, and roll on public streets and sidewalks without much public intervention, and perhaps, to onlookers' delight. Dogs are often present inside cars or in bicycle baskets, where they may be admired by gazers. However, transportation threatens dogs' safety and wellness because dogs may collide with vehicles or be injured by vehicle operators, such as conductors and sailors.

Americans may intentionally or accidentally kill dogs using various means, such as transportation, guns, drugs, knives, or concrete. Some jurisdictions permit dogs to be treated as nuisances, culled, and skinned; and in the majority of states, dogs legally and indiscriminately may be killed by humane methods. Often, agents of authority and children, who kill dogs, may be immunized by law. Police, for example, may be immunized by their employers and society for killing nipping puppies; and children may be excused as misbehavers or innocents. In a sense, treatment of children as ingénues represents how Americans treat dogs because the legal system is structured such that children typically are not held criminally responsible for cruelty.

Dogs cannot be held legally responsible for breaking the law or causing damages; and yet, they can be destroyed as a penalty for viciousness. However, because dogs are property, their owners are entitled to due process. This legal premise does not apply to wild animals, whose risk of spontaneously being killed increases when they share territories with humans or when domesticated puppies become overly interactive. Wild animals cannot be held civilly liable for damages; however, like dogs' owners, and exotic animals' owners may be civilly liable for damages. Dogs effectively may be entitled to payment, such as when their owners sue to recover damages or when they are beneficiaries of trusts providing for their care.

Dog grooming and training are practices connecting ancient and modern people to Americans from all walks of life. For example, women in American penitentiaries may become certified dog groomers, and dual-income childless couples may invest a significant amount of money in functional pampering for their dogs. Similarly, dog training connects diverse groups, such as veterans, delinquents, convicts, app developers, lawyers, disabled Americans, and children with neuroses and allergies. Dogs may be trained by incarcerated volunteers to search for escapees or wanted persons, some of whom have viciously or nonviolently involved dogs in drug smuggling, drug dealing, and gambling.

Dogs' work has undergirded and furthered human societies for hundreds of generations. They have worked in agriculture, as guards, as couriers, as spiritual touchstones, and in other roles; however, past and present societies have viewed dogs as enemies, food, and jokes, perhaps by individuals, who, unlike Americans, lack culturally-rooted appreciation for dogs. American love for dogs and their work is not uniform. Inconsistencies and particularities in American culture reflect global tendencies idiosyncratically to develop human–dog relationships and transform them into unique sets of customs, practices, roles, and rules. This trend is pronounced in religious rituals, politics, and art. It is also evidenced in the specialness conjured by the word "puppy," even though "pup" describes more than one dozen other species' babies, who may share some similarities with dogs.

Americans' adoption of puppy dogs into every realm of society is more than physical or legal; it's an adaptation to dogs. The United States would be unrecognizable without dogs and the influence dogs have had over the centuries. Americans identify themselves and their potential as individuals and as members of a young nation when they look into a puppy's eyes and believe that one day, with their help, that puppy will become a stalwart and wise ol' dog.

15.1 An American dog

Bibliography

02 N.C. Admin. Code 52J .0501 (2015).
4 Okl. Stat. Ann. §501 (2015).
11 Del. Code § 1325A (2015).
18 U.S.C. § 43 (2006).
19 U.S.C. § 1308 (2015).
21 U.S.C. § 801 (2006).
26 U.S.C. § 61 (2015).
42 U.S.C. § 1983 (2015).
49 U.S.C. § 41721 (2012).
510 Ill. Comp. Stat. Ann. 70/16.3 (2014).

(1990, August 17). Prison dogs get practice in inmate 'escapee' hunts. *Gainesville Sun*, Section 2B.

(2010, August 18). Airline: Heat could have caused puppies' deaths. *Chicago Tribune*, 9.

ABC 7. (2012, September 5). Police say drunk woman stuffed puppy down her pants. Retrieved from http://www.thedenverchannel.com/news/police-say-drunk-woman-stuffed-puppy-down-her-pants

ABC News. (n.d.). Hundreds of puppies smuggled across U.S.-Mexico border. Retrieved from http://abcnews.go.com/US/story?id=1425200

Abelson, M. (2009). Alvin Rosenthal, Leona Helmsley's dog-entrusted brother, buys $2 million apartment. *The Huffington Post*. Retrieved from http://www.huffingtonpost.com/2009/01/28/alvin-rosenthal-leona-hel_n_161575.html

Afoakwa, E. O. (2008). Cocoa and chocolate consumption – Are there aphrodisiac and other benefits for human health? *South African Journal of Clinical Nutrition, 21*(3), 107–113.

Agudelo, C. F., Filipejova, Z., & Schanilec, P. (2013). Chocolate ingestion-induced non-cardiogenic pulmonary oedema in a puppy: A case report. *Veterinarni Medicina, 58*(2), 109–112.

Ala. Code 1975 § 13A-11-241 (2015).

Alanez, T. (2005, February 15). Pair charged with abuse of puppies. *Los Angeles Times*. Retrieved from http://articles.latimes.com/2005/feb/15/local/me-pomeranian15

Allen-Bell, A. A. (2014). Activism unshackled & justice unchained: A call to make a human right out of one of the most calamitous human wrongs to have taken place on American soil. *Journal of Law & Social Deviance, 7*, 125–202.

American College of Allergy, Asthma & Immunology (ACAAI). (2012). High family income, hygiene habits can increase risk of allergies. Childhood Peanut Allergy. Retrieved from http://acaai.org/news/socioeconomic-status-linked-childhood-peanut-allergy

American Psychiatric Association. (2013). *Diagnostic and Statistical Manual of Mental Disorders* (5th ed.). Arlington, VA: American Psychiatric Publishing.

American Society for the Prevention of Cruelty to Animals (ASPCA). (2010, June 15). Dog-fighting DNA database breaks new ground in crackdown on animal cruelty. Retrieved from https://www.aspca.org/about-us/press-releases/dog-fighting-dna-database-breaks-new-ground-crackdown-animal-cruelty

———. (n.d.). Newborn puppy care. Retrieved from https://www.aspca.org/pet-care/dog-care/newborn-puppy-care

———. (n.d.). Pet statistics. Retrieved from https://www.aspca.org/about-us/faq/pet-statistics

Americans with Disabilities Act (ADA), 104 § 327 (1990).

Animal Crush Video Prohibition Act of 2010 (2010).

Animalist News. (2014, January 13). The zoo where people pet wild animals. Retrieved from https://www.youtube.com/watch?v=zTKkX0QEbmo

Animal People News. (2006). Dogs as drug mules. Retrieved from http://www.animalpeoplenews.org/06/06/dogsasDrugMules6.06.htm

Animal Planet. (2015). Puppy scares man to tears. Retrieved from http://www.animalplanet.com/tv-shows/my-extreme-animal-phobia/videos/puppy-scares-man-to-tears/

Animal Welfare Act, 9 C.F.R. § 3.6(c)(1–2) (2009).

Animal Wire. (2013, July 26). Alligator takes bulldog. Retrieved from https://www.youtube.com/watch?v=Cyiutq5ZKCI

Ansley, L. (2015, June 5). 5 times graffiti artist Banksy used dogs to get his message across. Three Million Dogs. Retrieved from http://wew.threemilliondogs.com/inspirational/5-times-graffiti-artist-banksy-used-dogs-to-get-his-message-across/6

Anxiety and Depression Association of America (ADAA). (2014). Facts & Statistics. Retrieved from http://www.adaa.org/about-adaa/press-room/facts-statistics

AOL. (2015, June 26). Top 5 tech gadgets for your pets. Retrieved from http://www.aol.com/article/2015/06/26/top-5-tech-gadgets-for-your-pets/21201951/

Armao, J. (2013, July 27). Truffle dog. *The Age.* Retrieved from https://www.youtube.com/watch?v=d2Z4LBtdc-4

Arteaga, L. (2013). The pattern of nipple use before weaning among littermates of the domestic dog. *Ethology,119*(1), 12–19.

Attwood, D. (2002). Fidel.

Associated Press (AP). (2015, June 24). Veterinarian arrested for smuggling heroin in puppies. *New York Post.* Retrieved from http://nypost.com/2015/06/24/veterinarian-arrested-for-smuggling-heroin-in-puppies/

Avis, S. P. (1999). Dog pack attack: Hunting humans. *American Journal of Forensic Medicine & Pathology, 20*(3), 243–246.

Bacchus, D., Garske, M., & Wood, M. (2014, January 4). Former Del Mar mayor killed by train while running after dog. NBC San Diego. Retrieved from http://www.nbcsandiego.com/news/local/Amtrak-Train-Hits-Pedestrian-Del-Mar-238657931.html

Badrul, A., et al. (2013). Contribution of illegal hunting, culling of pest species, road accidents and feral dogs to biodiversity loss in established oil-palm landscapes. *Wildlife Research, 40*(1), 1–9.

Baker, A. & Rashbaum, W. K. (2006, February 2). Heroin implants turned puppies into drug mules, U.S. says. *The New York Times.* Retrieved from http://www.nytimes.com/2006/02/02/nyregion/02puppy.html?_r=0

Baltimore County Government. (2014, April 2). Two charged in burglary of Thor the deaf puppy. Retrieved from http://www.baltimorecountymd.gov/news/policenews/iwatch/TwoChargedinBurglaryofThortheDeafPuppy

Banfield Hospital. (2015). Ask a vet. Retrieved from http://www.banfield.com/pet-health-resources/ask-a-vet/we-have-6-rottweiler-puppies

Barcroft Media. (2012, March 16). Dogs stolen by Thai criminal gangs and smuggled into Vietnam to be eaten. *The Huffington Post.* Retrieved from http://www.huffingtonpost.co.uk/2012/03/16/dogs-stolen-by-thai-criminal-gangs-and-smuggled-into-vietnam-to-be-eaten_n_1352773.html

Barcroft TV. (2010, October 19). Tiger and dog are best friends! Retrieved from https://www.youtube.com/watch?v=smYZ7nJp5wg

——. (2013, September). Living with tigers: Family share home with pet tigers. Retrieved from https://www.youtube.com/watch?v=xwidefc2wpc

Barker, S. B., et al. (2010). Exploratory study of stress-buffering response patterns from interaction with a therapy dog. *Anthrozoos, 23*(1), 79–91.

Basso, S. (n.d.). Why do some dogs become neurotic?. Retrieved from http://samthedogtrainer.com/articles/behavior-modification/why-do-some-dogs-become-neurotic/

Baxendale, S., et al. (2015). Risk factors in adolescents' involvement in violent behaviours. *Journal of Aggression, Conflict and Peace Research, 7*(1), 2.

Baxter v. Montana, 224 P.3d 1211 (2009).

Beach, F. A., Buehler, M. G., & Dunbar, I. F. (1983). Development of attraction to estrous females in male dogs. *Physiology & Behavior, 31*(3), 293–297.

Beckmann, C. & Shine, R. (2015). Do the numbers and locations of road-killed anuran carcasses accurately reflect impacts of vehicular traffic? *Journal of Wildlife Management, 79* (1), 92–101.

Bedard, P. (2015, February 2). PETA puts NBC Today show on notice over puppy mascot. *Washington Examiner.* Retrieved from http://www.washingtonexaminer.com/peta-puts-nbc-today-show-on-notice-over-puppy-mascot/article/2559654

Bellandi, D. (1990, September 8). USDA investigating deaths of 25 puppies left unattended on jet. *Los Angeles Times.* Retrieved from http://articles.latimes.com/1990-09-08/local/me-808_1_dead-puppies

Bennett, I. (2013). *Delinquent and Neurotic Children: A Comparative Study.* Oxon, UK: Routledge.

Berns, G. (2013, October 5). Dogs are people, too. *The New York Times.* Retrieved from http://www.nytimes.com/2013/10/06/opinion/sunday/dogs-are-people-too.html?_r=0

Bianchi, J. C. & Holland, R. W. (2014, September 15). *U.S. Patent No.*: US2015000612-A1. Washington, DC: U.S. Patent and Trademark Office.

Birbaumer, N., et al. (2005). Deficient fear conditioning in psychopathy: A functional magnetic resonance imaging study. *Archives of General Psychiatry, 62*(7), 799–805.

Bloomfield, M. (1905). *Cerberus, the Dog of Hades: The History of an Idea.* Chicago, IL: The Open Court Publishing Company.

Boortz, N. (2010, November 13). When service pets become a disservice: Your Saturday rude awakening. *The Atlanta Journal – Constitution.*

Boundless, R. (2011, June 20). Japan answers 7: Do Japanese people eat dogs and cats? Retrieved from https://www.youtube.com/watch?v=b1Zbv3T7JJU

Bowers, S. V. (2013). A perspective for Indiana: The use of "therapy dogs" in Indiana courtrooms: Why a dog might not be a defendant's best friend. *Indiana Law Review, 46,* 1289–1315.

Boya, U. O., Dotson, M. J., & Hyatt, E. M. (2012, May). Dimensions of the dog–human relationship: A segmentation approach. *Journal of Targeting, Measurement and Analysis for Marketing, 20,* 133–143.

Brant, J. & Bonaldi, T. (2011). Pet ownership at its highest level in two decades and pet owners are willing to pay when it comes to pet's health. American Pets Products Association. Retrieved from http://media.americanpetproducts.org/press.php?include=142818

Bratskeir, K. (2015, November 20). Soon Delta won't let you check a pet as baggage. *The Huffington Post.* Retrieved from http://www.huffingtonpost.com/entry/delta-airlines-pet-baggage-check_564f1cb2e4b0258edb30f2c5?ncid=txtlnkusaolp00000592

Braunstein, M. M. (n.d.). U.S. roads kill a million a day. *Culture Change, 8.*

British Broadcasting Corporation (BBC). (2015, October 3). Dogs 'victims of Greek debt crisis'. Retrieved from http://www.msn.com/en-us/news/world/dogs-victims-of-greek-debt-crisis/vi-AAf3p6I?ocid=mailsignout

Brito, R. (2013, September 27). Brazil man fights to keep trained tigers in his home. *Seattle Times.* Retrieved from http://www.seattletimes.com/nation-world/brazil-man-fights-to-keep-trained-tigers-in-his-home/

Brown, G. (2002). *Texas Gulag: The Chain Gang Years, 1875–1925.* New York, NY: Rowman & Littlefield Publishers.

Bryner, J. (2010, June 13). Good or bad, baby names have long-lasting effects. Live Science. Retrieved from http://www.livescience.com/6569-good-bad-baby-names-long-lasting-effects.html

Bueckner v. Hamel, 886 S.W.2d 368 (Tex. App. 1994).

Burnside, V. S. (2013, August 7). County jail escapee captured. *The Randolph Leader.* Retrieved from http://www.therandolphleader.com/news/article_53590ef4-ff5d-11e2-bff0-0019bb2963f4.html

Burwell v. Hobby Lobby, 573 U.S. ___ (2014).

Byszewski, E. T. (2003). Valuing companion animals in wrongful death cases: A survey of current court and legislative action and a suggestion for valuing pecuniary loss of companionship. *Animal Law, 9*, 215–241.

Cal. Code § 598a (2015).

—— § 597u-v (2014).

—— § 599d(a) (2014).

—— § 31102 (2015).

Carlin, G. (1996). Back in Town.

Casey, J. M. (1994). From agoraphobia to xenophobia: Phobias and other anxiety disorders under the Americans with Disabilities Act. *University of Puget Sound Law Review, 17*, 381–416.

Castillo, M. (2013, June 6). Hero dog Kabang cleared to go home with reconstructed nose. CBS News. Retrieved from http://www.cbsnews.com/news/hero-dog-kabang-cleared-to-go-home-with-reconstructed-nose/

Cebrián, R. B. (2010). Some Greek evidence for Indo-European youth contingents of shape shifters. *Journal of Indo-European Studies, 38*(3), 343–357.

Center for Disease Control (CDC). (n.d.). ICD code V10: Pedal cyclist injured in collision with pedestrian or animal. Underlying Cause of Death, 1999–2013 Request. Retrieved from http://wonder.cdc.gov/ucd-icd10.html

——. (n.d.). ICD code W53-W59 and X20-X29: Exposure to animate mechanical forces and Contact with venomous animals and plants. Underlying Cause of Death, 1999–2013 Request. Retrieved from http://wonder.cdc.gov/ucd-icd10.html

Chapman, C. (2009). Not your coffee table: An evaluation of companion animals as personal property. *Capital University Law Review, 38*, 187–227.

Chappell, B. (2014, December 23). Orangutan declared to have basic legal rights in Argentina. National Public Radio (NPR). Retrieved from http://www.npr.org/sections/thetwo-way/2014/12/23/372641268/orang-utan-declared-to-have-legal-rights-in-argentina

Chay, Y. (2010, January 4). Korea's pet care industry. GlobalTrade.net. Retrieved from http://www.globaltrade.net/f/market-research/text/South-Korea/Hygiene-Cosmetics-Health-Medical-Equipment-Korea-s-Pet-Care-Industry.html

Chitale, R. (2009, January 16). These dogs can hunt: Sniffing out peanuts. ABC News. Retrieved from http://abcnews.go.com/Health/AllergiesNews/story?id=6662959

Choi, S. (2015, October 2). Best dog cafe in Korea! Bau House Dog Café. Retrieved from https://www.youtube.com/watch?v=Sfyc_0GMqMc

Chowdhury, A. N., et al. (2003). Puppy pregnancy in humans: A culture-bound disorder in rural west Bengal, India. *The International Journal of Social Psychiatry, 49*(1), 35.

Christensen, J. (2013, January 4). Obamacare: A few changes coming in 2013. CNN. Retrieved from http://www.cnn.com/2013/01/04/health/obamacare-2013

Cibot, M., et al. (2015). Chimpanzees facing a dangerous situation: A high-traffic asphalted road in the Sebitoli area of Kibale National Park, Uganda. *American Journal of Primatology, 77*(8), 890–900.

Convention on International Trade in Endangered Species of Wild Fauna and Flora (CITES) (1963).

Clarke, R. (2007, April 25). Put Bush's 'puppy dog' terror theory to sleep. *New York Daily News.* Retrieved from http://www.nydailynews.com/opinion/put-bush-puppy-dog-terror-theory-sleep-article-1.209414

Claypool, L., LaLonde, L., & Alexander, T. (1990). Too many puppies. On *Frizzle Fry.* New York, NY: Caroline.

Compagno, L. J. V. (2001). Food & Agriculture Organization: *Sharks of the World, 1*(2).

Corbett, L. K. (2008). *Canis lupus ssp. dingo.* International Union for Conservation of Nature and Natural Resources (IUCN) Red List of Threatened Species 2008.

Coren, S. (2011, November 28). The art and science of naming a dog. *Psychology Today.* Retrieved from https://www.psychologytoday.com/blog/canine-corner/201111/the-art-and-science-naming-dog

——. (2012, July 2). Does your dog's name affect how people think of him? *Psychology Today.* Retrieved from https://www.psychologytoday.com/blog/canine-corner/201207/does-your-dogs-name-affect-how-people-think-him

Correctional Service Canada (CSC). (2013, December 6). Pet facilitated therapy in correctional institutions. Appendix I: An overview of pft programs in correctional institutions. Retrieved from http://www.csc-scc.gc.ca/publications/fsw/pet/pet-38-eng.shtml

Corso v. Crawford Dog & Cat Hospital, Inc., 415 N.Y.S. 2d 182 (1979).

Cowperthwaite, G. (2013). BlackFish.

CNN. (2012, January 17). Who consumes the most chocolate? Retrieved from http://thecnnfreedomproject.blogs.cnn.com/2012/01/17/who-consumes-the-most-chocolate/

Crothers, L. (2013). *Globalization and American Popular Culture.* New York, NY: Rowman & Littlefield Publishers.

Cunningham, B. & Seirup, D. (2014). Dogs on the Inside.

Cusack, C. M. (2011). Consensual insemination, an analysis of social deviance within gender, family, or the home (etudes 6), *Journal of Law & Social Deviance (2)*, 158–190.

——. (2012). Boob laws: An analysis of social deviance with in gender, family,

or the home (etudes 2).*Women's Rights Law Reporter, 33*, 197.
——. (2012). Two films, one law. *New York State Bar Association: Entertainment and Sports Law Journal, 23*, 3.
——. (2013). A feminist inquiry into intimate partner violence law, policy, policing, and possible prejudices in Alaska. *Journal of Law & Conflict Resolution, 5*, 24–32.
——. (2013). Comparative sexology: Nonconsensual insemination in the United States and the European Union. *Sexologies 23*, e19.
——. (2013). Feminism and husbandry: Drawing the fine line between mine and bovine. *Journal of Critical Animal Studies*, 11(1), 24.
——. (2013). *Medical and illicit drugs and the Caribbean.* Unpublished field research, Department of Criminal Justice and Human Services, Nova Southeastern University.
——. (2013). Nonconsensual insemination: A pilot study. *Online Journal of Social Science Research, 2*, 61–72.
——. (2013). *Worldly and wise: U.S. medical students in Cuba.* Unpublished research, Department of Criminal Justice and Human Services, Nova Southeastern University.
——. (2014). 50 state survey of prosecutors' willingness to prosecute nonconsensual insemination. *Family & Intimate Partner Violence Quarterly, 6*, 7–32.
——. (2014). In opposition of cultural institutionalization of speech following U.S. intervention into foreign governments. *Barry Law Review, 19*, 297–311.
——. (2015). *Animals and Criminal Justice.* Piscataway, NJ: Transaction Publishers.
——. (2015). *Animals, Deviance, and Sex.* Cambridge, UK: Cambridge Scholars Publishing.
——. (2015). *Criminal Justice Handbook on Masculinity, Male Aggression, and Sexuality.* Springfield, IL: Charles C Thomas.
——. (2015). *Hair and Justice: Sociolegal Significance of Hair in Criminal Justice, Constitutional Law, and Public Policy.* Springfield, IL: Charles C Thomas.
——. (2015). *Laws Relating to Sex, Pregnancy, and Infancy: Issues in Criminal Justice.* New York, NY: Palgrave Macmillan.
——. (2015). *Road kill species prevalence throughout southeastern, southwestern, and western states.* Unpublished field study. Department of Criminal Justice and Human Services, Nova Southeastern University.
——. (2015). *Fatalities from venomous and nonvenomous animals and insects.* Unpublished research, Department of Criminal Justice and Human Services, Nova Southeastern University.
Dalzell, T. (2008). *The Routledge Dictionary of Modern American Slang and Unconventional English.* New York, NY: Taylor & Francis.
Davis, T. (1995). Billy Madison.
Dayton, M. (2005, September 19). S.C COA rules no distress damages over dog's injuries. *South Carolina Lawyers Weekly.*

Death with Dignity Act, ORS 127.800-995 (1994).

——. RCW 70.245 (2008).

de Cervantes, M. (2003). *The Dialogue of the Dogs.* London, UK: Hesperus Press.

Declercq, E. R., et al. (2014). Major survey findings of listening to mothers III: Pregnancy and birth. *The Journal of Perinatal Education, 23*(1), 9–16.

Defabritiis, S. (2012). Barking up the wrong tree: Companion animals, emotional damages and the judiciary's failure to keep pace. *Northern Illinois University Law Review, 32,* 237–266.

Delta Cargo. (n.d.). Pet shipping. Retrieved from https://www.deltacargo.com/PetShipment.aspx

De Young, J. (2005). Toward a more equitable approach to causation in veterinary malpractice actions. *Hastings Women's Law Journal, 16,* 201–220.

Diamond, W. (2009, May 7). America's foreclosed pets. *Forbes.* Retrieved from http://www.forbes.com/2009/05/07/recession-dog-cat-horse-opinions-contributors-foreclosure-pets.html

Dillard, C. (2012). Empathy with animals: A litmus test for legal personhood? *Animal Law, 19,* 1–21.

Dining Addiction. (2013, June 12). Bau House Dog Café. Retrieved from http://www.diningaddiction.com/bau-house-dog-cafe/

Discovery TV. (2010, May 14). Dogs vs grizzly bears - weird, true & freaky. Retrieved from https://www.youtube.com/watch?v=Mkx1T4ckl0U

D'Oench, P. (2015, January 1). Woman accused of beating child, killing one-month-old puppy. CBS Miami. Retrieved from http://miami.cbslocal.com/2015/01/01/woman-accused-of-beating-child-killing-one-month-old-puppy/

Doerr v. Goldsmith, 2013 NY Slip Op 06442; 2015 NY Slip Op 04752 (NY Ct. App. June 9, 2015).

Doggone Express. (n.d.). Retrieved from http://doggoneexpress.com/

Dog killer loses job Ulster region. (2015, June 17). *The Sun,* 21.

Dog's Best Friend. (1958). *Marine Corps Gazette (Pre-1994), 42*(3), 51.

Dogs with Jobs. (2000). Cineflix Productions.

Dog Trainers Workshop. (n.d.). Puppy obedience: Let the fun begin! Retrieved from http://www.dogtrainersworkshop.com/connies-corner/puppy-obedience-let-the-fun-begin/

Dooley, R., et al. (2010, April 27). Baby pics boost altruism. Neuromarketing. Retrieved from http://www.neurosciencemarketing.com/blog/articles/baby-pics-boost-altruism.htm

Dotson, M. J. & Hyatt, E. M. (2008). Understanding dog–human companionship. *Journal of Business Research, 61*(5), 457–466.

Doucette, T. (2012, December 26). Puppy teaching puppy to go down stairs! Retrieved from https://www.youtube.com/watch?v=fDKDC_IUnOA

Dowd, R. (2014, June 26). Time to eliminate congress's yearly "dog fur" report? *The Fiscal Times.* Retrieved from http://www.thefiscaltimes.com/Articles/2014/06/26/Time-Eliminate-Congress-s-Yearly-Dog-Fur-Report

Drislane, L. E., Vaidyanathan, U., & Patrick, C. J. (2013). Reduced cortical call to arms differentiates psychopathy from antisocial personality disorder. *Psychological Medicine, 43*(4), 825–35.

Driving Dogs. (2012, December 9). Meet Porter. The world's first driving dog. Retrieved from https://www.youtube.com/watch?v=BWAK0J8Uhzk

Druery v. Texas, 225 S.W.3d 49 (2007).

Duckler, G. (2007). Animal wrongs: On holding animals to (and excusing them from) legal responsibility for their intentional acts. *Journal of Animal Law & Ethics, 2*, 91–121.

Dudley, W. G. (2013). Elizabeth's sea dogs. *Military History, 30*, 56-63.

Dyess v. Caraway, 190 So. 2d 666 (1966).

Dylan, J. (2003). American Wedding: American Pie III.

Edgemon, E. (2014, February 12). Animal activists smuggle dozens of stray dogs out of Sochi, Russia during Olympic Games. Al.com. Retrieved from http://blog.al.com/wire/2014/02/animal_activists_smuggle_dozen.html

Elliot, A. J. & Niesta, D. (2008). Romantic red: Red enhances men's attraction to women. *Journal of Personality and Social Psychology, 95*(5), 1150–1164.

Enchanted Learning. (n.d.). Names of males, females, babies, and groups of animals. Retrieved from http://www.enchantedlearning.com/subjects/animals/Animalbabies.shtml

End of Life Act, SB-128 (Cal. 2015).

Epstein, L. A. (2001). Resolving confusion in pet owner tort cases: Recognizing pets' anthropomorphic qualities under a property classification. *Southern Illinois University Law Journal, 26*, 31–51.

European Commission. (2015). Ban on Animal Testing. Retrieved from http://ec.europa.eu/growth/sectors/cosmetics/animal-testing/index_en.htm

Evans, R., Gauthier, D. K., & Forsyth, C. J. (1998). Dogfighting: Symbolic expression and validation of masculinity. *Sex Roles, 39*(11), 825–838.

Ewinger, J. (2012, August 20). Dogs were not tied to track and killed by train in Tremont area. Clevland.com. Retrieved from http://www.cleveland.com/metro/index.ssf/2012/08/dogs_were_not_tied_to_track_an.html

Fackler v. Genetzky, 595 N.W.2d 884, 892 (Neb. 1999).

Febres, J., et al. (2014). Adulthood animal abuse among men arrested for domestic violence. *Violence Against Women, 20*(9), 1059.

Federal Trade Commission (FTC). (2012, October 11). Public Comments for 16 CFR 301 Rules and Regulations under Fur Products Labeling Act. Retrieved from https://www.ftc.gov/sites/default/files/documents/public_comments/16-cfr-part-301-regulations-under-fur-products-labeling-act-ftc-matter-no.p074201-00034/00034-85303.pdf

Fiegl, A. (2012, December 11). Meet Migaloo, world's first "archaeology dog." *National Geographic*. Retrieved from http://news.nationalgeographic.com/news/2012/12/121210-archaeology-dogs-australia-conservation-canines/

Fla. Stat. § 828.1231 (2015).

Florida Department of Corrections. (n.d.). Timeline. Retrieved from http://www.dc.state.fl.us/oth/timeline/1927a.html

Fontenrose, J. E. (1981). *Orion: The Myth of the Hunter and the Huntress.* Berkeley, CA: University of California Publications.

Forrester, J. A. Holstege, C. P., & Forrester, J. D. (2012). Fatalities from venomous and nonvenomous animals in the United States (1999–2007), *Wilderness and Environmental Medicine, 23*(2), 146–152.

Fowler, B. (2015, September 2). Some top baby monitors lack basic security features. ABC News. Retrieved from http://abcnews.go.com/Technology/wireStory/report-top-baby-monitors-lack-basic-security-features-33480638

Fox, N. D., Sentivan, J. R., & Grieder, J. G. (2004, May 10). Negligent infliction of emotional distress —— pets. *New Jersey Lawyer*: Decisions; Unpublished Opinions; Appellate Division, *13*(19), 28.

Fox News. (2014, February 11). Animal activists smuggling stray dogs out of Sochi. Retrieved from http://www.foxnews.com/world/2014/02/11/animal-activists-smuggling-stray-dogs-out-sochi/

Freud, S. (1998). *Totem and Taboo.* P. Negri & J. Nords (Eds.). Mineola, NY: Dover Publications.

Friedenberg, S. G., et al. (2012). Seizures following head trauma in dogs: 259 cases (1999–2009). *Journal of the American Veterinary Medical Association, 241*(11), 1479–1483.

Friedman, E. (2008, March 5). Was killing the puppy a way of coping for one marine? ABC News. Retrieved from http://abcnews.go.com/Health/MindMoodNews/story?id=4387128

Friskies. (n.d.). Free games for cats from Friskies. Retrieved from https://www.gamesforcats.com/

Ga. Code Ann. § 27-3-63 (a)(9) (2015).

Gagnon, S. & Doré, F. Y. (1994). Cross-sectional study of object permanence in domestic puppies (canis familiaris). *Journal of Comparative Psychology, 108*(3), 220–232.

Galvani, W. (1994, October). Sea dogs. *American Heritage, 96.*

Gangestad, S. W. & Thornhill, R. (2008, May 7). Human oestrus. *Proceedings of the Royal Society B, 275* (1638).

Garcia, N., et al. (2012). Are protected areas truly protected? The impact of road traffic on vertebrate fauna. *Biodiversity and Conservation, 21*(11), 2761–2774.

Gaskill, M. (2013, May 16). Rise in roadkill requires new solutions. *Scientific American.* Retrieved from http://www.scientificamerican.com/article/roadkill-endangers-endangered-wildlife/

Gec, J. (2015, July 4). Brave dog Leo honored with monument in Serbian town. AOL. Retrieved from http://www.aol.com/article/2015/07/04/brave-dog-leo-honored-with-monument-in-serbian-town/21204935/

Gee, A. (2014, January 6). Pushinka: A cold war puppy the Kennedys loved. BBC. Retrieved from http://www.bbc.com/news/magazine-24837199

Gennis, S. (2014, June 7). Orange Is the New Black's Lea Delaria discusses that scene with the peanut butter. TV Guide. http://www.tvguide.com/news/orange-is-the-new-black-big-boo-peanut-butter-dog-lea-delaria-1082633/

Ghianni, T. (2015, January 19). Trayton Joiner, 2-year-old Kentucky boy, killed by train while walking with dog. *The Huffington Post*. Retrieved from http://www.huffingtonpost.com/2015/01/20/two-year-old-kentucky-boy_n_6504026.html

Giles, R. (2013, August 3). Alabama prison dogs aiding in search for jail escapee. WTVM. Retrieved from http://www.wtvm.com/story/23038255/s

Gilliam, D. (2015, July 6). Making bonds. *Florida Times-Union*. Section A-1.

Gips, M. A. (2001). Who let the dogs on? *Security Management, 45*(11), 10.

Glenza, J. (2015, January 28). Uber delivers puppies on-demand delighting Americans in 10 cities. *The Guardian*. Retrieved from http://www.theguardian.com/technology/2015/jan/28/uber-puppies-on-demand-denver-washington-dallas

Glocker M. L., et al. (2009). Baby schema modulates the brain reward system in nulliparous women. *Proceedings of the National Academy of Sciences, 106*(22), 9115–9119.

Gluckman v. American Airlines, Inc., 844 F. Supp. 151 (S.D.N.Y. 1994).

Goldberg, P. (2013). Courts and legislatures have kept the proper leash on pet injury lawsuits: Why rejecting emotion-based damages promotes the rule of law, modern values, and animal welfare. *Stanford Journal of Animal Law and Policy 6*, 30–80.

Goldschmidt, D. (2015, July 1). FDA moves to add warnings, child-proof packaging for liquid nicotine. CNN. Retrieved from http://www.cnn.com/2015/07/01/health/fda-liquid-nicotine/

Golgowski, N. (2013, September 12) Mother of a toddler fatally mauled by African dogs is to blame and shouldn't be allowed to sue: Zoo. *New York Daily News*. Retrieved from http://www.nydailynews.com/news/national/mom-blame-boy-mauled-death-zoo-article-1.1453399

Gonzales v. Oregon, 546 U.S. 243 (2006).

Good Morning America. (2014, February 14).How to adopt a stray dog from Sochi. Retrieved from http://abcnews.go.com/blogs/headlines/2014/02/how-to-adopt-a-stray-dog-from-sochi/

———. (n.d.). San Diego zoo's baby cheetah and puppy are best friends. Retrieved from http://abcnews.go.com/GMA/video/san-diego-zoos-baby-cheetah-puppy-best-friends-24088587

Gould, S. J. (1980). A biological homage to Mickey Mouse, pp. 95–107. *The Panda's Thumb: More Reflections in Natural History*. New York, NY: W.W. Norton.

Grace, K. (2013, August 23). How to teach a service dog to retrieve a beverage. Anything Pawsable. Retrieved from http://www.anything-pawsable.com/teach-a-service-dog-to-retrieve-a-beverage/#.VhfOX_l Viko

Grandell, P. (2010). Jeep: The Chihuahua "war dog." *Leatherneck, 93*(2), 28–29.

Grass, J. (2011, August 30). Woman punches bear to save her dog. *Juneau Empire*. Retrieved from http://juneauempire.com/local/2011-08-30/woman-punches-bear-save-her-dog

Gray, R. (2013, May 8). Dogs to get their iPaws as scientists build computers for animals. *The Telegraph*. Retrieved from http://www.telegraph.co.uk/lifestyle/pets/10044557/Dogs-to-get-their-iPaws-as-scientists-build-computers-for-animals.html

Grenoble, R. (2015, April 22). Georgia police shoot pit bull puppy that bit officer. *The Huffington Post*. Retrieved from http://www.huffingtonpost.com/2015/04/22/georgia-police-shoot-pit-bull-puppy_n_7089932.html

Griffiths, A. O. & Silberberg, A. (1975). Stray animals: Their impact on a community. *Modern Veterinary Practice, 56*(4), 255–6.

Grossman, J. (2007, September 18). Last words from the "queen of mean": Leona Helmsley's will, the challenges that are likely to be posed to it, and the likely fate of the world's second richest dog. FindLaw. Retrieved from http://writ.news.findlaw.com/grossman/20070918.html

Guarino, B. (2015, February 26). Joaquin Phoenix reveals the horrifying truth about dog leather. The Dodo. Retrieved from https://www.thedodo.com/joaquin-phoenix-dog-leather-1013107333.html

Hadge, M. (2014). All of the dog balloons in the Macy's Thanksgiving Day Parade – ever. Bark Post. Retrieved from http://barkpost.com/macys-thanksgiving-day-parade-dog-balloons/

Hammerschlag, N. (2015, July 8). Tiger shark sinks its teeth into scientific study. *National Geographic*. Retrieved from http://voices.nationalgeographic.com/2015/07/08/tiger-shark-sinks-its-teeth-into-scientific-study/

Hampton, J. (2011, May 12). Caring k-9s brighten lives, serve as advocates. *Claremore Daily Progress*.

Hanna, C. (2011, July 26). Nine-year-old boy faces animal cruelty charges for killing puppy. *Examiner*. Retrieved from http://www.examiner.com/article/nine-year-old-boy-faces-animal-cruelty-charges-for-killing-puppy

Harris v. Snelgrove, 290 Ga. 181 (2011).

Harro-Loit, H. & Ugur, K. (2011). Representation of death culture in the Estonian press. *Estonian Journal of Archaeology, 15*(2), 151–170.

Heimbuch, J. (2015, August 3). American dingo: America's only native wild dog. Mother Nature Network. Retrieved from http://www.mnn.com/earth-matters/animals/stories/meet-american-dingo-only-wild-dog-native-continent

Heinze, C. R., et al. (2014). Comparison of the nutrient composition of commercial dog milk replacers with that of dog milk. *Journal of the American Veterinary Medical Association, 244*(12), 1413–1422.

Heinz, F. (2011, June 28). Dead dogs tied to tracks, hit by train. NBC. Retrieved from http://www.nbcdfw.com/news/local/Dogs-Tied-to-Tracks-Killed-by-Train-124656224.html

Helmsley, L. M. (2005, July 15). Last will and testament of Leona M. Helmsley. Retrieved from http://www.nytimes.com/packages/pdf/nyre-gion/city_room/20070829_helmsleywill.pdf

Heine, S. (2009). *Bargaining for Salvation: Bob Dylan, a Zen Master?* New York, NY: Continuum Press.

Henry, B. (2015, June 25). Encinitas council votes to ban sale of 'puppy mill' pets. *The San Diego Union-Tribune.* Retrieved from http://www.sandiegouniontribune.com/news/2015/jun/25/encinitas-bans-puppy-mill-pet-sales/

Herek, S. (1996). 101 Dalmatians.

Hill, G. (2009). *A Hunter's Fireside Book: Tales of Dogs, Ducks, Birds & Guns.* New York, NY: Skyhorse Publishing.

Hodal, K. (2013, September 27). How eating dog became big business in Vietnam. *The Guardian.* Retrieved from http://www.theguardian.com/world/2013/sep/27/eating-dog-vietnam-thailand-kate-hodal

Hoffmann, W. A. & Human, L. H. (2003). Experiences, characteristics and treatment of women suffering from dog phobia. *Anthrozoos, 16*(1), 28–42.

Hope, H. S. (2015, January 12). Military working dogs deploy with Marines on ships. *Marine Corps Times.*

Hospodar, M. (2004). Aphrodisiac foods: Bringing heaven to earth. *Gastronomica, 4*(4), 82–93.

Housing Authority of the City of Norwalk v. Ross, SPNO 9206-A2880, 1993 Conn. Super. LEXIS 2467 (Sup. Ct. CT, July 19, 1993).

Howard v. Arkansas, CACR03-499, 2004 Ark. App. LEXIS 28 (2004).

Illinois Department of Corrections. (2013). Fiscal Year 2013 Annual Report. Retrieved from http://www.illinois.gov/idoc/reportsandstatistics/Documents/FY2013%20Annual%20Report.pdf

——. (2015, July 1). Decatur Correctional Center. Retrieved from https://www.illinois.gov/idoc/facilities/Pages/decaturcorrectionalcenter.aspx

The Huffington Post. (2015, September 5). Chilean police rescue malnour-ished child being breastfed by dog. Retrieved from http://www.huffingtonpost.com/entry/breastfeeding-dog-saves-toddler-child-chile_55eb2c98e4b093be51bbb359?ncid=txtlnkusaolp00000592

Illinois Prison Talk. (2008, November 14). How is Decatur Correctional. Retrieved from http://www.illinoisprisontalk.org/index.php?topic=60.0

Illinois v. Fair, 3-12-0371, 2014 IL App (3d) 120371-U (App. Ct. IL 3rd D. 2014).

Ingraham, C. (2015, June 16). Chart: The animals that are most likely to kill you this summer. *Washington Post.* Retrieved from http://www.washingtonpost.com/news/wonkblog/wp/2015/06/16/chart-the-animals-that-are-most-likely-to-kill-you-this-summer/

Inmates train puppies in Mich. (2014). *Corrections Today, 76*(2), 62.

Inquisitr. (2014, December 21). Pit bull shooting video: Cop Kevin Dupre shoots puppy dog on camera, police say it's 'justified'. Retrieved from http://www.inquisitr.com/1696670/pit-bull-shooting-video-cop-kevin-dupre-shoots-puppy-dog-on-camera-police-say-its-justified/#DHTvq7iQz dhbF7cY.99

———. (2015, March 7). Police halt train to rescue pit bull puppy shot and tied to railroad tracks. Retrieved from http://www.inquisitr.com/1904378/police-halt-train-to-rescue-pit-bull-puppy/#roMsLIA5vrTqC5jG.99

———. (2015, March 11). Ashley Johnston's puppy beheading video just 'kids being stupid'? Sheriff downplays dog killing. Retrieved from http://www.inquisitr.com/1917148/ashley-johnstons-puppy-beheading-video-is-just-two-kids-being-stupid-sheriff-downplays-dog-killing/#ciu5Y 2CIKMb4lkg2.99

In re O.J.v. Lynn T., No. G040271, 2008 Cal. App. Unpub. LEXIS 10359 (Ct. App. Cal. 4th D. Div. 3 2008).

Interfax: Russia & CIS Presidential Bulletin. (2012, July 30). Russia; Putin promises to send Siberian cat to Japanese governor in return for puppy.

———. (2012, September 13). Russia; Putin reciprocates puppy gift of Japanese governor with Siberian kitten.

Jackson, N. D. & Fahrig, L. (2011). Relative effects of road mortality and decreased connectivity on population genetic diversity. *Biological Conservation, 144*(12), 3143–3148.

Jamaican Proverb. (2014, October 8). Craven choke puppy. Retrieved from http://jamaicanpatwah.com/term/Craven-choke-Puppy/2071#. VZhZVPlViko

James, F. (2009, August 11). Dog charities sue for more Leona Helmsley wealth. National Public Radio (NPR). Retrieved from http://www.npr.org/sections/thetwo-way/2009/08/dog_charities_sue_for_greater. html

James, S. D. (2007, October 24). 300,000 imported puppies prompt rabies concerns. ABC News. Retrieved from http://abcnews.go.com/Health/story?id=3765973&page=1

———. (2011, June 10). Leona Helmsley's little rich dog trouble dies in luxury. ABC News. Retrieved from http://abcnews.go.com/US/leona-helmsleys-dog-trouble-richest-world-dies-12/story?id=13810168

Jenness, R. (1979). The composition of human milk. *Seminars in Perinatology, 3*(3), 225–239.

Jessica R. v. Arizona Department of Economic Security (ADES), No. 2 CA-JV 2008-0065, 2008 Ariz. App. Unpub. LEXIS 1577 (Ariz. Ct. App. 2008).

Jia, P. W. M. & Betts, A. V. G. (2010). A re-analysis of the Qiemu'erqieke (Shamirshak) cemeteries, Xinjiang, China. *The Journal of Indo-European Studies, 38*(3/4).

Johns, C. (2008). *Dogs: History, Myth, Art.* Cambridge, MA: Harvard University Press.

Johnson, M. S., Martin, M. W., & Henley, W. (2007). Results of pacemaker implantation in 104 dogs. *Journal of Small Animal Practice, 48*(1), 4–11.

Johnson, S. C., & Solomon, G. E. A. (1997). Why dogs have puppies and cats have kittens: The role of birth in young children's understanding of biological origins. *Child Development, 68*(3), 404–419.

Johnston, J. E. (2011, April 27). Children who are cruel to animals: When to worry. *Psychology Today.* Retrieved from https://www.psychology-today.com/blog/the-human-equation/201104/children-who-are-cruel-animals-when-worry

Jones, A. P., et al. (2009). Amygdala hypoactivity to fearful faces in boys with conduct problems and callous-unemotional traits. *The American Journal of Psychiatry, 166*(1), 95–102.

Jones v. Heidi, No. CV 12-10176-SVW, 2014 U.S. Dist. LEXIS 85943 (C.D. Cal. W. Div., March 31, 2014).

Jung, H. (2009, December 18). Buying a Christmas puppy? Think twice before you do. *People.* Retrieved from http://www.peoplepets.com/people/pets/article/0,,20493581,00.html

Kaatz, K. E. (2014). Those doggone police: Insufficient training, canine companion seizures, and Colorado's solution. *San Diego Law Review, 51,* 823–872.

Kaczor, B. (1995, August 29). Gator turns dogs into chow, but collars signal his doom. *Desert News.* Retrieved from http://www.deseretnews.com/article/436055/GATOR-TURNS-DOGS-INTO-CHOW-BUT-COLLARS-SIGNAL-HIS-DOOM.html?pg=all

Karimi, F. (2013, September 7). Dallas zoo brings in pet puppy to calm down cheetahs. CNN. Retrieved from http://www.cnn.com/2013/09/07/us/dallas-zoo-cheetah-cubs/

Kelch, T. G. (2014). Cultural solipsism, cultural lenses, universal principles, and animal advocacy. *Pace Environmental Law Review, 31,* 403–474.

Kemp, M. (2007, October 4). Russian science: A dog's life. *Nature, 449*(7162), 541.

Kenyon, S., Southwick, R., & Wynne, C. (2000). *Bears in the Backyard, Deer in the Driveway: The Importance of Hunting and Trapping in Helping Wildlife Professionals Manage Our Treasured Wildlife Resources.* Alexandria, VA: Southwick Associates.

Kern, S. (2012, January 31). Muslims declare jihad on dogs in Europe. Gatestone Institute. Retrieved from http://www.gatestoneinstitute.org/2796/muslims-ban-dogs-europe

King v. King, Bankruptcy Case No. 05-56485-C (W.D. Tex. February 21, 2006).

Kirby, A. (2015, June 16). Find Caramel: Stolen dog returned after online campaign goes viral. *The Telegraph.* Retrieved from http://www.telegraph.co.uk/news/uknews/crime/11677891/Find-Caramel-Stolen-dog-returned-after-online-campaign-goes-viral.html

Klee, M. T. (2013, August 18). iPad puppy training, really. Salon.com. Retrieved from http://www.salon.com/2013/08/18/daily_dot_dog_waiting_permission_partner/

Kneebone, G. M., Kneebone, R., & Gibson, R. A. (1985). Fatty acid composition of breast milk from three racial groups from Penang, Malaysia. *The American Journal of Clinical Nutrition, 41*(4), 765–9.

Knight, K. E., Ellis, C., & Simmons, S. B., (2014). Parental predictors of children's animal abuse: Findings from a national and intergenerational sample. *Journal of Interpersonal Violence, 29*(16), 3014.

Korea Rights Animal Advocates (KARA). (2012). Survey on the dog meat industry and possible measures to end the dog meat trade in South Korea. Retrieved from http://koreandogs.org/wp-content/uploads/2012/06/KARA-Dog-Meat-Report_English-1.pdf

Kottasova, I. (2015, July 12). Greece crisis: Sleeping on the streets of Athens. CNN. Retrieved from http://money.cnn.com/2015/07/12/ news/economy/greece-crisis-homeless/

KRDO. (2014, February 6). Woman breastfeeds puppy. Retrieved from http://www.krdo.com/news/breast-fed-puppy/24343536

Kringelbach, M. L., et al. (2008). A specific and rapid neural signature for parental instinct. LoS ONE, 3(2).

Kripke, S. A. (1991). *Naming and Necessity.* Hoboken, New Jersey: Wiley-Blackwell.

Kumar, S., et al. (2015). Inflation targeting does not anchor inflation expectations: Evidence from firms in New Zealand. Brookings Papers on Economic Activity, Fall 2015 Conference. Retrieved from http://www.brookings.edu/about/projects/bpea/papers/2015/kumar-et-al-inflation-targeting#recent/

Laens, I. J. (2015). Ignorance, indifference, inflation contribute to growing population of stray dogs, cats in Buenos Aires. *Global Press Journal.* Retrieved from http://globalpressjournal.com/americas/argentina/ignorance-indifference-inflation-contribute-growing-population-stray-dogs-cats#sthash.zTf8EMUV.dpuf

Lake, R. (2014). Breastmilk.

Lam, S. & Wu, M. (2011). Predicting Taiwanese adoption website members' intentions regarding on-line dog adoptions. *African Journal of Business Management, 5*(4), 1204–1210.

Langley, R. L. (2005). Animal-related fatalities in the United States-an update. *Wilderness & Environmental Medicine, 16*(2), 67–74.

Langley, R. L. & Morrow, W. E. (1997). Deaths resulting from animal attacks in the United States. *Wilderness & Environmental Medicine, 8*(1), 8–16.

Lanting, F. (n.d.). Islam, dogs, and personal rights. Sirius Dog. Retrieved from http://siriusdog.com/islam-dogs-and-personal-rights

Larson, G., et al. (2012). Rethinking dog domestication by integrating genetics, archeology, and biogeography. *Proceedings of the National Academy of Sciences, 109*(23), 8878–8883.

Lawson, H. (2012, November 3). Drunk man, 19, arrested after punching puppy in the face and throwing it against a tree. *Daily Mail.* Retrieved from http://www.dailymail.co.uk/news/article-2227212/Drunk-man-19-arrested-PUNCHING-puppy-face.html

League of Women Voters. (n.d.). Affordable care act myths and facts.

Retrieved from http://leaguelafayette.org/files/aca_mythsfacts120820.pdf

Lee, B. (2015, April 13). Fresno woman, 50, killed by train while trying to get dog. *The Fresno Bee.* Retrieved from http://www.fresnobee.com/news/local/article19651911.html

Leeman, L. (2010).One Lucky Elephant.

Life with Dogs, (2015, August 24). Police officer soothes dog who bit him. Retrieved from http://www.lifewithdogs.tv/2015/08/police-officer-soothes-dog-who-bit-him/

——. (2015, September 10). Dog bites puppy's tail to save him from speeding car. Retrieved from http://www.lifewithdogs.tv/2015/09/dog-bites-puppys-tail-to-save-him-from-speeding-car/

Lillich, C. (2013, April 11). Bloodhound brothers training to sniff out arsonists. Hawaii News Now. Retrieved from http://www.hawaiinewsnow.com/story/21948766/dogs-training-to-sniff-out-arsonists

Lippi, D. (2009). Chocolate and medicine: Dangerous liaisons? *Nutrition Journal, 25*(11–12), 1100–1103.

Liu, J. (2014, August 23). Dog on the tracks sparked a Hong Kong protest. BBC. Retrieved from http://www.bbc.com/news/blogs-china-blog-28892002

Lobell, J. A. & Powell, E. (2010). More than man's best friend. *Archeology, 63*(5). Retrieved from http://archive.archaeology.org/1009/dogs/

Lopez, R. J. (2014, January 8). Police recover puppy intended for cancer-stricken child. *Los Angeles Times.* Retrieved from http://articles.latimes.com/2014/jan/08/local/la-me-ln-police-recover-puppy-cancer-stricken-child-20140108

Los Angeles Times. (2006, September 7). Her assault weapon was a dead puppy. Retrieved from http://articles.latimes.com/2006/sep/07/nation/na-puppy7

Lou, E. (2015, July 5). Two women kicked off plane at Pearson after refusal to muzzle guide dogs. *Guelph Mercury.* Retrieved from http://www.guelphmercury.com/news-story/5709370-two-women-kicked-off-plane-at-pearson-after-refusal-to-muzzle-guide-dogs/

Loving v. Virginia, 388 U.S. 1 (1967).

Lustig v. Mondeau, 211 Fed. Appx. 364 (2006).

Lynch, A. (2015, June 29). This is awkward: Family dog learns to say 'mama' before the baby does. *Metro.* Retrieved from http://metro.co.uk/2015/06/29/this-is-awkward-family-dog-learns-to-say-mama-before-the-baby-does-5270670/

Malakoff, R. (n.d.). Pacemakers for veterinary patients. Massachusetts Society for the Prevention of Cruelty to Animals (MSPCA). Retrieved from http://www.mspca.org/vet-services/angell-boston/cardiology/pacemakers-for-veterinary.html?referrer=https://www.google.com/

Mark, J. J. (2014). Dogs in the Ancient World. *Ancient History Encyclopedia.* Retrieved from http://www.ancient.eu/article/184/

Marley, B. (1992). Craven choke puppy. On *Song of Freedom.* Kingston, Jamaica: Tuff Gong.

Masson, T. (2013, September 3). What won't a Louisiana alligator eat? *The Times-Picayune*. Retrieved from http://www.nola.com/outdoors/ index.ssf/2013/09/what_wont_a_louisiana_alligato.html

Mauritso, M. (2014, October 27). Black Labrador is known as Carlsbad courthouse dog. *Carlsbad Current-Argus*.

May, A. C., et al. (2013). Evidence-based behavioral treatment of dog phobia with young children: Two case examples. *Behavior Modification, 37*(1), 143–160.

Maynard, R. (2013). P.R.O.U.D. program rehabilitates shelter dogs. *Paw Street Journal*. Retrieved from http://www.kyhumane.org/a-second-chance-psj

McComb, D. (2010). Street dogs. Discover Buenos Aires. Retrieved from http://www.discoverbuenosaires.com/buenos-aires-street-dogs

McConnell, P. (2009, August 11). Dogs in Africa. Retrieved from http://www.patriciamcconnell.com/theotherendoftheleash/dogs-in-africa

McEwen, F. S., Moffitt, T. E., & Arseneault, L. (2014). Is childhood cruelty to animals a marker for physical maltreatment in a prospective cohort study of children? *Child Abuse & Neglect, 38*(3), 533.

McKelvey v. Alabama, 895 So.2d 1025 (2004).

Meade, R. (2014, September 18). Puppy vs. iPad. *Morning Express*. Retrieved from http://www.hlntv.com/video/2014/09/18/dog-fish-ipad

Mendes D. S. & Arias, B. (2012). Spinal cord injuries in dogs and cats: Prospective study of 57 cases. *Pesquisa Veterinaria Brasileira, 32*(12), 1304–1312.

Mendoza v. Whitehouse, No. C 07-01138 CW, 2008 U.S. Dist. LEXIS 63988 (N.D. Cal. August 21, 2008).

Menendez, B. (2012, August 28). Snakes on a plane! Menendez, Durbin, Lieberman welcome expanded measures to ensure safe air travel for animals. Retrieved from http://www.menendez.senate.gov/news-and-events/press/snakes-on-a-plane-menendez-durbin-lieberman-welcome-expanded-measures-to-ensure-safe-air-travel-for-animals

Meola, S. D., et al. (2012). Evaluation of trends in marijuana toxicosis in dogs living in a state with legalized medical marijuana: 125 dogs (2005–2010). *Journal of Veterinary Emergency and Critical Care, 22*(6), 690–696.

Mesquita, P., et al. (2015). Less charismatic animals are more likely to be 'road killed': Human attitudes towards small animals in Brazilian roads. *Biotemas, 28*(1), 85–90.

Milla, N., et al. (2014). Dry paths effectively reduce road mortality of small and medium-sized terrestrial vertebrates. *Journal of Environmental Management, 144*, 51–57.

Miller, G. D. (2008). Attitudes toward dogs in ancient Israel: A reassessment. *Journal for the Study of the Old Testament, 32*(4), 487–500.

Miller, G., Tybur, J. M., & Jordan, B. D. (2007). Ovulatory cycle effects on tip earnings by lap dancers: Economic evidence for human estrus? *Human Behavior, 28*(6), 375–381.

Mohatt, J., Bennett, S, M., & Walkup, J. T. (2014). Treatment of separation, generalized, and social anxiety disorders in youths. *American Journal of Psychiatry, 171*(7), 741–748.

Mondak, J., et al. (2010). Personality and civic engagement: An integrative framework for the study of trait effects on political behavior. *The American Political Science Review, 104*(1), 85–110.

Montana v. Kelley, 2005 MT 200 (2005).

Moon, T. (2013). Pack of stray dogs saves girl from rapist in Buenos Aires. *International Business Times.* Retrieved from http://www. ibtimes.co.uk/ stray-dogs-girl-12-rapist-buenos-aires-486499

Morán, L. (2013, March 20). Drug traffickers caught stuffing live dogs with drugs in smuggling scheme. *New York Daily News.* Retrieved from http://www.nydailynews.com/news/crime/drug-smugglers-stuffed-live-dogs-drugs-article-1.1293655

——. (2015, September 9). Police probe after woman is pictured taking grandson on 'dog-like' walk with arm leash. Retrieved from http://leemoranyahoo.tumblr.com/post/128701407907/police-probe-after-woman-is-pictured-taking

Morgan v. Kroupa, 702 A.2d 630 (1997).

Morse, D. (2014, October 8). Former police officer gets 12-month sentence for killing puppy. *Washington Post.* Retrieved from http://www.washingtonpost.com/local/crime/man-to-be-sentenced-for-killing-puppy-after-it-d efecated-on-carpet/2014/10/08/9aa530e2-4ed2-11e4-aa5e-7153e466a02d_story.html

Mothering. (2011, August 1). Mothering Forum. Retrieved from http://www.mothering.com/forum/27-breastfeeding/1323999-nursing-puppies.html

Mott, M. (n.d.). Human pacemakers offer hope to ailing dogs. Medicine Net. Retrieved from http://www.medicinenet.com/pets/dog-health/human_pacemakers_offer_hope_to_ailing_dogs.htm

——. (2005, October 19). Dogs used as shark bait on French island. *National Geographic News.* Retrieved from http://news.nationalgeographic. com/news/2005/10/1019_051019_dogs_sharks.html

——. (2006, January 30). Sick puppies smuggled from Mexico for sale in U.S. *National Geographic.* Retrieved from http://news.nationalgeographic. com/news/2006/01/0130_060130_puppies.html

MSN. (2015, June 15). Search for stolen puppy takes Facebook by storm. Retrieved from http://www.msn.com/en-us/video/animals/search-for-stolen-puppy-takes-facebook-by-storm/vi-BBlbzlD

Mueller, A. (2015, November 17). No more puppies in Budweiser Super Bowl ads. *St. Louis Business Journal.* Retrieved from http://www.ksdk.com/story/entertainment/television/2015/11/17/no-more-puppies-in-budweiser-super-bowl-ads/75933754/

Muramatsu, R. S., et al. (2015). Service dogs, psychiatric hospitalization, and the ADA. *Psychiatric Services, 66*(1), 87–89.

National Confectioners Association (NCA). (n.d.). *Sweet Insights,* 1–51. Retrieved from http://www.candyusa.com/files/SweetInsights/NCA%

20Sweet%20Insights%20-%20Chocolate%20Consumer%20-%20Final
.pdf

National Geographic Wild. (2014, August 18). And man created dog. Retrieved from https://www.youtube.com/watch?v=LQipLYeCqic

National Oceanic and Atmospheric Agency (NOAA). (n.d.). Fact sheet: Tiger shark. Retrieved from http://www.nmfs.noaa.gov/sharks/FS_Tiger.htm

———. (n.d.). Fisheries fact sheet. Retrieved from http://www.sharks-world.com/tiger_shark/

National Post's Financial Post & FP Investing. (2006, June 14). Jury to decide if $1US.6M will help ease a pet's untimely passing. *Financial Post*, 10.

Nature. (2013). Great zebra exodus.

NBC News. (2004, September 21). Puppy shoots Florida man, deputies say. Retrieved from http://www.nbcnews.com/id/5950304/ns/health-pet_health/t/puppy-shoots-florida-man-deputies-say/#.VgQDQN9Viko

Neb. Stat. Ann. § 28–318 (2015).

———. § 28–1010 (2015).

New Jersey v. Bryant, NO. A-1656-04T4, 2007 N.J. Super. Unpub. LEXIS 1794 (2007).

New York Estates, Powers and Trusts Law § 7-8.1 (2015).

Nixon, R. M. (1952, September 23). Checkers speech.

NJ Stat. 4:22-25.3 (2015).

———. 4:22-25.4 (2015).

Norton, E. (2014, May 27). Parenting rewires the male brain. *Science Magazine*. Retrieved from http://news.sciencemag.org/brain-behavior/2014/05/parenting-rewires-male-brain

Nowicki, S. A. (2014). You don't own me: Feral dogs and the question of ownership. *Animal Law, 21*, 1–27.

Obergefell v. Hodges, 576 U.S. ___ (2015).

Ohio v. Miller, NO. C-070691, 2008 Ohio App. LEXIS 4962 (Ct. App. Ohio 2008).

O'Neill v. Louisville Jefferson County Metro Government, 662 F.3d 723 (2011).

Orovitz, S. (2012). Free bird: No right to qualified immunity for police who retaliate against the middle finger gesture. *Journal of Law & Social Deviance, 3*, 1–77.

O. R. S. § 167.390(1) (2015).

Parker-Pope, T. (2008, March 7). Maternal instinct is wired into the brain. *The New York Times*. Retrieved from http://well.blogs.nytimes.com/2008/03/07/maternal-instinct-is-wired-into-the-brain/

Patient Choice and Control at End of Life Act (Act 39), 18 V.S.A. § 113 (2013).

Pedersen, A. (2009). The dog delusion. *The Humanist, 69*(6), 25–28.

Pelletiere, N. (2015, July 8). Vancouver man fights off wild cougar to save mini dachshund. Good Morning America. Retrieved from https://gma.yahoo.com/vancouver-man-fights-off-wild-cougar-save-mini-175236769———abc-news-pets.html

People for the Ethical Treatment of Animals (PETA). (n.d.). Joaquin Phoenix shares disturbing video. Retrieved from http://www.peta.org/ features/ joaquin-dog-leather-video/

———. (n.d.). 'No-kill' label slowly killing animals. Retrieved from http://www.peta.org/issues/companion-animal-issues/animal-shelters/kill-label-slowly-killing-animals/

People v. Peterson, C053458, 2007 Cal. App. Unpub. LEXIS 8134 (CA. Ct. App. 3rd D. 2007).

Perry, K. (2014, October 3). Pets bring out women's maternal instincts, brain scans suggest. *The Telegraph*. Retrieved from http://www.telegraph.co.uk/news/science/11140064/Pets-bring-out-womens-maternal-instincts-brain-scans-suggest.html

Pet Pace. (2014). Retrieved from http://petpace.com/_

Pew Research Center. (2015, November 3). U.S. public becoming les religious. Retrieved from http://www.pewforum.org/2015/11/03/chapter-1-importance-of-religion-and-religious-beliefs/

Physicians Committee for Responsible Medicine (PCRM). (2007). Illegal Experiments. *Good Medicine, 15*(4).

Phys.org. (2008, February 27). Parental instinct found in the brain. Retrieved from http://phys.org/news/2008-02-parental-instinct-brain.html

Pickert, K. (2011, January 17). Our puppies, ourselves. *Time, 177*, 1.

Pike v. Bruce Church, Inc., 397 U.S. 137 (1970).

Plowden, E. (2015, February 4). Homeless people protest for 'freedom from poverty'. The Bubble. Retrieved from http://www.bubblear.com/homeless-people-protest-freedom/

Poladian, C. (2015, June 26). Tihar festival in Nepal celebrates dogs with garland, not skewers. *International Business Times*. Retrieved from http://www.ibtimes.com/pulse/tihar-festival-nepal-celebrates-dogs-garland-not-skewers-photos-1986154

Pope Francis. (2013). A Pope for Everyone.

Popkin, H. A. S. (2008, November 14). The internet goes to the dogs. NBC News. Retrieved from http://www.nbcnews.com/id/27702300/ns/technology_and_science-tech_and_gadgets/t/internet-goes-dogs/#.Vk65w3ar Tio

Popular Archaeology. (2013, November 14). Study reveals more clues to origins of domesticated dog. Retrieved from http://popular-archaeology.com/issue/09012013/article/study-reveals-more-clues-to-origins-of-domesticated-dog

Presidential Pet Museum. (2013, July 22). JFK's dogs. Retrieved from http://presidentialpetmuseum.com/pets/jfk-dogs/

Price, J. (2001, March 1). Dog owner's lawyer says pets more than property. *Saint Paul Pioneer Press*, 2B.

Prison Pet Partnership (PPP). (n.d.). Boarding and grooming. Retrieved from http://www.prisonpetpartnership.org/_html/board-groom.html

Proctor, F. (2014). Amores perritos: Puppies, laughter and popular

Catholicism in Bourbon Mexico City. *Journal of Latin American Studies, 46*(1), 1–28.

Professional Services Close–Up. (2015). JetBlue opens the T5 rooftop.

Psych2go.net. (n.d.). Can baby "cuteness" trigger parental instincts? Retrieved from http://www.psych2go.net/can-baby-cuteness-trigger-parental-instincts/

Public Broadcasting Service (PBS). (2014, April 9). My Bionic Pet.

Puppy chow is better than Prozac: The true story of a man and the dog who saved his life. (2008). *Family Therapy, 35*(3), 191–192.

Puppies 'N Love v. City of Phoenix, No. CV-14-00073-PHX-DGC, 2015 U.S. Dist. LEXIS 97561 (D. Ariz. 2015).

Puppy Uniform Protection and Safety (PUPS) Act, S. 395, 113th Cong. (2013).

Radnedge, A. (2014, February 18). Puppy's overdose on e-cigarette 'could have killed a child'. *Metro.* Retrieved from http://metro.co.uk/2014/02/18/puppys-overdose-on-e-cigarette-could-have-killed-a-child-4309310/

Raiford, T. (2015, April 30). Did you know you can train your dogs to turn lights on and off? Puppy Toob. Retrieved from http://puppytoob.com/dog-training/know-can-train-dogs-turn-lights-off/#tk5hUt0m4S8DxrIX.99

Rainey, C. (2015, January 14). America is about to get its first dog café. Grub Café. Retrieved from http://www.grubstreet.com/2015/01/dog-cafe-opening-los-angeles.html

Read to Roo. (n.d.). Retrieved from http://www.readtoroo.com/media.php

Regulation (EC) No 1523/2007 (2007).

Reynolds, T. (2014, March 1). Dog adopted during Sochi Games still fighting. Yahoo. Retrieved from http://sports.yahoo.com/news/dog-adopted-during-sochi-games-203942261——spt.html

Roberts, H. (2013, July 10). Dogs 'used as cocaine mules by smuggling gang then killed to retrieve drugs they were forced to swallow'. *Daily Mail.* Retrieved from http://www.dailymail.co.uk/news/article-2359571/Dogs-used-cocaine-mules-smuggling-gang-killed-retrieve-drugs-forced-swallow.html

Robertson, L. (2015, July 7). Man thought he was raising two puppies turns out they're actually bears. Mashable. Retrieved from http://mashable.com/2015/07/07/man-thought-he-was-raising-two-puppies-turns-out-theyre-actually-bears/

Robinson, W. (n.d.). Terror attack at gugg Bilbao. ArtNet. Retrieved from http://www.artnet.com/magazine_pre2000/news/robinson/robinson10-14-97.asp

Roger, E., Gilad, B., & Ramp, D. (2012). Linking habitat suitability and road mortalities across geographic ranges. *Landscape Ecology, 27*(8), 1167–1181.

Rogozin, D. (2014, July 31). Twitter.com. Retrieved from https://twitter.com/DRogozin?ref_src=twsrc%5Etfw

Rosenthal, C. M. (2011, July 26). Nine-year-old accused of killing puppy. My San Antonio. Retrieved from http://blog.mysanantonio.com/animals/2011/07/nine-year-old-accused-of-killing-puppy/

Rostami, S. M., et al. (2014, June 12). Milk oligosaccharides over time of lactation from different dog breeds. PLoS ONE 9(6): e99824.

Rowling, J. K. (1997). *Harry Potter and the Philosopher's Stone.* London, UK: Bloomsbury.

Rubin, E. L. (2001). Puppy federalism and the blessings of America. *Annals of the American Academy of Political and Social Science, 574,* 37–51.

San Francisco Gate. (2015, November 4). Dogs rescued from South Korea meat farm sent to San Francisco. Retrieved from http://www.sfgate.com/bayarea/article/Dogs-rescued-from-South-Korea-meat-farm-sent-to-6611031.php

Sattar, M. & Reed, S. (2013, April 2). Dog meat trafficking disgusts health experts. Al Jazeera. Retrieved from http://www.aljazeera.com/indepth/features/2013/03/2013328132714178410.html

Salonia, A., et al. (2006). Chocolate and women's sexual health: An intriguing correlation. *Journal of Sexual Medicine, 3,* 476–482.

Sampson v. Commissioner of Internal Revenue, Docket No. 370–78, T.C. Memo 1982-276, (May 18, 1982).

Say No to Dog Meat. (2013). Dog Meat in Japan. Retrieved from http://saynotodogmeat.net/2013/12/06/dog-meat-in-japan/

S.C. Code §47-3-420 (2015).

Schoales, G. P. (1995). The Prosecution, 212–216. Retrieved from http://www.mlsd.net/~tlord/andersonville/03%20The%20prosecution.pdf

Self v. State, 420 So. 2d 792 (1981).

Senthilkumaran, S., et al. (2011). Hypersexuality in a 28-year-old woman with rabies. *Archives of Sexual Behavior, 40*(6), 1327–8.

Seps, C. D. (2010). Animal law evolution: Treating pets as persons in tort and custody disputes. *University of Illinois Law Review, 2010,* 1339–1373.

Serafino, L. (2011). No walk in the dog park: Drafting animal cruelty statutes to resolve double jeopardy concerns and eliminate unfettered prosecutorial discretion. *Tennessee Law Review, 78,* 1119–1169.

Service dogs: A way of life. (2009, June 10). Preventing and curing separation anxiety in service dogs. Retrieved from http://servicedogsawayoflife.blogspot.com/2009/06/preventing-and-curing-separation.html

Shadbolt, P. (2013, June 3). Smugglers drive Thailand's grim trade in dog meat. CNN. Retrieved from http://www.cnn.com/2013/06/02/world/asia/thailand-dogs/

Shakespeare, W. (2004). *As You Like It.* P. Werstine & B. A. Mowat (Eds.). Simon & Schuster.

Rasul v. Myers, 512 F.3d 644 (2008).

Travis v. Murray, 42 Misc. 3d 447 (2013).

Shapley v. Texas Department of Human Resources, 581 S.W.2d 250 (1979).

Sheffield v. State, 87 So.3d 607 (2010).

Show, C. (2012, March 22). Man 'got his dog so drunk on vodka it was four times over the legal limit and couldn't stand up'. *Daily Mail.* Retrieved from http://www.dailymail.co.uk/news/article-2118883/Man-got-dog-drunk-times-legal-limit-stand-up.html

Sirois, L. M. (2015). Recovering for the loss of a beloved pet: Rethinking the legal classification of companion animals and the requirements for loss of companionship tort damages. *University of Pennsylvania Law Review, 163*, 1199–1239.

Skylar, A. (2011, August 4). Baboons kidnap and raise feral dogs as pets. Animals like us. Retrieved from https://www.youtube.com/watch?v=U2lSZPTa3ho

Smith v. Texas, 05-06-01543-CR, 2007 Tex. App. LEXIS 6808 (Ct. App. Tex. 5th D. August 17, 2007).

Soffar v. Johnson, 237 F.3d 411 (2000).

Srinath, D. (2012). A new weapon in the obesity battle: Coordinated state attorneys general *parens patriae* consumer protection lawsuits. *Journal of Law & Social Deviance, 4*, 40–119.

Stanton, J. (2015, October 7). 'We will cut your filthy head': Child ISIS jihadi taunts 'Dog of Rome' Obama to submit to the 'Caliphate' or die in direct video threat. Daily Mail. Retrieved from http://www.dailymail.co.uk/news/article-3262979/We-cut-filthy-head-Child-ISIS-jihadi-taunts-Dog-Rome-Obama-submit-Caliphate-die-direct-video-threat.html#ixzz3nzUTB2vd

State of North Carolina Department of Correction Division of Prisons. (2010, June 6). *Policy and Procedure,* Chapter: E Section: .0605(b)(3)(ix), .0606(b).

State v. $36,560.00, 289 N.J. Super. 237, 261 (App. Div. 1996).

State v. Carrethers, M2001-01503-CCA-R3-CD, 2002 Tenn. Crim. App. LEXIS 832, (St. App. Tenn. July 17, 2002).

State v. Graham, M2012-02379-CCA-R3-CD, 2013 Tenn. Crim. App. LEXIS 841 (Ct. App. Tenn. August 13, 2013).

State v. James, 347 S.W.2d 211 (1961).

State v. Liendo, 797 N.W.2d 624, 2011 Iowa App. LEXIS 611 (Iowa Ct. App. 2011).

State v. Loper, 2003 Ohio App. LEXIS 2864 (Ct. App. 8th D. 2003).

State v. Rivera, CA2011-10-194, 2012-Ohio-3755 (Ct. App. Ohio, 12th D. 2012).

State v. Thurman, A13-2206, 2015 Minn. App. Unpub. LEXIS 117 (Ct. App. Minn. 2015).

Stevens-Scott, V. (2014, June 18). Buddy's baby crawling school. Retrieved from https://www.youtube.com/watch?v=Oql972Jht5k

Story, K. (2014, January 28). With kids' peanut allergy rise alert dogs are being trained. Examiner. Retrieved from http://www.examiner.com/article/with-kids-peanut-allergy-rise-alert-dogs-are-being-trained

Sun, X., et al. (2009). Does feigning amnesia impair subsequent recall? *Memory & Cognition, 37*(1), 81–9.

Sutherland, A. (2015, June 29). Puppy porta-potties are now a thing. *New*

York Post. Retrieved from http://nypost.com/2015/06/29/puppy-porta-potties-are-now-a-thing/

Sutyak, K. (2014, February 7). Woman: I breastfed puppy to save animal's life. Fox8. Retrieved from http://fox8.com/2014/02/07/woman-i-breastfed-puppy-to-save-animals-life/

Sweeney, C. (2010, March 25). Inside the black market: Puppy smuggling. *DVM360*. Retrieved from http://veterinarynews.dvm360.com/inside-black-market-puppy-smuggling

Tan, A. (2015, September 9). Patches the crossing guard dog 'fired' by school district. Yahoo. Retrieved from https://gma.yahoo.com/patches-crossing-guard-dog-fired-school-district-194751539——abc-news-pets.html

Taylor, S., et al. (2006). Vitamin D status as related to race and feeding type in preterm infants. *Breastfeeding Medicine, 1*(3), 156–63.

Teixeira, F. Z., et al. (2013). Are road-kill hotspots coincident among different vertebrate groups? *Oecologia Australis, 17*(1), 36–47.

——. (2013). Vertebrate road mortality estimates: Effects of sampling methods and carcass removal. *Biological Conservation, 157*, 317–323.

The Telegraph. (2014, August 11). British airways launches cute animals TV channel. Retrieved from http://www.telegraph.co.uk/travel/travel-news/11025513/British-Airways-launches-cute-animals-TV-channel.html

Temesi, A., Turcsan, B., & Miklosi, A. (2014). Measuring fear in dogs by questionnaires: An exploratory study toward a standardized inventory. *Applied Animal Behaviour Science, 161*, 121–130.

Tenn. Code Ann. § 44-17-403 (2014).

Texas Air & Space Museum. (2015). Retrieved from http://www.texas-airandspacemuseum.org/

The Big House to Your House. (n.d.). Retrieved from https://www.gofundme.com/bighouse

The Canadian Press. (2015, June 14). Ottawa man tweets search for dog lost by airline on Cuba-Montreal flight.

The Humane League of Philadelphia v. Berman and Company, 117363/09, 2010 N.Y. Misc. LEXIS 5395 (Sup. Ct. NY) [November 1, 2010]; 108 A.D.3d 417 (2013).

The Washington Post. (2014, May 3). Dog and Cat Fur Protection report. Retrieved from https://www.washingtonpost.com/apps/g/page/politics/dog-and-cat-fur-protection-report/998/

The Royal Dutch Guide Dog Foundation (KNGF). (2014, January 10). Retrieved from https://www.youtube.com/watch?v=WIlPFRsseQ8

Tiira, K. & Lohi, H. (2014). Reliability and validity of a questionnaire survey in canine anxiety research. *Applied Animal Behaviour Science, 155*, 82–92.

Tilikum v. SeaWorld Parks & Entertainment, 842 F. Supp. 2d 1259 (2012).

Timm, R. M., et al. (2004). Coyote attacks: An increasing suburban problem. *Proceedings of the Twenty-First Vertebrate Pest Conference*, 47–57.

Toolsidass, P. L. (2008). *Pets N Us*. Mumbai, India: Allied Publishers.

Travis v. Murray, 2013 NY Slip Op 23405, 42 Misc 3d 447 (Sup. Ct. New York County November 29, 2013).

Tricky. (2008). Puppy toy. On *Knowle West Boy*. London, UK: Domino Recording Company.

Udell, M. A. R., & Wynne, C. D. L. (2011). Reevaluating canine perspective-taking behavior. *Learning & Behavior, 39*(4), 318–323.

University of California (UC) Davis. (n.d.). Evidence collection. Veterinary Genetics Laboratory. Retrieved from https://www.vgl.ucdavis.edu/forensics/collection.php

———. (n.d.). Canine CODIS. Retrieved from https://www.vgl.ucdavis.edu/forensics/CANINECODIS.php

Underwood, J., et al. (2007), Reading the road: The influence of age and sex on child pedestrians' perceptions of road risk. *British Journal of Psychology, 98*, 93–110.

U.S. Const. amend. I

———. *amend. XIII.*

———. *art. I, § 10, clause 1.*

———. *art. I, § 8, clause 1.*

U.S. Customs and Border Protection (CBP). (2012). Dog and Cat Fur Protection Fiscal Year 2012 Report to Congress. U.S. Department of Homeland Security. Retrieved from https://assets.documentcloud.org/documents/1153439/dog-and-cat-fur-protection-fy-2012-cleared-and.pdf

U.S. News & World Report. (2013). Why dogs, unlike wolves, can be tamed. Retrieved from http://health.usnews.com/health-news/news/articles/2013/01/24/why-dogs-unlike-wolves-can-be-tamed

U.S. v. MacDonald, 779 F.2d 962 (4th Cir. N.C. 1985).

U.S. v. Mark, Criminal No. 2006–80, 2012 U.S. Dist. LEXIS 95130 (DVI July 10, 2012).

U.S. v. Ribeiro, 397 F.3d 43 (2005).

U.S. v. Skinner, 131 Fed. Appx. 650 (2005).

U.S. v. Washington, Case No: 13 CR 50048, 2014 U.S. Dist. LEXIS 57085 (N.D. Ill. April 24, 2014).

U.S. v. Wilson, 239 Fed. Appx. 260 (2007).

Uzoo. (2009, January 21). Dalmatian and tiger friends. Retrieved from https://www.youtube.com/watch?v=HreeOk9jpTs

Va. Code Ann. § 3.2-6589 (2008).

Vasilyeva, N. (2014, February 11). Sochi's stray dogs smuggled out of town by volunteers. *The Huffington Post.* Retrieved from http://www.huffingtonpost.com/2014/02/11/sochi-stray-dogs_n_4767638.html

Volo, D. D. (2015). Valentine's day. In *Daily Life through History*.

Waggin Tales. (2013). April newsletter. Retrieved from http://basset-tbhc.org/tbhc_newsletter/April_2013.pdf

Wagner, M. (2014, May 13). Michigan police shoot, kill couple's dog in their backyard: Owners. *New York Daily News.* Retrieved from http://www.nydailynews.com/news/national/mich-police-shoot-kill-dog-backyard-owners-article-1.1790492

Walker, W. E. (1993). Presidential transitions and the entrepreneurial presidency: Of lions, foxes, and puppy dogs. *Presidential Studies Quarterly, 23*(1), 57–75.

Walt Disney. (1955). Lady and the Tramp.

——. (1961). One Hundred and One Dalmatians.

Walters, G. D. & Noon, A. (2015). Family context and externalizing correlates of childhood animal cruelty in adjudicated delinquents. *Journal of Interpersonal Violence, 30*(8), 1369.

Wander Argentina. (n.d.). Buenos Aires launches new Animal Protection Agency. Retrieved from http://wander-argentina.org/2011/01/buenos-aires-launches-new-animal-protection-agency/

Washington State Correctional Center for Women. (n.d.). Prison Pet Partnership Program: Maximum Security Prison. Retrieved from http://prisonp.tripod.com/

Waters, J. (1972). Pink Flamingos.

Weaver, T. (2009). The ecology of globalization: The wolf at the global door. *Human Organization, 68*(4), 363–373.

Wells, D. L. & Hepper, P. G. (2012). The personality of "aggressive" and "non-aggressive" dog owners. *Personality and Individual Differences, 53*(6), 770–773.

Werb, J. (n.d.). The prison pet partnership program. *Modern Magazine.* Retrieved from http://moderndogmagazine.com/articles/prison-pet-partnership-program/273#sthash.WQYzKzhR.dpuf

Westenberg, K. (2014, September 21). From the travel desk. *Star Tribune,* G.2.

White, D. G. (1991). *Myths of the Dog-Man.* Chicago, IL: University of Chicago Press.

Whitehead, T. (2008, June 27). Sniffer dogs offend Muslims. *Express.* Retrieved from http://www.express.co.uk/news/uk/50071/Sniffer-dogs-offend-Muslims

Whiteman, H. (2012). Coroner rules dingo to blame for Australian baby's death. CNN. Retrieved from http://www.cnn.com/2012/06/11/world/asia/australia-dingo-inquest/index.html

Winter, S. & Gutteridge, N. (2015, August 3). RSPCA smashes cruel puppy trading gang: Sick dogs smuggled to UK and sold for huge profits. *Express.* Retrieved from http://www.express.co.uk/news/nature/595741/RSPCA-puppy-trading-gang-sick-dogs-smuggled-sold-profits

Wise Jamaican Proverbs. (2008, September 22). Crab'n choke puppy. Retrieved from http://wisejamaican.com/2008/09/

Wiseman, R. (2014, January 15). Never lose your wallet again. Retrieved from https://richardwiseman.wordpress.com/2014/01/15/never-lose-your-wallet-again/

Witz, B. (2013, November 15). Emotional support, with fur, draws complaints on planes. *The New York Times.* Retrieved from http://www.nytimes.com/2013/11/16/business/emotional-support-with-fur-draws-complaints-on-planes.html?_r=0

Wolf, J. E., et al. (2014). Need to train your rat? There is an app for that: A touchscreen behavioral evaluation system. *Behavior Research Methods 46*(1), 206–214.

Woodman v. Simmons, 342 Ore. 76 (2006).

W, R. W. (2004). Coast guard dogs fight terrorism. *United States Naval Institute. Proceedings, 130*(12), 78.

Yahoo Answers. (2011, June 16). My 7 year old son just killed our pet puppy. Should I be concerned? Retrieved from https://answers.yahoo.com/question/index?qid=20110616165443AAcFZrx&page=2

Yahoo. (2015, September 5). Dog lost in Yellowstone National Park found 42 days later. Retrieved from http://news.yahoo.com/dog-lost-yellow-stone-national-park-found-42-days-170624583.html

Yates, R. (2011). Criminalizing protests about animal abuse. Recent Irish experience in global context. *Crime, Law and Social Change, 55*(5), 469–482.

Yellen, L. (2013). North Side family says prized puppy was unjustly shot by cop. Fox 32. Retrieved from http://www.myfoxchicago.com/story/20251373/chicago-cop-shoots-puppy-with-world-champion-lineage-exclusive

Younger, J. (2010, July 5). Prison hounds are on job when folks are on the lam. *Arizona Daily Star*. Retrieved from http://tucson.com/news/local/crime/prison-hounds-are-on-job-when-folks-are-on-the/article_49a37ff7-29bb-55bb-965e-c3ce00b73829.html

Youtube.com. (2009, May 14). Bridgestone tire commercial——dog suicide. Retrieved from https://www.youtube.com/watch?v=QYv37OXXYH4

——. (2010, October 23). Awesome Labrador dog fetches a beer from fridge for owner! How cool!? Retrieved from https://www.youtube.com/watch?v=6W02C75-adA

——. (2014, May 8). Two dogs fight off intruding bear. Retrieved from https://www.youtube.com/watch?v=_oIqW2hbEcs

Zoo Borns. (n.d.). Baby animal names. Retrieved from http://www.zooborns.com/zooborns/baby-animal-names.html

Index